"Kent Hughes and even more the Word of God that he has faithfully preached are worthy of this astonishing array of contributors. I rejoice that the ripple effect of one man's allegiance to the Bible has pushed so many new waves of blessing out of their hearts and into these pages."

—John Piper, pastor for preaching and vision,
Bethlehem Baptist Church, Minneapolis

"That Kent Hughes can inspire contributions of such quality tells us something of the esteem in which he and his ministry are held. Here in these papers lasting treasure is to be found—in rare wisdom, fresh thinking, and occasional plain speaking. Highly recommended by one who has been uncommonly impressed and helped."

—Dick Lucas, rector emeritus, St. Helen's Church, Bishopsgate

"A book packed with preaching wisdom to honor one of this generation's greatest expositors of Scripture. Kent Hughes is rightly honored, but God's Word is ever-more highly honored in this special book."

—Bryan Chapell, president, Covenant Seminary;
author of *Christ-centered Preaching: Redeeming the Expository Sermon*

"*Preach the Word: Essays on Expository Preaching: In Honor of Dr. R. Kent Hughes* is not just a treasure trove for preachers; it provides what amounts to a refresher course in pastoral theology. Faithful ministers frequently pause to reflect, 'What am I doing and why am I doing it and what does God want me to be doing and how does he want me to be doing it?' This book will prove a tremendously helpful conversation partner for this kind of all-important reflection and self-evaluation. I warmly commend it to all who are serious about doing biblical pastoral ministry today."

—Ligon Duncan, senior minister,
First Presbyterian Church, Jackson, Mississippi;
president, Alliance of Confessing Evangelicals;
chairman, Council on Biblical Manhood and Womanhood

PREACH THE WORD

PREACH THE WORD

Essays on Expository Preaching:
In Honor of R. Kent Hughes

Leland Ryken
and Todd A. Wilson, Editors

CROSSWAY BOOKS
WHEATON, ILLINOIS

Library of Congress Cataloging-in-Publication Data
    Preach the Word: essays on expository preaching in honor of R. Kent Hughes /
    Leland Ryken and Todd Wilson, editors.
        p. cm.
    Includes index.
    ISBN 978-1-58134-926-9 (hc)
    1. Preaching. I. Hughes, R. Kent. II. Ryken, Leland. III. Wilson, Todd A.,
    1976– IV. Title.

    BV4211.3.P725   2007
    251—dc22

                                                 2007016848

TS		15	14	13	12	11	10	09	08	07
		9	8	7	6	5	4	3	2	1

For Kent and Barbara Hughes

Contents

Contributors

Wallace Benn, Bishop of Lewes, Church of England

D. A. Carson, Research Professor of New Testament, Trinity Evangelical Divinity School

Jon M. Dennis, Associate Senior Pastor, Holy Trinity Church, Chicago

Wayne Grudem, Research Professor of Bible and Theology, Phoenix Seminary

Randy Gruendyke, Campus Pastor, Taylor University

David Helm, Senior Pastor, Holy Trinity Church, Chicago

Paul House, Associate Dean; Professor of Divinity, Beeson Divinity School

David Jackman, Director, Cornhill Training Course, London

Phillip Jensen, Dean, St. Andrew's Cathedral, Sydney

Duane Litfin, President, Wheaton College

John MacArthur, Pastor, Grace Community Church, Sun Valley, California

J. I. Packer, Board of Govenor's Professor of Theology, Regent College, Vancouver

Leland Ryken, Clyde S. Kilby Professor of English, Wheaton College

Philip Ryken, Senior Minister, Tenth Presbyterian Church, Philadelphia

Todd A. Wilson, Associate Pastor of Adult Training and Ministries, College Church, Wheaton, Illinois

Bruce Winter, Director, Institute for Early Christianity in the Greco-Roman World, Tyndale House, Cambridge

List of Illustrations

Introduction

Todd A. Wilson

What could be more full of meaning?—for the pulpit is ever this earth's foremost part; all the rest comes in its rear; the pulpit leads the world. From thence it is that the storm of God's quick wrath is first descried, and the bow must bear the earliest brunt. From thence it is that the God of breezes fair or foul is first invoked for favorable winds. Yes, the world's a ship on its passage out, and not a voyage complete; and the pulpit is its prow.

—Herman Melville, *Moby Dick*

For nearly four decades R. Kent Hughes has devoted himself to expository preaching. Believing that not just the world but also the church is on its passage out and not a voyage complete, he has made the pulpit its prow—and the priority of his ministry. This year marked not only Kent's sixty-fifth birthday, but also his retirement from the position of senior pastor of College Church in Wheaton, a post he held for over a quarter of a century. To mark this occasion and pay tribute to his life and legacy, we assembled this collection of essays written by Kent's friends and colleagues. Our primary goal has been to produce a volume of good essays on the subject of expository preaching and a book that Kent himself would enjoy reading, because it covers the topics that are dearest to his preaching heart.

Celebratory volumes like this are usually reserved for those in academic guilds and are seldom produced for pastors. However, we thought it entirely fitting to honor Kent in this way because of his substantial contribution to raising the standard of expository preaching in North America and beyond. His own distinguished pulpit ministry, his nu-

1

merous expositional commentaries and published writings, and his extensive training of other preachers have done much to strengthen pulpits across this country and around the world—and we believe the evangelical church is the better for it!

This project has brought together a diverse group of contributors. Not all are North American. Nearly half are from Australia and the United Kingdom. Nor are all pastors or preachers. In fact, we have essays from college and seminary professors, a university chaplain, a college president, and urban church planters. This attests to the scope of Kent's influence, his professional ties extending to several continents and a variety of ministry spheres. This diversity also attests to the fact that expository preaching is more than the fascination of a particular wing of North American evangelicalism or the interest solely of pastors and preachers. As this collection testifies, interest in expository preaching crosses national and vocational lines; indeed it is a concern for all who love the church and desire to see her flourish.

Our desire is that this volume serve as a useful resource for many. The privilege of expository preaching, its challenges and hermeneutical presuppositions, biblical and historical examples of such preaching, the priority of training the next generation—these are the leading themes addressed in the pages to follow. Students will find this an inspiring introduction to the great art and science of expository preaching. Those employed in the training of future pastors and preachers will find a good overview of the subject. Congregants will gain insight into some of the delights and difficulties attending pulpit ministry and thus be encouraged to pray more empathetically and strategically for their shepherds. And pastors and preachers will, we trust, find fresh encouragement in these essays and be challenged to make the pulpit the prow of their ministries!

Preach the Word: An Overview

Every editor anxiously wonders whether a collection of essays will in the end form a coherent book. To our delight this volume has come together not only in a way that provides good coverage of the subject at hand, but also with essays that reiterate many of the same themes, thus giving the volume an overall unity and coherence. We have grouped these sixteen essays under four broad headings. By way of introduction, I would like to offer you, our readers, a brief yet enticing preview of each of the sections in the hope of whetting your appetites.

Interpretive Principles and Practices

"What you believe about the Bible determines everything," Kent Hughes was fond of saying to me as a College Church intern nearly a decade ago. He meant this not just in general terms, but specifically as it relates to preaching. If you believe the Bible to be the Word of God written, God's words in human words, it should shape your entire approach to preaching. In other words, there are specific interpretive principles and practices that ought to flow naturally from one's conviction about God's Word. In this first section, our contributors invite us to reflect upon some of them: things such as listening carefully to the text of Scripture, approaching the study of a passage inductively, appreciating the historical dimensions of a biblical text, seeking to preach both Old and New Testaments as Christian Scripture, and being sensitive to the various genres of the Bible.

It should become clear as one reads these essays that if expository preaching is to be done well, certain habits of study need to be developed and certain pitfalls, both practical and theoretical, need to be avoided. However, as important as right interpretation and interpretive methodology are for preaching, the ultimate criterion of success is faithfulness. This section of essays thus concludes on the right note with pastor John MacArthur helping us to hear once more Paul's charge to Timothy: "Do your best to present yourself to God as one approved, a worker who has no need to be ashamed, rightly handling the word of truth" (2 Tim. 2:15).

Biblical and Historical Paradigms

Thomas Kuhn's *Structure of Scientific Revolutions* is arguably the most oft-cited work of the twentieth century. It is also responsible for injecting into our everyday parlance the term "paradigm." A paradigm is a model. Our second section of essays provides us with a few paradigms, a few models for modern-day preachers. The first is a biblical one, the model of the rugged and indefatigable apostle Paul. Both Bruce Winter and Duane Litfin explore aspects of Paul's gospel proclamation and set him up, as it were, as a pastoral paradigm for twenty-first-century preachers. Then, drawing upon the rich legacy of history, Wallace Benn and J. I. Packer offer us a glimpse into the lives of the great Puritan pastor Richard Baxter and the towering Anglican divine Charles Simeon. Baxter provides us, as Benn demonstrates, with a model of how the preacher's pastoral care for his flock can enhance, rather than detract from, his work in the pulpit. And Packer's reflections on Simeon's life paint for us not only an impressive picture of an exemplary preacher and homiletician, but a moving portrait of a life and ministry characterized by earnestness over the long haul.

Contemporary Challenges and Aims

Expository preaching has never been easy. Indeed, as Don Carson rightly points out, challenges have confronted the pulpit in every generation. That being said, as this third section of essays recognizes, there are some distinctive challenges in the twenty-first century: multiculturalism; rising biblical illiteracy; shifting epistemology; increasing social, cultural, and technological complexity; rapid change; and a dearth of models and mentoring.

These are some of the challenges. But if this is what preachers are up against, what should they be trying to accomplish? En route to an answer Phillip Jensen reminds us of the theological basis and rationale for preaching. In simplest terms, preaching is communicating God's Word in human words. Or to borrow from the apostle Peter, it is speaking the very "oracles of God" (1 Pet. 4:11). Don Carson defines it with the single, felicitous phrase: "re-revelation." Hence, preaching is nothing less than God re-revealing himself through the exposition of his sacred Word. Quite an ennobling vision of what transpires in the pulpit! As to the aims, then, of preaching in the twenty-first century, Philip Ryken rightly points in a threefold direction: through the proclamation of the Word, expository preachers must seek the reformation of the church, the reconciliation of the world, and the glorification of God in Christ Jesus. Anything less is less than truly *biblical* preaching, that is, preaching with Scripture-informed aims and ends.

Training and Example

Who is responsible for training future preachers? When hearing this question, our thoughts tend to run toward the seminary. And not without good reason, since for over a century now, the seminary has been the primary conduit of formal ministerial training for pastors and preachers; and this situation is not likely to change anytime in the near future. So it is incumbent upon the church to think seriously about what seminary education ought to look like. To this end, Peter Jensen, dean of Moore College, Sydney, Australia, provides an incisive and sobering analysis of the state of seminary education today, bedeviled as it is by increasing fragmentation, specialization, and generalization. However, his is not simply a song of lament. Rather, the burden of Jensen's essay is to challenge seminaries to prioritize the training of *preachers* amidst everything else they do. As Jensen contends, "It is the business of the whole faculty and the whole curriculum to produce preachers." Or to put it concretely, the sermon is the aim of the seminary.

Of course, seminaries are not the only ones who should produce preachers. The church is ultimately responsible to raise up her own shepherds. Thus in every generation the church must set itself anew to the task of raising up its own. But what might this look like in our day and age? Setting his proposal against the backdrop of the preacher-led Puritan movement in Tudor England, David Helm identifies several twenty-first-century strategies to help raise up not just a few but a whole generation of gospel preachers. This inspiring proposal is complemented by Jon Dennis's seasoned reflection upon Paul's charge to his pastoral understudy, Timothy: "Preach the Word!" (2 Tim. 4:2), which Dennis suggests provides us with a call and a model for training and deploying gospel ministers.

This entire collection of essays concludes, then, where it ought: with a warm, engaging and indeed fascinating sketch of Kent Hughes's life and ministry. Randall Gruendyke, longtime friend and former associate of Kent's at College Church, has done a great service in putting Kent's story down on paper. Such an exercise, however, serves more than the public record; it provides us with a *living example* of faithfulness to one's calling and faithfulness to one's Lord. We all need examples—preachers not least. May the reader see in this story an inspiring portrait of how the Pauline paradox of grace and discipline (1 Cor. 15:10) came to expression in the life of one godly and much-beloved pastor!

The Pulpit Leads the World

These are tumultuous and indeed unsettling times. As the rising tide of post-Christian secularism threatens to capsize the evangelical church and as many foul breezes rip across her deck, it is the pulpit that should be out in front, leading, navigating, warning of danger, signaling hope. Regrettably, however, it is the pulpit that is all too often relegated to the rear, pastors choosing instead to lead with all the rest. As a result, many churches are left adrift in a sea of moral and theological confusion, tossed to and fro by every wind of doctrine, by human cunning, by craftiness in deceitful schemes. Furthermore, as the pulpit recedes from the prow of many ministries, the church of Jesus Christ forfeits her divinely appointed means of bringing sinners to the Savior—and the world suffers.

This collection of essays on expository preaching, a labor of love and tribute to our friend and colleague Kent Hughes, is offered in hopeful anticipation of fairer days. So too we pray for favorable winds and a rising tide—a new generation of gospel preachers who heed the example of our honoree by ordering their lives and ministries around the conviction that the pulpit is ever the earth's foremost part; all the rest comes in its rear; the pulpit leads the world.

Soli Deo Gloria!

PART ONE

INTERPRETIVE PRINCIPLES AND PRACTICES

The Hermeneutical Distinctives of Expository Preaching

David Jackman

No one can seek to be a preacher of God's Word on a regular basis today without becoming acutely conscious of the cultural barriers, challenges, and constraints of our contemporary culture. As the tide of anti-Christian secularism appears to be assuming tsunami proportions, all Bible preachers are made supremely aware of our own inadequacies, vulnerability, and weakness, no matter how apparently fruitful and outwardly effective those ministries may be. It would be tempting to imagine that we are called to preach at a particularly difficult time in the church's history, or that God can only use men of prodigious talent in the face of such overwhelming opposition. But we would be wrong. There is indeed "nothing new under the sun."

Expository Preaching: The Difficulty of the Task

In 1592, William Perkins, an English Puritan scholar-pastor and a fellow of Christ's College, Cambridge, wrote a book entitled *The Art of Prophesying*. Only thirty-four years of age, Perkins lamented the scarcity of true biblical ministers—a truth that he claimed was self-evident from the experience of all ages. His complaint was that few men of quality and ability seek out the calling of the preaching ministry. Moreover, even of those who have the titles, very few really deserve the honorable names of messenger (*angelos*) and interpreter. Even at the ascendancy of Puritan influence, in the last decade of the Elizabethan era, it was apparently still very difficult to find godly pastors who could exercise effective expository ministries.

Perkins identified three causes of this dilemma. First, he cited the contempt with which the calling is treated, recognizing that biblical ministry will always be hated by the world since by its very nature it reveals human sin and unmasks hypocrisy. Second, Perkins drew attention to the immense difficulty of discharging the duties of the ministry well. The charge of the cure of souls was (and is) an overwhelming responsibility. The pastor-teacher must speak to God on behalf of the people, as well as speaking to the people on behalf of God, and who is sufficient for these things? Lastly, Perkins focused on the inadequacy of financial recompense and its accompanying status. Who would accept the contempt and the difficulties for such a paucity of reward? Small wonder, he said, that the sharpest minds of the day turn to the law as their chosen profession. And that was over four hundred years ago!

The Contemporary Context

The issues besetting a biblical teaching ministry today are nothing new, though they are more accentuated. While the Reformation era regarded preaching as "the source and spring of Christian faith," it is now marginalized and increasingly jettisoned. The hostility of the culture has always been a "given," but the skepticism and rejection of sound biblical teaching at the heart of the local church's life of ministry—from within the congregation itself—is perhaps a defining aspect of the current crisis. It is, of course, evidence of the world's waves swamping and threatening the very viability of the church's boat. A worldly church is always going to reject the clarity of biblical revelation. Such people "will not endure sound teaching, but having itching ears they will accumulate for themselves teachers to suit their own passions, and will turn away from listening to the truth and wander off into myths" (2 Tim. 4:3–4). These can be the myths of atheistic humanism or the psychiatrist's couch, the flattering spin of the politicians and the advertisers, or the hard-nosed ethos of corporate capitalism and the culture of success. They are all around us, and they are the powerful siren songs of our unbelieving world.

So, when we are told that biblical preaching is presumptuous, or naïve, or ineffective, or all three, we know that the ocean is truly within the boat and that it will soon be sunk unless the preachers begin bailing. That is why a biblical ministry, such as College Church has enjoyed under our esteemed brother Kent these many years, stands as a beacon light in the darkness and crosscurrents of contemporary confusion. We salute a ministry devoted to "the truth, the whole truth, and nothing but the truth" and thank God for the countless lives influenced from that pulpit in both the spoken and the written word, and the numerous ministries put back on track by this powerful example and model. At the heart of this ministry lies the conviction that it is the Word of God in the hands of the Spirit of God that accomplishes the work of God—through the preacher, the man of God.

The Proclamation Trust

That same conviction lies at the heart of the ministry of The Proclamation Trust in the United Kingdom that, in informal partnership with the Simeon Trust in the United States, seeks to bring about the renaissance and development of biblical expository preaching, characterized by careful listening to God in his Word and its powerful application to the lives of both the preacher and his hearers, with penetrating, practical relevance.

John Stott has often spoken of effective preaching as a bridge, firmly grounded at either end, both in the biblical text, with all its unchanging truth, and in the contemporary world, with all its urgent need as expressed in darkened understanding and hardened hearts (Eph. 4:18). Both firm groundings are certainly characteristic of the ministry of Dick Lucas, in which The Proclamation Trust had its origins.

Founded in 1986, the Trust at its inception could already look back over twenty-five years of extraordinary growth and fruitfulness. Dick Lucas was appointed in 1961 as rector of St. Helen's Bishopsgate in the heart of the business community of the city of London. Building on lunchtime services for those working in "the Square Mile," extending to Bible study and discipleship groups, St. Helen's added Sunday evening services for students and young graduates and in due course a families' work on Sunday mornings, so that over the years, countless numbers of people heard the Word of the Lord. For many, this led to their conversion to Christ and for even more the nurture and growth of a vigorous life of discipleship.

The simple purpose of The Proclamation Trust is to train and equip a new generation of biblical preachers to do that same work, dependent on the same Spirit to use the same Word to multiply gospel growth across the land and around the world. This is carried out through two main programs. The first is an annual schedule of preaching conferences for ministers, lay preachers, and seminarians, culminating each year in June with the Evangelical Ministers Assembly at St. Helen's, which draws together as many as nine hundred Christian workers from all over the United Kingdom, Europe, and beyond. The second is a full-time study program for one academic year called the Cornhill Training Course, which concentrates on providing practical tools for biblical expository ministry.

The Hermeneutical Principles of Expository Preaching

These tools constitute the foundational hermeneutic on which expository proclamation of biblical truth can be most effectively built. They are very basic, and one might be tempted to think all too obvious, but experience has shown over the years that such principles have not been widely taught or assimilated. In the midst of the highly demanding academic agenda of the seminary, very little time can be given to the practicalities of biblical preaching. As a result, young ministers tend on the one hand to read academic essays to their congregations and simply relate their textual exegesis or, on the other, to move into an "inspirational" mode that is basically exhortation frequently disconnected from the plain meaning of Scripture. Either way, "the hungry sheep look up and are not fed" (to borrow Milton's formulation in his poem "Lycidas"). But there is no valid alternative plan for the nourishment of God's flock other than for the under-shepherds to feed them with the rich pastures of God's Word. So, how can we encourage each other to keep working at this most demanding, but also most rewarding, of ministry responsibilities?

Listening to the Biblical Text

Everything depends upon our detailed, careful, and disciplined reading of the text. Effective preaching, as Eugene Peterson has pointed out in his excellent book *Working the Angles*, begins with "passionate hearers, not cool analysts." Our problem is that the skills of literary analysis we have been taught often seem to deprive us of any sense of immediacy, or even intimacy, in hearing the living Word of the living God through the paragraphs, sentences, and individual words of Scripture. The text needs to be seen not as an object to be analyzed, dissected, or even "mastered" so that we can then begin to "do something with the Bible." Rather, we need to hear it as the urgent, present-tense message of the present-tense God (I AM) through our minds to our hearts to energize our wills in faith and obedience. Then the Bible is doing something with, in, and to us. If the preacher's life is being changed through his encounter with God in the "living and enduring Word" (1 Pet. 1:23 NIV), he really does have a message to proclaim, not simply from the written page but from the heart.

This is why prayer is so central to the process of preparation. We are entirely dependent on God's Spirit to open our blind eyes, unstop our deaf ears, and soften our hardened hearts, so at every stage in preparing to preach we seek the author's help to rightly hear and handle his Word of truth. From the first reading of the text to the final words of the sermon, we are entirely dependent on the gracious work of the Spirit, in preacher and hearers alike, to bring understanding, to generate faith, and to empower obedience.

Learning to listen by opening our eyes is one of the key skills for the biblical preacher to develop. We need to see what is really there and what is not. Like a person with hearing difficulties, we need to strain to catch every detail of vocabulary and nuance of tone in our Lord's conversation with us in the unique and specific parts of Scripture. But the problem with a written text, which increases the more familiar we think we are with it, is our tendency to skim-read it in order to find what we already know is there. We then deal with general ideas rather than give attention to detail, and the resulting sermons exist in a world of theological abstraction. So much preaching is bland and predictable because there has been no move toward studying the text beyond its general themes and familiar ideas to the uniqueness of this particular Word of the Lord. The preacher has been content with a superficial, surface reading in which he has viewed the text through the prescription lenses of his own evangelical framework. This means that he has been in control of the text, assessing it, dissecting it, allowing it to illustrate the principles of his framework that he is determined to preach, but not permitting the text to be in the driver's seat, controlling the sermon.

What needs to be happening in the preparation process is for the text to be challenging our framework, and this is achieved by questioning. Obviously, our first question will always be, "What precisely is this text saying?" But then there are other key questions with which we can sharpen our listening skills. For example, "Why does the biblical author say it in these words?" This may alert us to specialist vocabulary that often opens up major themes in the rest of the book of which our preaching passage is a part. Or it may challenge our pastoral rules of thumb, or even our doctrinal formulations. Additionally, we can ask, "Why is the author saying it to these people (his original readers)?" This raises the whole issue of contexts, both historical and theological, both of the book in the Bible and the passage in the book. Finally, "Why does the author say it here, at this particular point in his work?" This is an inquiry about the literary context, which helps us to build a picture of the development of the book's major teaching themes, which will also greatly help with application of the passage to the context of today.

These questions help to discipline us to read the passage with our antennae up, specifically on the lookout for the challenges and surprises. Anything that pulls me up short and makes me say, "I wouldn't have said that" or "I wouldn't have used those words" is a great step forward in helping me listen to the message of this particular text. My presuppositions are being challenged and my habitual ways of thinking are being reshaped as the text, with its own specific content, questions my framework.

Approaching a Text Inductively

Like a lens sharpening the focus, careful observation of this sort enables the reader to probe beneath the immediate surface meaning of the text to begin to grapple with its intended purpose and significance. That is what produces clarity in exposition and gives the sermon an edge to penetrate beyond confused half-understanding and generalized notions. It enables the unique richness of the detail of a passage to have its intended effect, and when that happens the Bible really does speak. But it doesn't happen without a good deal of effort and hard work. The reason for this is that we all read the Bible through our own presuppositions. Inevitably, we cannot approach any text without inputting our own cultural conditioning into our reading of it. We have a particular background. We live at a particular time in history. Our past experience, values, and priorities have all combined to build up a personal, individual framework of thought and behavior, convictions and attitudes, that makes each of us the unique people we are. But this framework can be the enemy of careful observation.

The danger is that certain words or ideas in the text will trigger ideas in the preacher's memory bank that are then downloaded and uncritically included in a sermon. So we end up preaching our framework rather than the biblical text, unless the Bible text is questioning our framework every time we are preparing. It is not that framework preaching is wrong if the framework is itself biblically orthodox. What is said will probably be true, but the preaching will soon become reductionist and predictable. The problem is that such preaching does not challenge the church, and it will not change the world. It becomes impository of the preacher's word upon the text, which has to dance to the preacher's tune—the agenda that he has constructed—rather than being expository of the fundamental meaning of the Bible, with all its necessary challenges and unsettling disturbance to our inherently sinful, this-worldly patterns of thought and behavior. In John Stott's words, it is the function of biblical preaching both "to disturb the comfortable and then to comfort the disturbed." And that process begins with the preacher in his preparation.

There is an old saying that a text out of context is merely a pretext. Its truth is constantly demonstrated in many a pulpit, where the preacher's "angle" on the subject becomes the key constituent of the sermon, irrespective of why the text was originally written or even what it actually teaches. But it is a very important inference from our evangelical doctrine of Scripture that God's revelation will itself provide us with divinely given authoritative keys as to how to unpack and use its contents. Our submission to Scripture, as a vital part of our submission to Scripture's Lord, means that we must be prepared to teach the Bible not only in its truth-content but also to use its own distinctive methodologies. We must cut with the grain of the biblical text. This should affect our preaching schedules and the shape of the pulpit diet for our congregations, as much as it does the contents of an individual sermon.

Much of the benefit that has flowed so consistently from the College Church pulpit is attributable to the systematic consecutive exposition of Scripture, book by book, as the solid "given" of the preaching ministry. We should study and preach the Bible book by book since this is how God has provided it for us. Indeed, there is a real sense in which the whole Bible is one book, comprised of its sixty-six separate but clearly integrated units, each one having its own specific purpose and major themes. The principle of the "melodic line," or the theme tune of every book, is an important tool to work with. What does this particular book contribute to the one great story of salvation history, as God's plan to rescue humanity from its rebellion and to reconcile rebels to himself is worked out through the ages and comes to its culmination and fulfillment in Christ? What would we *not* know if this book were not included in the sixty-six? What is its distinctive value and message? What is the tune it plays?

The Journey to the World of the Biblical Text

This is where the preacher will need to travel back to the original setting and context of the first hearers in order to bring the unchanging meaning of this particular book or passage with penetration and obvious relevance into the world of today. It might seem strange to say that we must travel to first-century Corinth or Galatia in order to hear the Word of the living God for twenty-first-century London or Chicago, but it is absolutely true. If we do not wrestle with what our text meant to *them*, when it was first spoken or written, we shall never be able to apply its message with any sort of accuracy or penetration to our hearers today. This does not mean that we all need to be scholars in the original languages or in the biblical historical background, though we are thankful to God for those who are, and we can benefit greatly from their labors. But it is the genius of a teaching ministry, with time set apart for the study of the Scripture, to enable those who listen to the preaching to be as close to the situation of the original readers as it is possible to be so as to remove as many barriers to understanding as we can.

The expository preacher wants always to be giving the Bible back into the hands of the congregation. The Bible is not the preserve of the expert but the Word of God for everybody, everywhere. However, it does come to us in the form of words spoken by and to people in human history. There is a particularity about all its contents, tying its origin to a particular time and place, to specific spokesmen, and its purposes to particular groups of recipients. Yet what is revealed is of eternal significance and validity precisely because it is the "forever" Word of the infinite and eternal God, working in and from its original historical context but transcending those limitations as it addresses the whole human race across planet earth at every point of time.

God did not produce a book of rules or a set of systematized theological propositions, though both can rightly be adduced from the Bible. Its fundamental format is neither abstract nor theoretical. God spoke to real people in real situations. He intervened in space-time history, explaining his actions before and interpreting them afterwards. Scripture is the story of the loving purposes of God in our redemption from paradise lost in Eden, to the appearance of the holy city, the New Jerusalem, and the establishment of God's eternal kingdom. But if we don't get right what the revelation of Scripture meant to its original recipients, we shall certainly not get right its meaning and significance for us today.

The Genres of the Bible

That is why we must take seriously the different types of biblical literature through which God speaks still—poetry, historical narrative, prophecy, proverbial sayings, apocalypse, parables, allegories, sermons, letters, theological arguments, and so on. They are very different styles of writing with specific patterns and accepted conventions governing their use and referencing their meaning. In recent years a good deal of attention has been given to genre studies, so that each type of biblical writing is properly understood within its own framework of reference. This too will be an important set of tools for the biblical preacher to be able to own and use.

One of the most obvious examples would be the symbolic language of the apocalyptic tradition in Jewish literature, exemplified for us in books like Daniel, Zechariah, or Revelation. To read the numerical and other symbolic ingredients "in the flat" as literal facts or events would be to misunderstand how the genre works. This is not to devalue or avoid the plain meaning of Scripture in any way, but rather to recognize that its truth is not literal where the writing is metaphorical or symbolic, where that literary convention is being employed. After all, I have yet to meet anyone who imagines that Isaiah 55:12 will have a literal fulfillment: "The mountains and the hills before you shall break forth into singing, and all the trees of the field shall clap their hands"! However, we are not always so aware of how the genres work in other areas of the Bible.

To understand something of the chiastic structure of Hebrew thinking can be a great help in getting to the heart of a detailed Old Testament narrative or to the main burden of a prophetic oracle. With the central point as the focus of the passage, all that precedes and follows it augments or explains its significance. At the heart of a conflict narrative there is usually a key turning point that resolves the issue and after which everything is different. To see that as the major teaching point can unlock all the details of the story to accomplish their intended purpose. To realize that a prophetic oracle can have more than one point of fulfillment or level of significance can enable the message of the prophet to come alive to us today. We do need to explore what it meant to the people of God when the oracle was first delivered, and we do need to realize that what it reveals of God is unchangeably true. But we cannot simply put the contemporary Christian congregation into the same position as Old Testament Israel. Both are covenant peoples, but what is the significance of the coming of Christ and of the new and better covenant? And what of the prophecy remains to be fulfilled through Christ in the eternal kingdom, beyond the present gospel age? As Martin Luther said, "We can only read the Bible forwards, but we have to understand it backwards." We must always read the Old Testament in the light of the New if we are not to reinstitute sacramental religion or look for the rebuilding of the temple in Jerusalem. Recognizing the different types of gospel materials, understanding the intricacies of apostolic theological argument, looking for the affective, emotional ingredients of biblical poetry—these and other genre-specific tools will be a great help to the Bible preacher in allowing the text to speak for itself in its own authentic voice.

All too often, evangelical preaching has put every text through the same mincing machine of a particular systematized theology so that its content is dissected and laid out in terms of doctrinal propositions with ethical applications, in an identical way, irrespective of whether the original was poetry or prose, proverb or parable. This can give expository preaching a bad name because its content is abstract and predictable, which often becomes irrelevant and boring to the hearers. It also fails to recognize that the God of the Bible, whose love of variety and end-less ingenuity are reflected in his physical creation, is hardly likely to reveal himself with any less diversity in his inspired written text. Good expositors learn to work with the literary distinctives of the genres and not to iron them out into a standard, flattened three-point sermon. We need to learn how to value and benefit from the intricate arguments and precise vocabulary of the epistle, the twist in a parable, the punch line of a gospel pronouncement story, the provocation of a wisdom say-ing, the turning point of a narrative, the multiple fulfillment levels of a prophecy, and the emotive, affective ingredients of a poem.

The Return Journey: Applying the Biblical Text

Every expositor knows that once the meaning of the biblical text has been stated and explained, its application to the contemporary hearers still remains to be spelled out. Some preachers assert that this is the sovereign work of the Holy Spirit and not for us to try to accomplish. But the pattern of the New Testament epistles strongly underlines the practical application of the propositional teaching content, and while we know we cannot ourselves root God's Word into anyone's life, we should surely expect the Holy Spirit graciously to do this work as we apply the Word to our current situations. Application that is faithful and authentic is largely stimulated by context. To understand the original significance helps us to direct God's truth in its life-changing power with penetrating accuracy into our own lives and the lives of those who listen to us.

This process does not start with us in the modern world but with the given text. The Bible is not provided to answer the spiritual whims and fancies of the twenty-first century. We can and do come to it with our own cultural questions. But the good expositor is more interested in asking the Bible's questions, which, since they are God's questions, are going to be much more important and far more significant than any we, in our ignorance and spiritual blindness, could ever pose. To do the contextual work faithfully at the biblical end will ensure that the unchanging text is truly heard in the modern world, with all its potency to teach, rebuke, correct, and train in righteousness. Then it really is the Word that is doing its characteristic work. And that work really is the Lord's.

The biblical method of application has another great advantage. It delivers us from the tyranny of the currently fashionable norms of our own particular Christian subculture. So often in preaching, the application is mass-produced out of the current orthodoxies and enthusiasms of the wider church scene. The latest book, the newest ideas, the most exciting models are bolted onto a biblical text with very little authenticity. Because such applications are usually in the form of obligation: "We ought to . . .", followed by the challenge, "so *are* you . . . ?" they quickly develop into legalism and soulless duty. The emphasis is then more and more on doing Christian things (giving, praying, witnessing) so that grace is effectively evacuated from the preaching. Attention becomes focused on the present—on me and my world, on my current concerns, or on our congregation and its growth and prosperity. It is almost as though there is no great eternal plan and no universal church. We become entirely obsessed with our own concerns, the prisoners of our inflated egos.

There is a dangerous and immediate consequence of this contemporary sort of preaching. The hearers soon become adept at screening out the all-too-predictable challenges that masquerade as application. Successful life-changing application, however, is launched from the text in its original context and flies under the radar screen with an irresistible power. When the text surprises me, so that my response is "so, *that's* what it means . . . of course!" then the Word is really at work. The mind is persuaded by the truth and the heart is softened to receive it and put it into practice. Finally, the will is energized to active obedience, to make the necessary life changes in thought and behavior, in the power of that same Holy Spirit who has been communicating through his inspired Word.

The Heart of Expository Preaching

These are some of the skills we seek to develop in the courses, conferences, and media products of The Proclamation Trust. They are not new, nor are they complex, but they are largely neglected and sadly underpracticed. Of course, they call for hard work, which demands time, energy, and application, and these, in turn, are things that many preachers have decided are not a priority in their schedule. I believe it is greatly to the detriment of our churches. This collection of essays celebrates a different set of values, modeled consistently over the many years of Kent's ministry as he has put the Word of God in the hands of the Spirit of God to accomplish his own unique, Christ-glorifying work. Such preaching priorities badly need to be reclaimed across our enfeebled Western churches.

Homiletics, the introduction of novel multimedia presentations, or any other new techniques are not where we need to look for a revival of the Word of God in our culture. We need to look to preaching that has developed from listening passionately to Scripture and to preachers who incarnate that truth in their lives and seek to channel it to their hearers. We shall all do it differently, since, in Phillips Brookes's famous definition, preaching is "truth through personality." But we need to pray and work for an army of young preachers to be raised up by God to reclaim the pulpits of Western culture for faithful, penetrating, and life-changing proclamation of God's Word as "the truth, the whole truth, and nothing but the truth."

Effective exposition finds its origin and power not so much in clever sermon construction, as in detailed, obedient listening to God's voice in the text. The Bible really must be in the driver's seat, dictating the content of the message, its contemporary application, and even its shape. When we serve God's Word in this way we come to realize that the Bible is a book about God long before it is a book about us, and that its strongest relevance and most urgent application is to teach us how to live rightly in the light of his unchanging nature. There will, of course, be parallels between God's old covenant dealings with Israel and his new covenant dealing with us, the universal church, which is the body of Christ. We shall find many similarities between ourselves and the men and women we meet in the Bible's pages. But we shall come to recognize that we are not the focus of the story, and that we should not read our circumstances or experiences into theirs. This is God's book, and it is about God first before it is our book about our relationship with him. Consecutive biblical exposition seeks to guard and propagate these revelatory distinctives in every generation to the greater glory of God and for the blessing of his people and the rest of his world.

In a wonderful insight into his own ministry priorities and goals, the apostle Paul revealed to the Colossians the nature of the stewardship that God had given to him for the church. It was "to make the word of God fully known, the mystery hidden for ages and generations but now revealed to his saints. To them God chose to make known how great among the Gentiles are the riches of the glory of this mystery, which is Christ in you, the hope of glory" (Col. 1:25–27). This is the contemporary preacher's task in the only valid and authentic apostolic succession—that of the gospel, focused and fulfilled in Christ, who is in the believer now and the guarantee of glory to come. So Paul continues, "Him we proclaim, warning everyone and teaching everyone with all wisdom, that we may present everyone mature in Christ. For this I toil, struggling with all his energy that he powerfully works within me" (vv. 28–29). That is the goal. Those are the resources. This is the cost. As we thank God for a wonderful example of such apostolic ministry at College Church through our brother Kent, let us dedicate ourselves to that kind of prayer and hard work, so that through the agency of the Simeon Trust and others whom the Lord will yet raise up, this kind of ministry will be multiplied across the world in the coming days far beyond all that we might ask, or even imagine, as the Word does the work.

2

Written for Our Example: Preaching Old Testament Narratives

Paul House

One of the joys and burdens of expository preaching, as Kent Hughes practices, is that this approach requires preachers to construct sermons from the whole Bible, both Old Testament and New Testament. When my wife, Heather, and I became members of College Church in 2001, Dr. Hughes was preaching through Genesis, and he was doing a marvelous job. More than once in personal conversations he mentioned how hard he worked to know exactly how to present the elements of the Genesis narratives. I think that the struggles of this gifted veteran preacher indicate that Old Testament narrative constitutes one of the more difficult genres for expository preachers to use in their pulpit ministries. This assertion may sound odd at first, since these narratives reveal many compelling characters involved in key moments in Israelite and world history, which is in fact salvation history. But I have found such difficulty to be the case as I have explored the wider world of conservative Christian circles. Indeed, I have found it fairly rare to find preachers proclaiming these portions of Scripture at all,[1] despite the large number of narrative passages in the Old Testament.

There are some fairly legitimate reasons why preachers hesitate to preach from these passages with any regularity. Some preachers may think that there are other passages that are more important for their churches to consider. Also, some expositors may find it hard to derive effective applications from these passages, because the texts themselves do not always divulge how they apply to believers. As a result, some preachers find themselves simply retelling the story or retelling the story and offering simplistic moralistic comparisons between the people in the text and their people. Furthermore, several of the narrative books are quite long, making it difficult to sustain a passage-by-passage series for the amount of time it takes to preach through the entire book. Finally, some of the individual stories in narrative are likewise very lengthy, even when divided into scenes, and current congregations are rarely trained to read and focus on long sections of the Bible.

I believe that there are at least three fundamental systemic problems that must be addressed before preaching from Old Testament narratives becomes more common. First, even many conservative expositors have been trained to wonder if the Old Testament is worth the effort, since it is much easier to "apply the New Testament to hearers' lives." In my opinion, it is important for preachers to consider whether this is the proper way to understand our relationship to the Bible. Second, although conservative expositors believe quite rightly that the Bible is inerrant, they do not always act as if they believe the entire Bible is useful for Christian living. They need to recall some key principles about the Bible's origins and purposes. Third, many expositors are not clear as to how the Old Testament participates in the Bible's grand narrative. They are not sure how to conceive of the Bible as a unity and therefore lack a grasp of the Bible's wholeness.

This essay seeks to address these difficulties by examining our attitude toward the connection between Scripture and life, by offering some key principles concerning the Old Testament's usefulness, and by exploring the Bible's overall narrative structure. No amount of ex-

---

1. I served as a pastor for many years before and after entering Christian higher education in 1986. To be quite honest, I preached only sporadically from Old Testament narratives before being asked to write a commentary on 1 and 2 Kings in 1991. Besides Dr. Hughes's messages on Genesis, which I heard while serving at Wheaton College during 2001 to 2004, I have recently been gratified to hear sermons on Genesis preached by Dr. Harry Reeder at Briarwood Presbyterian Church in Birmingham, Alabama. Having visited forty to fifty conservative churches of various denominations over the past three years, I have found it unusual to hear any expository preaching of the type Dr. Hughes practices and have not heard any sermons on Old Testament narratives other than those preached by Dr. Reeder.

cellent commentaries, published sermons, handbooks, and articles on how to analyze these texts will result in more attention to these largely neglected passages, though such works are needed. Indeed, high quality works of these types have existed for some time. Without a fundamental change of perspective, it is unlikely a larger number of preachers will use the wonderful tools at their disposal for unlocking the riches of Old Testament narrative.

Old Testament Narratives and Application

One of the most repeated and yet ultimately unbiblical notions among Christians is the idea that preaching the Old Testament as God's Word for today must be treated as a particular type of *legitimate* problem to solve. Stated simply, preachers and hearers often act as if the Old Testament has something special to prove before it should be heard as Christian Scripture. Like many other teachers, preachers, and commentators, for years I offered rationales for reading, hearing, and studying the Old Testament based on an unwitting acquiescence to this belief. I did so with the good intention, or so I conceived it, of helping students and parishioners "apply the Bible to their lives." I wanted them to benefit from the Old Testament in ways I had appreciated it in my own life.

After years of trying to explain why the Old Testament matters for believers, I came to two basic conclusions. First, the New Testament writers do not treat the Old Testament as a problem to be solved but rather as God-breathed sacred writing (Scripture) to be obeyed (2 Tim. 3:16; see below). Second, when I incorrectly treated the Old Testament as the problem instead of putting upon my hearers a responsibility to obey the Old Testament, I actually made it harder for my students and parishioners to come to terms with the whole Word of God. Even though many Christians believe that the Old Testament must prove itself relevant before they are ready to consider it, it is unhelpful to these people to condone what is after all an erroneous and ultimately rebellious presupposition. Instead of accepting a common misconception, we are well advised to help people replace their incorrect presupposition with correct ones and then aid them in reading the Bible effectively.

The most important presupposition to give people today is that we, not the Bible, have something to prove. As Christopher Wright has argued, all of us must learn that the Christian life is not a matter of our becoming convinced of the benefits associated with "applying the Bible to our lives." Rather, we must realize and we must preach the opposite.

Through the power of the Holy Spirit we must learn and help others learn to "apply our lives to the Bible." God and his Word—not our lives and minds—comprise the horizon of reality and authority. We are required to conform to the Scriptures; they are not required to conform to us.[2]

Preachers must see their task as aiding their congregations in the process of applying their lives to the whole Bible. They must lead hearers to ask God in what ways he wishes their lives to matter by obeying his Word. In this way, they can obey God and learn what Paul means when he writes in 1 Corinthians that the Old Testament was written "for our sake" (9:10), "as examples for us" (10:6), and "for our instruction" (10:11). Without this starting point, preachers may be unaware that they are presenting the Word of God in a way that leaves hearers thinking they may pick and choose the parts they consider most valuable, or the parts that a preacher or teacher has redeemed from the ash heap by proving them worthy of consideration.

The Usefulness of Old Testament Narrative

Once the horizon of reality and obedience are fixed, those who preach from Old Testament narrative should keep some basic steadying principles about the Old Testament's accuracy and usefulness in mind. These principles will encourage new preachers to approach any biblical text with the assurance that it is something their congregations need. These principles may help veteran expository preachers avoid capitulating to the temptation to ignore the Old Testament in their preaching program. They might even keep both old and new preachers from shelving expository preaching of narratives for trendier, yet less biblically saturated and thus ultimately less helpful, approaches to preaching these passages.

I derive these principles from Paul's assertions about the Scriptures in 2 Timothy 3:16 because it is a classic statement of how the Bible coheres with the consistency of God's character and testifies to his helpful dealings with his people as revealed in the Bible. I also use principles from the New Testament at this point, because these writers were, like us, Christians seeking to preach and obey God's Word written as found in what we call the Old Testament. The passage is as follows: "All Scripture is breathed out by God and profitable for teaching, for reproof, for correction, and for training in righteousness."

---

2. Christopher Wright made these points in his sermon entitled "The View from God's Throne," an exposition of Rev. 4:1–11, which he preached at College Church, Wheaton, Illinois, on November 7, 2004.

In this passage Paul states his twofold conviction that the Bible is perfect and pure on the one hand and therefore useful on the other. This conviction is also found in key Old Testament passages (such as Ps. 19:7–14) that summarize the nature of Scripture. Paul's comments to Timothy about the Scriptures comprise a summary statement of how New Testament writers viewed the Old Testament, including its narratives, when they preached from its contents, for Jesus and Peter also agree with Paul's statements about the Scriptures (John 5:39; 2 Pet. 1:20–21).

Paul tells Timothy that "all Scripture is breathed out by God" (2 Tim. 3:16). There is little doubt that by "all Scripture" Paul means at least the whole Old Testament. He may also include at least some of what we know as the New Testament. After all, Peter calls Paul's letters part of "the Scriptures" (2 Pet. 3:16), so Paul may have had a similar opinion of Peter's writing and/or that of other apostles. William Mounce observes that the phrase "breathed out by God" indicates "the origin of every single element of the OT comes from God."[3] D. B. Knox adds that God's being the Bible's source means that the "Holy Scripture, since it is the word of God, is true in respect to all the things that God is saying through it. It will be infallible, that is to say, utterly reliable; it cannot be broken or proved wrong; it must be fulfilled."[4] In other words, the Old Testament is coherent and completely trustworthy, or inerrant, in every aspect of what it teaches because it comes from God, who is completely coherent and trustworthy.[5]

This last conclusion means, among other things, that the Old Testament cannot contradict itself. As Jesus says, "Scripture cannot be broken" (John 10:35), by which he means Scripture is not pitted against itself in interpretation. Furthermore, the Old Testament cannot be contradictory to the New Testament, since God's character lies behind both. As Article 7 of the 39 Articles of the Anglican Communion asserts, "The Old Testament is not contrary to the New: for both in the Old and New Testament everlasting life is offered to Mankind by Christ, who is the only mediator between God and Man. Wherefore they are not to be heard, which feign that the old Fathers did look only for transitory promises." The Article then distinguishes between the moral and ceremonial law,

---

3. William D. Mounce, *Pastoral Epistles*, World Biblical Commentary 46 (Nashville: Thomas Nelson, 2000), 566.

4. D. B. Knox, *Selected Works: Volume 1, The Doctrine of God*, ed. Tony Payne (Sydney: Matthias Media, 2000), 331.

5. See the excellent development of this thesis in Mounce, *Pastoral Epistles*, 566–70. See also Carl F. H. Henry, *God, Revelation and Authority* (1976; rprt. Wheaton, IL: Crossway, 1999), 69–76.

noting the Christian's duty to obey the moral law and implying that the ceremonial law has much to teach us as well.

Paul does not stop his exhortation to Timothy with his comments on the Bible's origins, coherence, and truthfulness. He proceeds to address the reasons God gave a revelation that so closely adheres to his own nature. Since the Scriptures are "breathed out by God," they are "profitable for teaching, for reproof, for correction, and for training in righteousness." God's perfect Word was given so that God's people could learn to obey him. Mounce writes that the word translated "teaching" (cf. 1 Tim. 1:10) is a technical term in the Pastoral Epistles "for the doctrinal formulation of Scripture (cf. especially 1 Tim. 4:13). It, not myths, is the basis of Timothy's ministry, as Paul emphasizes elsewhere (cf. Rom. 15:4)."[6] Mounce adds, "Scripture is the standard of truth, the pattern of truth (2 Tim. 1:13). Timothy is to guard it (2 Tim. 1:14) by using it to convict error."[7] Thus, "teaching" indicates the totality of what the Bible teaches on all subjects it addresses. This "teaching" constitutes the Bible's definition and application of key themes such as sin, salvation, the people of God, judgment of sin, and the coming of the kingdom of God at the end of world history.

This teaching is profitable for offering "reproof" to the people of God. The Greek word translated as "reproof" (*elegmos*) does not appear elsewhere in the New Testament, though 1 Timothy 5:20 and 2 Timothy 4:2 use cognates. Though it is possible that the term means "the conviction of false doctrine," as Mounce believes,[8] there may be other options related to this definition that are more precise. I. Howard Marshall writes that the term means "getting a person to realize that they have done wrong," and cites the Septuagint translation of Numbers 5:18–22 as evidence for his comment.[9] There *elegmos* appears when the water in the prescribed ritual is defined. Thus, in 5:18–19, the phrase translated "water of bitterness" in the English Standard Version could be translated "water of reproof." The ritual has a clear reproving purpose, so the latter translation is defensible.

Marshall could have added the fact that the Septuagint translation of Leviticus 19:17 includes *elegmos* in its description of how to treat one's neighbor. Moses tells Israel to avoid slander (19:16) and hating a neighbor in one's heart (19:17). Instead, one should reprove a neighbor openly and honestly (19:17) as a way of proving love for that neighbor

---

6. Mounce, *Pastoral Epistles*, 570.

7. Ibid.

8. Ibid.

9. I. Howard Marshall, *The Pastoral Epistles*, International Critical Commentary (Edinburgh: T. & T. Clark, 1999), 795.

(19:18). The context of Leviticus 19:16–18 coincides with Paul's context nicely, since both describe how to aid others in walking with God. It seems likely that Paul tells Timothy that the Bible does what Leviticus 19:17 encourages Israel to do: speak to the person in a reasonable and loving manner so that behavior can change, love can shape the relationship, and fellowship can continue. "Teaching," or "doctrine," supports and demands as much.

The Bible's teaching is also profitable "for correction." This is the only appearance of this word in the New Testament. Marshall writes that its basic lexical meaning is "correction, restoration, improvement," and that the flow of the passage from "reproof" to "correction" is a natural progression from the conviction of sin "to the recovery of the sinner to a better life."[10] T. D. Lea adds, "The term . . . suggests that Scripture helps individuals to restore their doctrine or personal practice to a right state before God. Correction is one means God uses in order to restore people to spiritual positions they have forfeited. This emphasis frequently appears in the wilderness experience of Israel (see Deut. 8:2–3, 5)."[11] Thus, when the Bible offers "correction," it is not simply for the purpose of addressing someone's faults to point out wrongdoing. Rather, it is for the purpose of changing behavior in order to restore that person to a proper relationship with God. The Bible both points out error and offers examples of how errors may be expunged and right living before God renewed.

Finally, the Scriptures are profitable for "training in righteousness." The word translated "training," *paideia*, involves discipline, correction, and instruction for the purpose of educating a person in a path of life.[12] It "means the rule of a good and holy life."[13] As Lea summarizes the matter, "A final use of Scripture is to provide moral training that leads to righteous living. This positive purpose is expressed by a term (*paideia*) that also appears in Ephesians 6:4 ("training"). There it denotes a system of discipline used by a parent to develop a Christian character in a child. Here it describes a system of discipline in Scripture that leads to a holy life-style."[14] The Bible does not simply offer a set of rules to be consulted in every situation, though it does include commands. Instead, it accepts the fact that a set of rules cannot address every situation that might

---

10. Ibid.

11. T. D. Lea and H. P. Griffin Jr., *1, 2 Timothy, Titus*, New American Commentary 34 (Nashville: Broadman, 1992), 237.

12. Marshall, *The Pastoral Epistles*, 795–96.

13. John Calvin, *Commentaries on the Epistles to Timothy, Titus, and Philemon*, trans. William Pringle (1854; repr., Grand Rapids, MI: Baker, 1996), 250. Calvin published the lecture from which this quotation is taken in 1556.

14. Lea and Griffin, *1, 2 Timothy, Titus*, 237.

arise in one's lifetime and emphasizes a biblically informed pattern of living that believers embrace and practice. Persons who have learned this principle have embraced the exhortation John Calvin offers at the end of his sermon on 2 Samuel 1:21–27: "In the end, let us learn how to govern ourselves in such a manner that he may rule over us, and have complete mastery and superiority. And may we not only be governed by the written laws, but may we have such obedience to his Word that it may cause us to conform ourselves entirely to it."[15]

Paul strongly implies that the Bible divulges a way of life that requires reading, reflection, the reception of teaching, hard thinking, application, and experience. This way of life is deepened in community and by the presence of teachers instructing in both formal and informal settings. These teachers may differ in a variety of ways, but they must all be deeply committed to the fact that the Bible trains them and their pupils in a specific pattern.

As has been implied in the preceding paragraphs, this specific pattern of training is "in righteousness." Mounce notes that here this term "is not only a gift bestowed but also a virtue to be sought (cf. 1 Tim. 6:11; 2 Tim. 2:22), the latter being emphasized in the PE [Pastoral Epistles] owing to their practical emphasis."[16] The context does not indicate that the believer's pattern of life is a training leading to the reception of righteousness by that person's merits but rather the development of a pattern of life in which a believer learns to practice "righteous behavior (cf. Eph. 4:24)."[17] The same source that lies behind the Scriptures empowers the believer to live in such a manner: The Holy Spirit.

When believers hear the Bible preached, they have the opportunity to learn God-breathed patterns of teaching (doctrine). When necessary, this teaching reproves them as one reproves a neighbor one loves (Lev. 19:16–18). Believers who open their minds and lives to reproof then have the chance to have their beliefs and behavior corrected and their relationship with God and God's people restored. Those who make a habit of gaining doctrine, reproof, and correction from the Bible and from biblical preachers learn permanent patterns that they practice in order to maintain righteous ways of living. In short, they have begun to gain what God wishes them to gain from the Bible. The preacher's task is to help hearers arrive at this point regularly and to a growing extent over a lifetime of Christian service. What preachers must never doubt is that

---

15. John Calvin, *Sermons on 2 Samuel: Chapters 1–13*, trans. Douglas Kelly (Edinburgh: Banner of Truth, 1992), 47. The quotation comes from Calvin's sermon on 2 Sam. 1:21–27 entitled "Calmness in All Circumstances," which was preached June 2, 1562.

16. Mounce, *Pastoral Epistles*, 570.

17. Marshall, *The Pastoral Epistles*, 796.

all Scripture is part of this development of healthy Christian belief and behavior. They do not have to make the Old Testament part of this process; it is already part of the process by divine inspiration and declaration.

The Narrative Shape of the Old Testament in Apostolic Preaching

Preachers need a sense of the Bible's wholeness if they are to present any portion of the Bible in both its immediate and broader context. Part of this wholeness lies in the Scriptures' common story line. This story line includes key characters, events, and themes that span from creation to new creation, as William Dumbrell has observed.[18] These elements provide the data from which the Bible's theological wholeness comes. Therefore, preachers do not need to shape the Bible into a coherent narrative; they simply need to recognize the narrative the Bible provides for itself.

One way of seeing the Bible's narrative wholeness is to examine the apostolic preaching described in Acts, for these sermons often include a grand narrative that traces the Christian story from Old Testament times until the time the sermon is preached.[19] Such recounting of the great events of salvation history is in continuity with the several similar summaries that appear in every segment of the Old Testament. I have surveyed some of those Old Testament passages elsewhere, so I will not analyze them here.[20] Rather, I will note the ways that Stephen and Paul use this grand narrative to address three very different audiences. My goal is to encourage expository preachers to see that the Bible itself divulges the larger narrative to which shorter narratives contribute and also to encourage them to use narratives to help hearers live the Christian life.

Acts 7:2–54: Stephen's Narrative of Rebellious Israelites

In Acts 6:5 Luke identifies Stephen as one of the men chosen to handle the daily distribution of aid to widows and describes him as "full

---

18. See his *The Search for Order: Biblical Eschatology in Focus* (Grand Rapids, MI: Eerdmans, 1994).

19. The two classic works on this subject are C. H. Dodd, *The Apostolic Preaching and Its Developments* (New York: Harper, 1936) and William Mounce, *The Essential Nature of New Testament Preaching* (Grand Rapids, MI: Eerdmans, 1960).

20. See Paul R. House, "Examining the Narratives of Old Testament Narrative," *Westminster Theological Journal* 67, no. 2 (Fall 2005): 229–46.

of faith and the Holy Spirit." In 6:8 Luke adds that Stephen was "full of grace and power" and that he was "doing great wonders and signs among the people." This ministry led to disputes with the temple council (6:9–15). When asked by the high priest to give the council an account of his beliefs (7:1) to answer the accusation brought against him, that he taught that Jesus would destroy the temple (6:14), Stephen offered a message that explained his commitment to Jesus (7:2–53).

This message begins with Abraham (7:2–8), a logical choice since the audience was Jewish, probably dominated by Sadducees and politically motivated clerics, and quite aware of the biblical story line. At least some of this group were therefore likely to have considered the Pentateuch the only binding Scripture, and they were quite interested in Stephen's views on the temple's purpose and future (6:14). Stephen continues by recounting episodes in the lives of the patriarchs and Moses (7:9–44) before turning to the tabernacle and Solomon's temple. This summary of Israel's story is punctuated by comments about negative events, such as the jealousy of Joseph's brothers (7:9), the majority of Israel's rejection of Moses (7:35, 39), and the golden calf incident (7:40–43). Stephen adds his belief that the temple is important, yet not the place where the Creator actually dwells (7:44–50). He then concludes by connecting his hearers to the wicked people of the past, noting that their fathers killed the prophets and they have killed the Messiah, "the Righteous One" (7:51–52). He accuses them of not obeying the law they say was "delivered by angels" (7:53). Of course, his sermon leads to his martyrdom (7:54–60).

In this narrative-driven sermon, Stephen makes several important choices. He does not stray beyond the Scriptures his audience accepts as coming from God. He chooses episodes from Israel's story that address the subject the council set before him, yet in a way that includes examples of the sort of rebellion he believes them guilty of currently. He ends with Jesus but assumes that his listeners know his beliefs about the recent death and resurrection of Jesus. He does not feel the need to include Jesus in Old Testament stories that do not address the Messiah, but he does preach to that point in history, for it is the climax of the story. He conceives of Israel's rebellion and its manifestation in his day as a terrible, yet highly instructive, narrative. He certainly uses this narrative to attempt to teach, reprove, correct, and train his hearers in the ways of Scripture. There is no record of anyone accepting his message, but in an excellent bit of foreshadowing Luke notes that a young man named Saul heard the sermon (7:58).

Acts 13:13–49: Paul's Narrative of God's Message of Salvation

During his first missionary journey, Paul preached in the synagogue at Antioch of Pisidia. His audience consisted of Jews and God-fearers (13:16, 26) who worshiped there regularly, so it is likely he expected from the crowd a fair amount of biblical knowledge. He did not address persons with little or no understanding of the Old Testament, as he did in Lystra (14:8–18) and Athens (17:16–34; see below). Indeed, he spoke in a context in which passages from the Law and Prophets had already been read (13:15). Like Stephen in Acts 7:2–54, he tailored his message to the audience at hand through means of presenting an overarching narrative that included his hearers.

Paul begins by mentioning briefly the patriarchs, the exodus, and Israel's wilderness years (13:17–18). Next, he proceeds to summarize the conquest of Canaan and the era of the judges so that he can reach the point of Israel's request for a king (13:19–21a). Paul then introduces David as the king through whom God gave Israel a Savior, whom he identifies as Jesus (13:21b–23). Interestingly, he includes in his narrative a statement about John the Baptist's testimony to Jesus (13:24–25), which may indicate that some in the congregation had knowledge of John's ministry or had even received "the baptism of John" (Acts 18:25). If so, Paul wants these people to understand that what the Old Testament and John promised had come to pass.

Having set the stage for the major portion of his sermon, Paul proceeds to present Jesus' life and ministry for the purpose of pressing upon the congregation their need to believe the "message of this salvation" (13:26). First, he asserts that the leaders in Jerusalem did not accept Jesus because they did not understand the Scriptures. In an extreme irony, they did not understand the Scriptures, but they "fulfilled them by condemning him" (13:27). Second, Paul claims that though Jesus was not worthy of death, the ones who did not understand the Scriptures asked the Roman official Pilate to crucify him. Pilate obliged, and afterwards Jesus was buried (13:28–29).

Third, Paul proceeds to the irreplaceable core of the Christian message: the resurrection.[21] He proclaims, "But God raised him from the dead, and for many days he appeared to those who had come up with him from Galilee to Jerusalem, who are now his witnesses to the people" (13:30–31; see 1 Cor. 15:3–7). The import of this fact is that Paul brings them "the news" (the gospel), the divine proclamation, that God has

---

21. In 1 Cor. 15:1–58 Paul states quite plainly that without the resurrection, Christianity is a false religion that tells lies about God. Also, every one of the apostolic messages includes the resurrection.

fulfilled his promise of sending a messiah and raising him from the dead. Paul cites Psalms 2 and 16 to confirm his point (13:32–35). He says Jesus' resurrection makes him the greatest figure in Israel's history, for it places him above David (13:36–37) and Moses (13:39).

Fourth, Paul explains the meaning of the story he has related. Hearers should know that through Jesus, forgiveness of sins is possible (13:38). What "the law of Moses" could not do (because it was not its purpose), Jesus has done. He has removed sin forever (13:38–39). Thus, the congregation must believe (13:38) and not harden its hearts at this message, the very danger the prophet Habakkuk, whom Paul quotes, warned Israel to avoid (13:40–41; Hab. 1:5). Unbelief will lead them to "perish" (13:41), for judgment approaches, just as it did in Habakkuk's day. What makes Paul's news "good news" is that his "news is not only of the judgment but more significantly of salvation in that judgment."[22] Paul's hearers can avoid repeating the negative aspects of the narrative Paul presents. They can participate in a new ending to the story they have heard.

Interestingly, the story Luke tells about Paul telling the biblical story continues in the description of the people's reaction to the message. Apparently many persons believed, or at least wished very much to hear more (13:42–43). So Paul preached the next Sabbath, drawing large crowds (13:44) but also much criticism and opposition. Luke writes, "But when the Jews saw the crowds, they were filled with jealousy and began to contradict what was spoken by Paul, reviling him" (13:45).

Given this response, Paul claims that God's Word had to be proclaimed to Jews first, but the Jews' rejection of the message, which amounted to a repetition of the negative parts of Israelite history, means it is time to take the message to the Gentiles (13:46). God has made the apostles servants of the Suffering Servant, so they must do what he came to do: be "a light for the Gentiles, that [they] may bring salvation to the ends of the earth" (13:47; citing Isa. 49:6). The story of God's salvation of people from sin and judgment must go "to the ends of the earth," and the apostles and their team members are God's means of doing just that. The reaction to Paul's ending of the narrative is threefold: "as many as were appointed to eternal life believed" (13:48), the Word of God spread throughout that region (13:49), and those who did not believe persecuted the apostles, driving them from the area (13:50–51).

There are several important implications of Paul's sermon for today's preachers. First, like Stephen, the apostle Paul conceived of salvation history as a connected series of events that explain what happened in

---

22. D. B. Knox, *Selected Works: Volume 3, The Christian Life,* ed. Tony Payne and Karen Beilharz (Sydney: Matthias Media, 2006), 40.

world and Israelite history as depicted in God's Word. Jesus and his apostles and their ministries to Israel and the Gentiles are the latest installment of that story, but these are not unexpected or illegitimate additions to the story, for the Scriptures had already stated that they would minister God's news of redemption from sin and judgment. Second, Paul uses the Scriptures to teach, reprove, correct, and train his hearers in God's ways. He wants them to realize what God has done, believe it, and move forward in the grace of God, which is following Jesus. Third, Paul has no qualms about drawing analogies between his audience and the people described in the Old Testament. He feels very comfortable applying their lives to Scripture. Fourth, Jesus is at the center of the narrative, yet he is not the whole narrative. He is also not inserted into every phase of the narrative. Abraham, Moses, David, and Paul have their parts as well. These other characters and their story are sub-stories within the great story. Not telling their stories impoverishes an understanding of Jesus' story and of the story of final redemption and resurrection that Jesus will complete. Inserting Jesus at the wrong places can lead to a diminishing of what he achieved. Of course, leaving Jesus out would leave an unfinished story that lacks the possibility of the sort of good news Paul offers.

Acts 17:22-31: Paul's Narrative of the Creator and the Resurrection

This brief passage is often used to demonstrate ways to present the gospel to persons who do not have extensive backgrounds in Christianity. This emphasis is appropriate, since Paul speaks to "Epicurean and Stoic philosophers" (17:18) and those they assemble (17:19) to hear his new (to them) teaching. The narrative he shapes for this audience begins at a different place from the one he gives in the synagogue in Acts 13:13–41, but it ends at the same place as the one offered to a more biblically literate audience.

Having perceived their religious, yet idolatrous, context, Paul begins his recounting of the biblical narrative with creation. He identifies "the unknown god" to which the Athenians have erected an altar (17:22–23) as the creator of the universe (17:24). The Creator is a spirit, does not live in a temple, and does not need sacrifices to survive (17:24–25). The Creator made all of humanity from one man, and the Creator rules all people (17:26). All that Paul has said so far coincides with the Old Testament's theology of creation, which in turn fuels the Old Testament's insistence that there is only one living and true God.

Paul then asserts that the import of his creation doctrine is that people should seek and find this Creator, who alone is God (17:27). He claims God is not far away but, rather, quite close, as some of their philosophers and poets have written (17:28). In order to find the Creator, people must reject notions and rituals that connect him to images (17:29). They must turn away from such notions ("repent"), for God has fixed a day of judgment, has chosen a man to be the judge on that day, and has raised that man from the dead to assure people of his intentions (17:30–31).

Paul's message to the Athenians shares some key aspects of the narrative he and Stephen have already preached in Acts and displays one clear difference. Like the other messages, it moves from a beginning point to a clear conclusion. It seeks to move hearers to faith in Jesus. It includes judgment and the resurrection as indispensable components of the Christian message. It begins where the hearers are in relationship to their understanding of the Bible and their need for salvation. It differs in where it begins, for it starts with the audience's belief in creation, asserts the biblical doctrine of creation, and concludes with what will eventually happen to creation. Paul's use of creation here is not a theological innovation, for his hearers in Acts 13 would have agreed with his account of creation theology based on their knowledge of passages like Genesis 1–2, Isaiah 40–48, and Jeremiah 10:1–16.

Conclusion

Expository preachers should take their sense of the Bible's grand narrative from these descriptions of early Christian preaching. Stephen and Paul preached an account of salvation history that encompasses God's good work from creation to final judgment. This work includes the covenants with Israel and the nations that were given to Abraham, Moses, and David. It includes the sending of Jesus the Messiah and his life, death, and resurrection. It includes a coming judgment that all persons must face. Stephen and Paul also stressed the necessity of hearers' displaying a right response to God's message that can be summarized as believing in Jesus, which means believing in all that has been said about Jesus. Their message required those who believed to join the community of those who believed and to live according to that community's standards.[23] This

---

23. Graeme Goldsworthy treats this emphasis in his stressing of God's people living in God's kingdom in his *Gospel and Kingdom: A Christian Interpretation of the Old Testament* (Carlisle: Paternoster, 1994).

believing response was rooted in their belief in the resurrection and its connection to judgment.[24] Other themes were included in their preaching, but these comprise the core of the biblical narrative.

Preachers should keep this sweeping narrative in mind as they preach through any narrative segment of the Bible. They will then be in a position to do what Stephen and Paul did, which was to apply the lives of their hearers to the biblical narrative in a manner that instructed, reproved, corrected, and trained those who believed their message, which was indeed God's message. They will be prepared to mine the text at hand for life-changing teaching and to set that text in its proper place in the overall biblical story line. They will be prepared to preach about Jesus from any text without inserting Jesus into texts that do not mention him or the messianic promise.

Preaching the Old Testament with Confidence

Embracing the principles I have outlined in this essay will not solve all the expositor's problems related to preaching Old Testament narratives. There will still be hard exegetical work to do. Translations from the Hebrew, as well as fruitful analysis of the passage's genre, structure, theology, and chief means of instructing, reproving, correcting, and training still must be attained from the text. Congregations must still be taught to read, hear, and engage in longer passages of the Bible. Preachers must still read, reflect, and pray. In other words, the sort of struggle Kent Hughes had in preaching Genesis will continue in the lives of careful and caring expositors. There is no easy road in this process.

In this essay I have encouraged preachers to believe that the effort is definitely worth the price they will pay and that to believe these principles is a first step to paying this price. I have asserted that what preachers have in the Old Testament narratives is truly astounding. They have God's promise that what they share with their hearers is breathed out by the Holy Spirit, the same Holy Spirit who convicts hearts and teaches believers. They have the great purpose of being God's instrument for training God's people in the path of faithful living. They have a great narrative that incorporates all human beings and all human history into a story that leads sinners to be saved and believers to sanctification. They have many great examples of smaller narratives that fit into this grand narrative that can help hearers in personal ways. They have a means of seeing how the Bible is a unified literary and theological

---

24. So Knox is justified to call preachers back to preaching judgment as the necessary prelude to preaching forgiveness. See *Selected Works: Volume 1*, 189–203.

work. Since such is the case, preachers may have the confidence that as they preach the whole Bible, they will see God do his work in his people through his Word. In short, I think we must not let an unstated lack of faith in God's Word become a stumbling block for preaching all of God's true, helpful Word so that disciples may apply their lives to its large and small narratives.

3

The Bible as Literature and Expository Preaching

Leland Ryken

I am persuaded that without knowledge of literature pure theology cannot at all endure, just as heretofore, when letters [the old name for literature] have declined and lain prostrate, theology, too, has wretchedly fallen and lain prostrate; nay, I see that there has never been a great revelation of the Word of God unless He has first prepared the way by the rise and prosperity of languages and letters, as though they were John the Baptists. . . . Certainly it is my desire that there shall be as many poets and rhetoricians as possible, because I see that by these studies, as by no other means, people are wonderfully fitted for the grasping of sacred truth and for handling it skillfully and happily. —Martin Luther*

What does literature have to do with expository preaching?" That is what a preacher asked with incredulity when I told him that I was coauthoring a book on expository preaching. In my mind, it remains a question that should never have been asked. I have also pondered *why* the question arose.

What the question signals is an inadequate understanding of literature and literary analysis. As an extension of that, when I encounter resistance to the idea of the Bible as literature, the objections almost always turn out to be based on incorrect views of what it means that a piece of writing is literature. The procedures of what literary scholars call "explication of the text" (*explication de texte*) and the methodology of an expository sermon are nearly identical. The only difference is that a sermon adds certain elements to a literary explication of a text. As Kent Hughes expressed it to me informally, all biblical exposition is literary analysis.

The burden of the present essay is to assert that although good expository preachers intuitively practice an incipient literary criticism, they could enhance their expository sermons significantly if they would add even a modicum of self-conscious literary analysis to their methodology. By expository preaching I mean preaching in which the central feature is the preacher's choosing a text that is neither too short nor too long to be completely analyzed in a single sermon. Two further features of such preaching are that it (1) keeps its focus on the announced text instead of escaping from it to other material, and (2) interacts with the chosen text in terms of the kind of writing that it is instead of immediately extracting a series of theological propositions from it.

With the foregoing as a point of departure, I will devote the remainder of my discussion to the following four subjects: first, if we are to approach the Bible as literature, we need to understand what it *means* that the Bible is literature. Second, we need to go beyond mere acknowledgement that the Bible is literary to an understanding and practice of what it means to *approach* the Bible as literature. Third, we need to take an honest look at ways in which preachers have generally neglected an important tool of biblical exposition by their indifference to literary analysis of the Bible. Finally, I will outline the advantages that can come through a commitment to correct this current neglect.

The Bible as Literature

Three primary modes of writing converge in the Bible—theological, historical, and literary. Overwhelmingly, theology and history are embodied in literary forms. A crucial hermeneutical principle thus needs to be established right at the outset: meaning is communicated *through form,* starting with the very words of a text but reaching beyond that to considerations of literary genre and style. We cannot properly speak about the theological or moral content of a story or poem (for example) without first interacting with the story or poem.

Literary form exists prior to content in the sense that no content exists apart from the form in which it is embodied. As a result, the first responsibility of a reader or interpreter is to assimilate the form of a discourse. Without the literary form, the content does not even exist.

The concept of literary form needs to be construed very broadly here. Anything having to do with *how* a biblical author has expressed his message constitutes literary form. Further, we can profitably ponder the implications of the statement of fiction writer Flannery O'Connor that storytellers speak "*with* character and action, not *about* character and action."[1] What this means is that biblical writers do not simply tell us *about* Abraham's life, the daily routine of a shepherd (Psalm 23), and the indulgent lifestyle of the wealthy of Amos's time (Amos 6:4–6), but *by means of* these things about God, people, and life.

The Idea of "the Bible as Literature"

The idea of the Bible as literature began with the Bible itself. The writers of the Bible refer with technical precision to a whole range of literary genres in which they write—proverb, saying, chronicle, complaint [lament psalm], oracle, apocalypse, parable, song, epistle, and many another.

Furthermore, some of the forms that we find in the Bible correspond to the literary forms current in the authors' surrounding cultures. For example, the Ten Commandments are cast into the form of suzerain treaties that ancient Near Eastern kings imposed on their subjects, and the New Testament epistles, despite unique features, show many affinities to Greek and Roman letters of the same era.

Mainly, though, we can look to the Bible itself to see the extent to which it is a literary book. Virtually every page of the Bible is replete with literary technique, and to possess the individual texts of the Bible fully, we need to read the Bible as literature, just as we need to read it theologically and (in the narrative parts) historically.

With these preliminary principles in place, I will delineate three features that make up the overarching genre that we know as literature. To keep my discussion manageable, I will illustrate all of my generalizations from the story of Cain (Gen. 4:1–16).

The Voice of Human Experience

Literature is identifiable first of all by its subject matter. The subject of literature is human experience, rendered concretely. We can profitably contrast literary writing to expository (informational) writing on this point. The staple of expository discourse is the propositional statement, often tending toward abstraction or generality. The sixth

---

1. Sally and Robert Fitzgerald, eds., *Mystery and Manners* (New York: Farrar, Straus & Giroux, 1957), 76 (emphasis in original).

40

commandment is an example of expository discourse: "You shall not murder" (Ex. 20:13).

Literature, by contrast, is incarnational in the sense that it embodies ideas and meaning in the form of characters, settings, actions, and images. It aims to get a reader to share an experience, not primarily to grasp ideas. The truth that literature imparts is thus partly *truthfulness to human experience*, not simply ideas that are true. The sixth commandment gives us the precept; the story of Cain gives us the example, without using the abstraction "murder" we should note, and without the injunction that we are to refrain from murder.

There is a certain irreducible quality to a literary text in the sense that a propositional summary of it—an idea that we extract from the particulars—never adequately represents the meaning of the text. Flannery O'Connor expressed this in terms that virtually all literary critics would accept: "the whole story is the meaning, because it is an experience, not an abstraction."[2]

Because literature is truthful to human experience, it is universal. History and the news tell us what *happened*, whereas literature tells us what *happens*—what is true for all people in all places and times. Of course a text can do both of these, and the Bible does so, but to the extent to which it is literary, a text is filled with recognizable human experience.

The story of Cain, despite the ostensible remoteness of the text from the modern world, contains an abundance of recognizable human experience. Part of what is up to date is the *literary* categories that we find in the story: murder story; detective story; crime and punishment. Because the focus of the story is family living, many of the recognizable experiences are domestic in nature: domestic violence; the problem child and the model child; the parents who are disillusioned by the failure of their early hopes for their children; the domineering older sibling; the victimized younger sibling; sibling rivalry. Moral and spiritual experience are also represented: giving in to temptation; envy; harboring a grudge; lack of self-control; moral indifference ("Am I my brother's keeper?"); murder; guilt. An additional cluster consists of attitudes toward authority: defiance; lying toward a (divine) parent; anger at having gotten caught; being forced to submit to the judgment administered by an authority figure. There are also experiences that fall loosely under the rubric of social and psychological experience: self-pity; the hardened criminal without regret; the outcast; the futile attempt to cover up a crime.

---

2. Sally and Robert Fitzgerald, eds., *Mystery and Manners*, 73.

We need to hear the voice of authentic human experience from the pulpit, and an incorrect stereotype is that expository preaching does not give it, whereas topical preaching does, especially when couched in the confessional mode. For the expository preacher, the avenue toward giving voice to authentic human experience lies in the literary nature of the Bible. To gain relevance, all a preacher needs to do is explicate the human experiences that are embedded in the literary parts of the Bible.

Literary Genres

The most customary way to define literature is by the external genres (types or kinds of writing) in which its content is expressed. The two main genres in the Bible are narrative and poetry. Numerous categories cluster under each of these. Narrative subtypes, for example, include hero story, gospel, epic, tragedy, comedy (a U-shaped plot with a happy ending), and parable. Specific poetic genres keep multiplying as well: lyric, lament psalm, praise psalm, love poem, nature poem, epithalamion (wedding poem), and many others.

But those are only the tip of the iceberg. In addition to narrative and poetry, we find prophecy, visionary writing, apocalypse, pastoral, encomium, oratory, drama (the book of Job), satire, and epistle. Then if we add more specific forms like travel story, dramatic monologue, doom song, and Christ hymn, the number of literary genres in the Bible readily exceeds one hundred. C. S. Lewis has said famously that "there is a . . . sense in which the Bible, since it is after all literature, cannot properly be read except as literature; and the different parts of it as the different sorts of literature they are."[3]

The importance of genre to biblical interpretation is that genres have their own methods of procedure and rules of interpretation. An awareness of genre should program our encounter with a text, alerting us to what we can expect to find. Additionally, considerations of genre should govern the terms in which we interact with a text, so that with narrative, for example, we know that we are on the right track if we pay attention to plot, setting, and character.

There is too much to say about these things in the story of Cain to attempt a full explication. In every verse of the story, setting plays an important role, and this emerges if we use the formula "_____ scene" or "scene of _____." Thus the story begins with a

---

3. C. S. Lewis, *Reflections on the Psalms* (New York: Macmillan, 1958), 3.

sex scene and a birth scene. It is followed by a work scene, a scene of worship, a counseling scene, a judgment scene, a scene of wandering, and so forth. According to verse 7, most profoundly the stage on which the action occurs is the soul of Cain.

The plot of this story of crime and punishment focuses on the character of the criminal Cain. The sequence is as follows: the criminal's family, vocational, and religious background (vv. 1–4a); the motive for the crime (vv. 4b–5); the criminal's counseling history (vv. 6–7); the circumstances of the crime (v. 8); the arrest, interrogation, and sentencing (vv. 9–12); the appeal and modification of the sentence (vv. 13–15); serving the sentence (v. 16). Well-made plots are a seamless progression, and this story illustrates it.

When we turn to characterization, the cast of primary characters is two—God and Cain. Abel is the exemplary human character, but he is an accessory character who occasions the main action but does not actively participate in it. The protagonist of the story—the "first struggler" (literal meaning of *protagonist*) with whom we go through the action—is Cain, and the key to his characterization is that the story is an ever-expanding exposure of his bad actions and attitudes. The authority figure in the story is God, and the chief attributes that we can trace are his benevolence toward Cain and his judgment of the sinner.

A biblical scholar who caught the vision for a literary approach to the Bible has written regarding Bible stories, "A story is a story is a story. It cannot be boiled down to a meaning," that is, adequately treated at the level of theological abstraction.[4] A person listening to an expository sermon on the story of Cain should be aware from start to finish that the text being explicated is a narrative, not a theological treatise. The text exists to be relived in its fullness, not dipped into as a source of proof texts for moral and theological generalizations.

Literary Resources of Language

Literature also uses distinctive resources of language that set it apart from ordinary expository discourse. The most obvious example is poetry, inasmuch as poets speak a language all their own, consisting of images and figures of speech. The most important of the special resources of language that push a text into the category of literature include the following: imagery, metaphor, simile, symbol, allusion, irony, wordplay,

---

4. John Drury, *Luke* (New York: Macmillan, 1973), 217.

43

hyperbole, apostrophe (direct address to someone or something absent as though present), personification, paradox, and pun.

Some of these linguistic resources are present in the story of Cain. In an evocative metaphor (or personification), sin is pictured as a predatory monster ready to pounce on Cain (v. 7). Cain's rhetorical question, "Am I my brother's keeper?" (v. 9), rises to the level of aphorism, as does Cain's statement, "My punishment is greater than I can bear" (v. 13). The blood of Abel is personified, as is the ground (vv. 10–11). Rhetorical formulas include the curse (v. 11) and the number formula "sevenfold" (v. 15). The story ends with irony and wordplay, inasmuch as the land in which Cain "settled" is Nod, which means "wandering" (v. 16). More generally, the story exploits the resources of suspense, as we are repeatedly led to wonder whether Cain will respond appropriately to the opportunities that God puts before him to conquer his bent toward making wrong choices.

The expository preacher, like the literary critic, approaches a biblical text on the premise that whatever was important enough for the writer to include in a text is important to the expositor as well. If rhetoric, style, and special resources of language leap out at us from virtually every page of the Bible, we need to take note of them and do something with them when expounding the Bible.

Approaching the Bible as Literature

Many Bible expositors would assent to all that I have said about the literary nature of the Bible, only to ignore it when they stand in the pulpit. Mere assent to the idea that the Bible is a literary anthology has not produced a literary approach to the Bible. The payoff *should* have been straightforward; by definition, a literary approach to the Bible is one that does justice to the literary aspects of the Bible as I have outlined them. The following is a brief checklist.

First, literary analysis brings out the universal human experiences embodied in a passage. Literature is the human race's testimony to its own experience. It does not consist primarily of ideas but instead the accurate portrayal of human experience as lived in the world. The test of whether an expository preacher has dealt adequately with a text at this level is simple: if listeners have been led to see their own experiences in the text and its exposition, the expositor has interacted with the subject matter in keeping with its literary nature.

Second, a literary analysis of a text identifies the genre and interacts with the text in terms appropriate to that genre. This means that (for example) with a story, an expositor talks about plot conflict moving to resolution, story patterns such as ordeal or the temptation motif, characterization, and the role of setting in the action. Such interaction does justice to the specificity of a text. It does not reduce every passage to a set of theological propositions, and it avoids making every exposition seem as though the Bible consists of only one type of writing.

Third, interaction with a biblical text has been appropriately literary if the expositor has identified and commented on such linguistic and rhetorical features of the text as patterning, figurative language, and the style in which a biblical author has couched his content. If those aspects of a text were unimportant to an author, he would not have incorporated them into his writing. But inasmuch as the biblical writers did incorporate these features, they are worthy of attention.

Of course preachers need to be relieved of anxieties about the idea of the Bible as literature before they can be expected to endorse literary analysis as part of their expository preaching. Let me allay possible anxieties by asserting the following:

- As noted above, the idea of the Bible as literature is implicit in the Bible itself and can be inferred from some of the generic names that biblical writers apply to their writings. The idea of the Bible as literature is not a concoction of modernity.

- Such towering figures from the past as Augustine, Luther, and Calvin did not doubt that the Bible has literary features. To speak of the Bible as literature is to put oneself in good and respectable company.

- To speak of the Bible as literature need not imply theological liberalism. Among the ranks of those who conduct literary criticism of the Bible, one can find exactly the same range of evangelical orthodoxy and theological liberalism that one finds in biblical scholarship at large. The literary study of the Bible can and should begin where any other kind of biblical study begins—by accepting as true everything that biblical writers say about the Bible.

- While fictionality is a common characteristic of literature, it is not a necessary feature of it. The literary nature of a text depends on the writer's selectivity and molding of material and the presence of artistry and stylistic excellence, regardless of whether the content is factual history/biography or made up.

- A literary approach to the Bible need not imply *only* a literary approach, any more than a historical approach implies *only* a concern with history or a theological approach *only* an interest in theology.

- In regard to the theological approach, we need to remind ourselves that such an approach is no guarantee of accuracy or truthfulness. Scholars taking a theological approach to the Bible have sometimes strayed as far from the truth as some literary and historical scholars have strayed. To theologize is not inherently "safe," as many Christians incorrectly assume. The privileging of theology over other ways of handling the Bible has provided a false and dangerous sense of security.

- To view the Bible as literature does not by itself impair one's belief in the inspiration of biblical writers by the Holy Spirit. Our beginning premise must be that everything that we find in the Bible came by inspiration and was safeguarded by the Holy Spirit. If, then, we find an abundance of literary forms in the Bible, we should conclude that God inspired those literary forms, reminding ourselves at the same time that there is no content apart from the forms in which it is embodied.

Contemporary Expository Preaching and the Bible as Literature

If we measure contemporary expository preaching by the hermeneutical principles that I have outlined (all of them variations on the main principle of doing justice to the literary characteristics that the Bible actually displays), I would say with regret that the record is one of widespread neglect. It is largely a history of missed opportunities, though not in an absolute sense, of course.

With close attentiveness and a lot of filling in of gaps, a listener with literary sensitivities can often pick up snatches of character analysis and exploration of the dynamics of plot in biblical stories. By supplying some missing terminology, a listener can see that the meanings of images and figurative language have been unpacked in biblical poetry (though attendees at evangelical church services are unlikely to hear sermons preached on the poetic parts of the Bible, which is itself a symptom of inattention to the literary nature of the Bible). But why should it require a person with literary sophistication to pick up the latent clues that a preacher is expounding a literary text in keeping with the kind of text that it is? Attentiveness to the literary dimension of the Bible should be foregrounded in expository sermons.

If we ask how much has been lost by the inattentiveness of many expository preachers to the literary features of the Bible, I believe that the loss has been immense. We are in a situation similar to that of the church in Roger Bacon's day (thirteenth century). Bacon claimed that the church had done a good job of communicating the theological content of the Bible but had failed to make the literal level of the biblical text come alive in people's imaginations.

In an online course on the Bible as literature that I teach for the general public, a recent posting by an enrollee asked this question: "Why do most preachers choose to remain silent about engaging with the Bible as literature?" The answers are multiple.

Most preachers have never been committed to the idea that the Bible is literature. Many of them know at a subsurface level that the Bible is literary, but it has never gained the sovereignty of their minds, and in fact it has not excited enough interest to prompt them to explore what promise a literary approach to the Bible might afford in their preaching.

Furthermore, preachers are the product of their seminary or graduate school education. They handle the Bible as their education taught them. With few exceptions, the teaching they received was deficient in regard to the literary dimension of the Bible. For the most part, seminaries pay lip service to the idea of the Bible as literature. Students may be introduced to literary approaches to the Bible as part of a menu of approaches, but the goal is simply to ensure that students have been exposed to these approaches. It was never the intention of professors that students would actually apply these approaches in a systematic and regular way when they entered the ministry. Lacking models for applying literary methods of analysis to the Bible, preachers have naturally not regarded such analysis as having practical importance to them.

Finally, preachers (again prompted by their education) have assumed that traditional ways of handling the Bible by seminary professors and graduates are all that are necessary. After all, biblical scholars and preachers are the ones to whom lay people have entrusted the task of interpreting the Bible. What need does the guild have to seek input beyond itself?

But the whole premise here is faulty. In any sphere of life, it makes sense to seek the help of experts when undertaking a project. If I intend to build a deck on the back of my house, I am well advised to purchase a book on the subject and perhaps hire the services of a deck builder. If I need to give a theological talk to a Sunday school class, it behooves me to look closely at how theologians deal with their material, and perhaps to interact with a pastor on whether I am expressing the material as a theologian would.

If we ask who is most expert in literary analysis of a work of literature, my answer is that the people who know most about literary analysis are English teachers who teach literature day-in and day-out in high school and college classrooms. Preachers have not sought the help of people who know the most about literary analysis. Literary scholars are rarely given a seat at the table of hermeneutical and homiletic theory and practice.

What Literary Analysis Can Add to Expository Preaching

What, then, can literary analysis add to expository preaching? I would hope that my answers will make the prospect of incorporating a literary approach into expository preaching appealing to expository preachers. As I outline the advantages, it will be apparent that by literary criticism I mean traditional literary criticism, not the bewildering and highly technical critical approaches that have dominated upper-level literary scholarship for the past four decades. I do not envision anything more technical than the methods of analysis that are instilled in any good high school or college literature course.

First, then, a literary approach to a biblical text provides the best possible antidote to a nearly universal tendency of seminary graduates to translate biblical texts into a series of abstract theological propositions. Theologically educated preachers do not see this tendency as a problem because they love theological discourse. Nonetheless, the immediate move toward theological abstraction *is* a problem if the goals are those of expository preaching.

The aim of expository preaching is to unfold a biblical passage—to relive the passage—from beginning to end and in keeping with the kind of writing that it is. Only a tiny percentage of the Bible is couched as theological exposition. There is, indeed, a place for spinning out a series of moral and theological propositions in an expository sermon, but that place is *after* the text has been experienced as a piece of writing and never as a substitute for reliving the text in terms of the kind of writing that it is. A literary approach to a biblical text can serve as a warden to block a common practice of viewing virtually every passage in the Bible primarily as a collection of theological or moral ideas. Many people who value the Bible most highly as a spiritual authority experience the Bible in large part as a repository of proof texts for theological ideas—quite contrary to the actual form in which the Bible comes to us, namely, a literary anthology.

The positive counterpart to this negative function of preventing immediate theological and moral reductionism is that application of the tools of literary analysis to literary texts opens the door to improved precision in identifying what is in a biblical text. For example, if stories are comprised of plot, setting, and characters, interaction with those three elements will yield a better grasp of a biblical story than when a preacher does not speak of the elements of narrative.

Again, if poets speak a language of images and figures of speech, a sermon that refuses to name these literary features and unpack the meanings of the figurative language will in some measure be cutting against the grain. If a satiric passage by definition has one or more objects of attack and a stated or implied norm by which the criticism is conducted, not speaking of these things is a missed opportunity in the quest to make listeners see the passage as it really is in itself. The hermeneutical principle of which I speak is not peripheral but central to expository preaching, namely, doing justice to the specificity of a text.

Literary criticism also offers a methodology for interacting with the Bible that can be taught and passed on to congregants. Hermeneutical methods that dominate in seminary and graduate education are so sophisticated that preachers legitimately despair of passing them on to their parishioners. The result is that most preachers do not even think in terms of educating their listeners into the methods of biblical analysis as they preach their sermons. When preachers stand in the pulpit on Sunday mornings, their whole bent is directed to sharing the *product* of their work in the study during the week. The *process* of analyzing the Bible is not even on preachers' radar screens as something to mention from the pulpit.

This adds up to a missed opportunity of gigantic proportions. One of the byproducts of expository preaching ought to be a congregation adept at handling the Bible inductively. A mere two or three minutes of interspersed tips for interpreting the Bible in every expository sermon would yield spectacular results. After a year, church members would know that plots are based on one or more conflicts that move toward resolution by the end of the story, and that stories need to be broken into a sequence of episodes or scenes, and that the word *metaphor* is based on two Greek words meaning "to carry over," with the result that we need to carry over the meanings of a metaphor from level A (the statement itself) to level B (the actual subject of the passage).

A literary approach to biblical interpretation also offers a foolproof way to keep expository preaching rooted in common human experience and therefore relevant to everyday life. This is true because an axiom of literary criticism is that the subject of literature is human experience portrayed concretely. I recall an occasion when after I had completed conducting a workshop on teaching the Bible, one of my students in the workshop (a preacher) told me that the most important new idea that he would carry away from the workshop was that the Bible embodies human experience. He confided to me that it had never occurred to him that the Bible is a book of human experience.

Many (perhaps most) expository preachers are so captivated by theological abstraction and (even more) by the interlocking story of salvation history that pervades the Bible that the orientation of their sermons is to whisk us away from the everyday world to a world of theological abstraction. When we stare at a biblical text, we should most immediately see aspects of human experience that the author has placed before us, and only at a later stage should we see theological ideas. We should not set these up as rivals, since a complete treatment of a biblical text should include both. But a literary approach can help ensure that we first see the human experiences that have been embodied in a text.

When expository preachers adopt the methods of literary criticism, they at once enlarge the arsenal of terms and analytic tools at their disposal. Most of these terms and tools would, moreover, represent a fresh approach for both preacher and congregation. Stagnation can enter even the best expository preaching. Literary criticism is not a gimmick for innovation; it is a centuries-old way of dealing with literary texts dating all the way back to Aristotle's *Poetics*. The language of plot and characterization and metaphor and irony is in the active vocabulary of anyone who had a bona fide literature course in high school or college, and in any case terms like these cannot be said to be totally unfamiliar to, or beyond the reach of, the ordinary person.

A particular strength of literary criticism is its emphasis on literary wholes and on the unity of texts. A pioneer in the modern Bible-as-literature movement correctly stated that "no principle of literary study is more important than that of grasping clearly a literary work as a single whole."[5] The primary reason that the dean of an international correspondence graduate school asked me to write a hermeneutics course on the Bible as literature (required of all students enrolled at the school) is that in his thinking my literary approach to the Bible does the best job of showing the unity of Bible passages.

A final gift that the literary approach can bequeath to expository preachers is that it opens the door to preaching from the whole span

---

5. Richard G. Moulton, *The Modern Reader's Bible* (New York, 1895), 1719.

of the Bible. A preacher once shared that although he would often read psalms to people in the hospital, he would avoid preaching from them because he did "not know what to do with them." Mastering the literary genres of the Bible shows anyone "what to do" with Bible passages.

We can profitably pause for a moment longer on this matter of preachers' selection of Bible passages for their sermons. In some evangelical circles, preachers find it hard to conceive of preaching from anything other than the Epistles. As we all know, the Epistles are ostensibly the most idea-laden section of the Bible. There is no good reason why evangelical preachers should gravitate so overwhelmingly to the Epistles for their sermons—and why they should refuse to interact with them as letters when they do. God gave us the entire Bible with the intention that we would use it—in our sermons as well as elsewhere. Accepting a literary approach to the Bible is a way out of a longstanding evangelical fixation with the Epistles.

Why a Literary Approach Should Not be Considered Optional

The incorporation of a literary approach is not simply desirable, as I have argued above, but it is essential. I can make that claim in confidence because once we embrace the hermeneutical principles that undergird expository preaching, literary analysis is automatically included in the repertoire.

The most important of these hermeneutical principles is a commitment to close reading of a biblical text. The moment we embrace close reading, several concomitants at once become operative, as follows:

- Close reading implies that an expositor does justice to the specificity of a text. It should go without saying, then, that if the text is literary in nature, an expositor cannot deal with the particulars of a text without identifying and interpreting the literary details.

- Pointing in the same direction, it is an established hermeneutical principle that a piece of writing needs to be analyzed in terms appropriate to the genre in which it is written. After all that has been written about the Bible as literature, it would be logical for preachers to acknowledge the literary nature of the Bible. Therefore, if passages need to be analyzed in keeping with their genre, it is self-evident that a literary passage requires literary analysis.

- The goal of expository preaching is to relive a text as fully as possible, and ordinarily to do so in a sequential manner from the beginning of the passage to the end. Literary scholars call this explication of a text. Expository preaching on a literary text adds theological analysis and application to ordinary literary explication, but in other ways literary explication and exposition of a text are not just similar—they are identical.

- Finally, evangelical hermeneutics has championed the idea of authorial intention. The only tenable conclusion is that everything that biblical writers put into their writing is intended for a purpose. If they wrote in literary genres rather than expository ones, and if stylistic and rhetorical techniques spring forth from virtually every page of the Bible, it stands to reason that biblical writers intended that expositors do something with the literary dimension of their writing.

No matter how strong the case is in regard to literary analysis of a text as part of expository preaching, however, little progress can be expected until two fallacies are acknowledged and repudiated. The first fallacy is that biblical scholars and preachers are the only ones who have something to bring to the table in regard to biblical exposition. While preachers would not consciously assent to such a viewpoint, their practice shows it to be largely true. How often are literary critics or their books on interpretation and the Bible given a place in our churches and workshops? The unstated assumption is that all necessary hermeneutical methodology lies with the guild of seminary professors and their graduates.

The second fallacy is that the literary aspects of the Bible are "only" the form in which the content of the Bible is expressed. The prevalent viewpoint in evangelical circles is that the literary dimension of the Bible, if it is acknowledged at all, is regarded as an optional activity to be pursued if we have time or interest to engage in it after we have assimilated the message or content of a biblical passage.

But this practice violates a very obvious principle of communication, namely, that content is communicated *through form*. There can be no message without the form in which it is embodied, starting with language itself but including many additional aspects of form (broadly defined to include everything having to do with *how* an author expresses content). We cannot extract meaning from a literary text in the Bible without first interacting with aspects of literary form.

In short, forms like story, poetry, proverb, and vision (to name just a few) are the forms *through which* biblical content is mediated. If the writing of the Bible is the product of divine inspiration—if it represents what the Holy Spirit prompted the authors to write as they were carried along (2 Pet. 1:21)—then the only possible conclusion is that the literary forms of the Bible have been inspired by God and need to be granted an importance congruent with that inspiration.

In the epigraph that I placed at the head of this essay, Martin Luther makes extravagant claims for the ability of "English major types" (my colloquial epithet) to handle the Bible skillfully. Luther's statement is doubtless at an extreme end of the continuum. But for as long as any of us can remember, professors and graduates of seminaries have been at the opposite extreme on the continuum. They have given scarcely a thought to the possibility that English major types can bring something valuable to the enterprise of expository preaching. The resources for correcting this omission are ready at hand. All that is required is a willingness to take the step.

4

Right and Wrong Interpretation of the Bible: Some Suggestions for Pastors and Bible Teachers

Wayne Grudem

Throughout many years of ministry, Kent Hughes has been known as a faithful and accurate interpreter of the Word of God, both in his pulpit ministry week after week at College Church in Wheaton and in his numerous publications. In fact, I would point to Kent as someone whose ministry models the kind of faithful interpretation of Scripture that I will discuss in this essay.

I write as a friend who worked with Kent for many years on the board of the Council for Biblical Manhood and Womanhood, who worked with Kent on the translation team for the English Standard Version, and who still serves with Kent on the board of Crossway Books. From many years of friendship, I am quite sure that Kent would agree with much or all of what I am about to say here. In fact, I suspect that he may have taught many of these things to his pastoral interns over the years! But I offer these comments here in Kent's honor, because I think they represent much of what his life has been about.

My purpose here is to offer some words of advice on right and wrong interpretation of the Bible. I hope these words may help seminary students and pastors and other Bible teachers as they seek to interpret the text rightly and then to teach it week after week to their congregations. Many of the following comments have grown out of twenty-five years of seminary teaching (six years teaching New Testament, then nineteen teaching systematic theology). As I have watched seminary students over the years, they first become excited about all there is to learn about biblical interpretation, then some become discouraged that there is too much to learn, and then a few may even tend to despair, wondering if they can ever know *anything* about the text when so many different opinions have been written about it over the centuries. The amount of information available, and the number of viewpoints on any passage, can become overwhelming unless we keep them in proper perspective.

To keep students from discouragement, I have tended to tell them over the years that the purpose of seminary training is to help them *do better* something *they already do quite well* as mature Christians: understand the meaning of the Bible. That is because I believe God gave us his Word in such a form that ordinary people could, in general, understand it rightly. That is the doctrine of "clarity" of Scripture. "The testimony of the LORD is sure, making wise the simple" (Ps.19:7).

So these comments are intended to help people become better interpreters. I have couched my comments as suggestions that may be helpful for pastors and Bible teachers. They include much of what I tell seminary students about how to interpret the Bible, though I hope that others will be helped by these comments as well.

General Principles for Right Interpretation

1) *Spend your earliest and best time reading the text of the Bible itself.* I'm afraid that too often pastors and scholars can fall into the trap of spending 90 percent of their time reading commentaries *about the text* and then spend only the last 10 percent of their time reading *the text of the Bible itself.* But when that happens, people tend only to see problems and disputed meanings in every phrase rather than seeing the clear and strong message of the text itself. I therefore tell students (only partly in jest) that the three most important rules for interpreting the Bible are: (1) Read it. (2) Read it again. (3) Read it again.

The words of Scripture are the product of the infinitely wise, omniscient mind of God. There is much more depth of meaning in them than any human being will ever be able to understand. That is why I have found, and millions of Christians throughout history have found, that increased depth of understanding comes from repeated reading and rereading of a single passage of Scripture, pondering each word and phrase, sometimes even slowly reading the text aloud. Since this is God's Word, it is especially important that we do this while consciously being in the presence of God, asking him to help us understand his Word rightly, to see connections to other parts of Scripture, and to see proper application to life.

Time and again I have found that the most powerful sections of my own sermons have come from times when God has first spoken deeply to my heart through the words of the Bible itself, and I have been so moved that I have experienced tears of awe and reverence, or tears of sorrow and repentance, or times of great joy and laughter and rejoicing at the greatness of God. Commentaries do not speak to my heart in this way. Now please do not misunderstand me. I own many commentaries (not as many as Kent, however, for I have seen his library!), and I have even written one myself (on 1 Peter). When I get "stuck" and simply can't figure out the meaning of a passage, I will read a number of commentaries and gain helpful insights. And when I have finished spending extensive time with a text of Scripture on its own, *after that* I will read through some commentaries to see if I have missed anything or made any foolish mistakes. But I cannot do that first, or I simply get lost in endless detours and byways that should not be my primary concern.

So I encourage pastors and Bible teachers: spend your earliest and best time with the text of Scripture itself and with a notepad and pen in your hand. For those who know only English, spending time with a good English translation (such as the English Standard Version) will be wonderfully rewarding. But for those who know Hebrew and Greek, spending time in the original text, doing some word studies, and checking the meaning of some words in lexicons will add richness and accuracy and depth at this point.

I remember many years ago when I traveled to Wheaton and had an appointment to meet with Kent Hughes in his office. His secretary let me in a minute or two before Kent arrived, and when I walked in I saw a well-marked Greek New Testament open and propped up in a bookstand on his desk where Kent was preparing his sermon for the following Sunday. Seeing that told me that this was a pastor who still used his Greek text, and who still was serious about feeding his people the solid meat of the Word of God week after week. He spent time with the text of the Bible itself. I think this is what Psalm 1:2 encourages us to do when it talks about the blessed man: "His delight is in the law of the LORD, and on his law he meditates day and night."

2) *The interpretation of Scripture is not a magical or mysterious process, because Scripture was written in the ordinary language of the day.* Sometimes seminary students have a false impression that when they come to seminary they will be given some "secret tools" for getting hidden meaning from the text that other people couldn't find there. But this is not true, because the Bible was written for ordinary people, and it was written in the ordinary language of the people to whom it was first given. That is why Moses could command all the people of Israel, "These words that I command you today shall be on your heart. You shall teach them diligently to your children, and shall talk of them when you sit in your house, and when you walk by the way, and when you lie down, and when you rise" (Deut. 6:6–7).

That means that when we are seeking to understand the Bible, we are not seeking some secret "new revelation" that will give us better insight into the text. Nor are we looking for some secret numerical code in which the Bible has a mysterious message that can be found by counting backwards every seventeenth letter, and if that doesn't work, every eighteenth letter, then if that doesn't work, then programming the computer to count backwards every eighty-sixth letter, or eighty-seventh letter, until some mysterious message about Napoleon suddenly appears! This is simply not the way that God caused Scripture to be written, and not the way he expects his people to read and understand it. Certainly the original readers did not think they had to read it this way.

No, what we are looking for as we read Scripture is *understanding*. We seek to know what the words and the phrases *mean*, and we seek to understand how they relate to the next phrase and the next sentence and the next. We seek to understand the purpose of a sentence in the whole of the paragraph, or the whole of the chapter, or the whole of the book. In all this we are asking God to give us *understanding*. We want to know *why* a sentence means one thing and not another; and we believe that the reasons for a certain meaning will be there in the text if we look for them until we find them.

3) *Every interpreter has only four sources of information about the text.* This is related to the previous point. There are only four kinds of information (as far as I know) that any interpreter can use in understanding the text and in arguing for that understanding in an attempt to persuade others. The four sources of information are these:

a) *The meanings of individual words and sentences.* Of course we need to understand the meanings of words correctly, and then the meanings of the sentences in which they occur. Words can have a range of meanings (that is why a dictionary entry will list several meanings for a word), but that range is not unlimited. In fact, for every word in the original Greek or Hebrew text of the Bible, there was *a recognized range of meanings* that the original speakers shared. If one person didn't know what another person's words meant, the two could not have communicated with each other! I realize that the context can help us decide *among the possible meanings* for a word, but context doesn't give a word an entirely different meaning than it had everywhere else (that is why Greek and Hebrew dictionaries are useful in giving us the range of meanings).

In seeking to understand Greek and Hebrew words, I have found that doing a "word study" (that is, looking at the way a word is used in various verses of the Bible) gives me a much better appreciation of the actual range of meaning of a word, and helps me understand more vividly and accurately the precise meaning of the word and also the kind of contexts in which the word is used.

b) *The place of the statement in its context.* What is the purpose of a verse or a sentence? Is it to support a previous statement? Or is it stating something with which the author is going to disagree? Is it a statement made by someone whom the author will later say was wrong (such as the statements of Job's three friends)?

c) *The overall teaching of Scripture.* Because I believe that the entire Bible is the product not just of human authors but also of God himself, and that "men spoke from God as they were carried along by the Holy Spirit" (2 Pet. 1:21), I also believe that the entire Bible, rightly understood, will be internally consistent. It will not have contradictory teachings. In fact, the psalmist says, "the *sum* of your word is truth" (Ps. 119:160), and the word here translated "sum" (Hebrew *ro'sh*) in this context means something very close to what the word "sum" means in English—it is the result you get when all of God's words are added together. When all of God's words are considered together, they are not contradictory, but they constitute "truth."

Certainly it is a good discipline, in interpreting any text, to seek first to understand it in the immediate context of the book in which it occurs and what we know of that author's situation and viewpoint. But I think it is right for us also to remember that a correct interpretation will not ultimately contradict what other passages of Scripture say. Therefore I may struggle for a time attempting to find out what James means when he writes, "You see that a person is *justified by works* and not by faith alone" (James 2:24), but I am certain that, whatever James means, he cannot be directly contradicting Paul when he writes, "We know that a person is *not justified by works* of the law but through faith in Jesus Christ" (Gal. 2:16). To take another example, I may need to struggle for a time working on the details of Hebrews 6:4–8, trying to understand the meaning of this: "For it is impossible, in the case of those who have once been enlightened, who have tasted the heavenly gift, and have shared in the Holy Spirit, . . . and then have fallen away, to restore them again to repentance" (Heb. 6:4–6). Does this mean that some people who are truly born again can actually lose their salvation? People come up with different solutions to this question, but two answers that I do not think possible are: (1) Hebrews teaches that people who have been genuinely born again can lose their salvation, and (2) John and Paul and Peter teach that genuine believers cannot lose their faith.

Of course, liberal New Testament scholars have no problem at all saying that different New Testament authors taught contradictory viewpoints of doctrinal questions. In fact, they *expect* this to happen because they think of the Bible as merely a human book, recording the religious experiences and ideas of human beings who lived long ago. But I disagree with that viewpoint, and I do not think that the Bible contains direct contradictions in its teaching. Therefore I must work more carefully at interpreting the individual passages until I find a solution that does not contradict other passages of Scripture.

Of course, my own ideas of "what the rest of the Bible teaches" might at some point be incorrect, and I may need to go back to those other passages and reexamine them to see if I need to change my mind about the teaching of the rest of the Bible. One verse influences our understanding of the whole, and our understanding of the whole influences our understanding of one verse, so there is a back-and-forth thought process as we seek to get it all right. But on many doctrinal matters the teaching of Scripture is so extensive and so clear that I think it very unlikely that we have misunderstood it through the whole history of the church. All this is to say that the overall teaching of Scripture is something that we must keep in mind in order to interpret Scripture rightly.

d) *Some information about the historical and cultural background.* Good commentaries and reference books on archeology and geography and extrabiblical history can be very useful in this regard. Jewish literature after the time of the Old Testament and Christian literature after the time of the New Testament can also be useful and can enrich our understanding of the historical background, the surrounding culture, the precise meanings of some words used in the Bible, and so forth.

However, while this material is *often helpful,* I think *it is seldom necessary* in order to understand the passage correctly, at least in its central meaning. And too much of what I have read about supposed "background information" I have found to be largely speculative or inaccurate. It is important therefore to have some reliable, standard reference works such as the *International Standard Bible Encyclopedia*[1]

---

1. Geoffrey Bromiley, ed., *International Standard Bible Encyclopedia*, 4 vols. (Grand Rapids, MI: Eerdmans, 1988).

or the *Oxford Classical Dictionary*[2] or the *New International Dictionary of the Christian Church.*[3] In addition, it is often helpful to look at the primary documents from ancient Jewish and Greek literature (Josephus, Philo, rabbinic literature, Dead Sea Scrolls, apostolic Fathers, etc.) in English translation where that is easily available.

Sometimes this extrabiblical material makes a text much more vivid and forceful. I remember reading about Samson, when he was in Gaza and the men of the city were waiting to ambush him and kill him, that at midnight, "he arose and took hold of the doors of the gate of the city and the two posts, and pulled them up, bar and all, and put them on his shoulders and carried them to the top of the hill that is in front of Hebron" (Judg. 16:3). I knew this was an impressive feat, since the gate of an ancient city was massive and was made as strong as could be to defend against enemy attacks. But I wondered how far he carried the gate. How far was Hebron from Gaza? I looked at a Bible atlas and found that the distance was over thirty miles! When I found out that bit of background information, I understood more clearly why the men of Gaza decided not to mess with Samson.

Summary

So those are the four sources of information:

a) The meanings of individual words and sentences;
b) The place of the statement in its context;
c) The overall teaching of Scripture;
d) Some information about the historical and cultural background.

That's all there is. There isn't some other "secret" arsenal of information that only Bible scholars in dusty libraries have access to. And when we realize this, then the task of interpretation seems more manageable and able to be done with some degree of accuracy and confidence.

4) *Look for reasons rather than mere opinions to give support to an interpretation, and use reasons rather than mere opinions to attempt to persuade others.* Too often I think interpreters have a tendency to count commentaries, and if six commentaries favor interpretation A, while only two commentaries favor interpretation B, they think that A must be the right interpretation. But that is just counting opinions. That is not weighing the reasons for those opinions. Maybe the six commentaries are all

---

2. Simon Hornblower and Antony Spawforth, eds., *Oxford Classical Dictionary*, (Oxford: Oxford University Press, 2003).

3. Earle E. Cairns and J. D. Douglas, eds., *New International Dictionary of the Christian Church*, (Grand Rapids, MI: Zondervan, 2001).

based on the work of one respected writer, and maybe that writer got it wrong. (For example, I found that several commentaries on 1 Peter were written with too much dependence on E. G. Selwyn without realizing that he had made a number of mistakes both in information and in judgment.)

Far better is the approach that looks for the *reasons* a commentator gives for his interpretation. Then it is up to us, as interpreters, to decide whether those reasons are persuasive. Perhaps we see things in the text that those commentaries just overlooked. Or perhaps they are based on assumptions that we cannot agree with (such as a liberal assumption that there are contradictions and historical inaccuracies in what the Bible says).

I think that a good pastor or Bible teacher will take the same approach with his congregation. He won't just say, "In my opinion the verse means X," but will rather give the *reasons* for his understanding. He will say something like, "I think the text means X and not Y because this same word occurs three verses earlier and has the same meaning, and because meaning X supports the author's purpose in this chapter, which we see in this other verse." A good Bible teacher will be able to summarize those arguments briefly and clearly and express them in a way that the hearers can understand, so that they can follow the argument in their own English texts as well.

5) *There is only one meaning for each text (though there are many applications).* To take an example we used earlier, either Hebrews 6 means that genuine Christians can lose their salvation, or it doesn't mean that genuine Christians can lose their salvation. It doesn't mean both! This is because (as I mentioned earlier) God's word is truthful and internally consistent in every part. Every time we see Jesus or Paul reasoning from an Old Testament verse and saying something like, "It does not mean A, B, C, but it means D, E, F," we see them appealing to a conviction that a text means one thing and not something else. (See, for example, Matt. 22:32; Acts 2:25–35; Rom. 9:6–8).

The *Westminster Confession of Faith* includes a classic statement of this when it says:

> The infallible rule of interpretation of Scripture is the Scripture itself: and therefore, when there is a question about the true and full sense of any Scripture (*which is not manifold, but one*), it must be searched and known by other places that speak more clearly (*Westminster Confession of Faith* 1.9; italics added).

I admit that the meaning of a passage can be complex and multilayered because of the richness and depth of Scripture. But there is still only one correct meaning.

What is that meaning? It is the meaning that the *original authors* of Scriptures intended. In most cases that is the same as the intent of the *human* author of Scripture, but there are times when the *Divine* Author, who knows the end from the beginning, has more in mind than the human author understands (1 Peter 1:10–12 indicates that was generally true of the Old Testament authors when they were predicting the coming Messiah).

As for multiple applications, there are of course many millions of different situations to which any given Scripture might apply. And we should grow in skill in applying Scripture rightly. But it still has just one meaning at any one point.

6) *Notice the kind of literature in which the verse is found.* The Bible has different kinds of literature. It contains historical narrative, poetry, doctrinal argument, collections of wisdom sayings, prophetic speeches, and visionary or "apocalyptic" literature. Although all the words of Scripture are "breathed out by God and profitable for teaching" (2 Tim. 3:16), we understand it better when we realize that poetic literature often speaks in imagery rather than with literal description and realize that wisdom literature often makes generalizations about things that are usually true with regard to human conduct (without claiming that they are true in every single instance in every person's life), and so forth. Each type of text should be understood according to the kind of literature it is.

But here is a word of caution as well: too often I have found that scholars get carried away with "parallels" to similar kinds of literature outside the Bible. They can end up saying things such as, "This set of laws from Moses is just like the laws found in Hammurabi's law code in ancient Babylon, and therefore the biblical law must be saying the same thing," and then they use Hammurabi as the deciding factor in interpreting the text of the Old Testament. Or a New Testament scholar might say something like, "This set of moral standards in Paul's epistles is just like the 'household codes' in ancient Greek or Roman society, and therefore Paul must be upholding the same moral principles as found in those 'household codes.'" But in both cases the parallels have been overdrawn, because the interpreter has failed to realize that the Bible has both similarities to and differences from other literature of its time. Certainly we would expect the moral standards given by God to be higher and purer than the moral standards of the surrounding cultures.

7) *Notice whether the text approves or disapproves or merely reports a person's actions.* For example, Genesis records a number of events that God does not approve of. Jacob lied to his father, Isaac, in order to get Esau's blessing (Gen. 27:19, 24), but that does not mean it is right to lie. And "Rachel stole her father's household gods" (Gen. 31:19), but that does not mean that God approves of what Rachel did! It reports that Jacob told Esau he would come to him "in Seir" (Gen. 33:14), but the subsequent verses show he had no intention of doing this but went another direction to Succoth (v. 17). Joshua reports that Rahab told a lie to save the Israelite spies (Josh. 2:4–6), but I doubt that the author means to encourage readers to tell lies in difficult situations. (Although Hebrews 11:31 commends Rahab for her faith and for welcoming the spies, and James 2:25 commends her for receiving the spies and sending them out by another way, the Bible nowhere explicitly approves of Rahab's lie, which violates the ninth commandment. Moreover, it is doubtful that the author of Joshua intends us to take the uninstructed moral conduct of a Canaanite prostitute as an example for how to live a morally blameless life.)

The question of whether an action is morally right or wrong, or is approved by God or not, should be determined by the explicit teachings of Scripture regarding moral conduct, not merely by appeal to narrative examples where it is unclear whether God approves of the character's action or not.

8) *Be careful not to generalize specific statements and apply them to fundamentally different situations.* Too often I have heard people in a Bible study take some verse where Jesus is criticizing the Pharisees and make an immediate application to "our evangelical leaders today," thereby implying that many evangelical leaders are, like the Pharisees, hypocrites, or given to excessive pride or greed, or accustomed to placing human traditions above the Word of God, and so forth.

But these easy connections between the Pharisees and modern evangelical leaders fail to make the most important distinction: the Pharisees who opposed Jesus were not born again and did not (by and large) have a genuine personal relationship with God or a genuine spiritual life within. They were unregenerate religious leaders, for Jesus said they were "like whitewashed tombs, which outwardly appear beautiful, but within are full of dead people's bones and all uncleanness," and he told them, "You also outwardly appear righteous to others, but within you are full of hypocrisy and lawlessness" (Matt. 23:27–28). Therefore, anybody who makes a direct parallel between the Pharisees who opposed Jesus and modern evangelical leaders should first be prepared to say that he thinks that these modern evangelical leaders are not genuinely born again, that they are not really Christians at all.

I realize, of course, that we can all take warning from observing the sinful conduct of various people in the Bible, and there are surely appropriate warnings against pride and hypocrisy that we all should take from reading about the Pharisees. But to say that we all should be warned not to become like the Pharisees is far different from assuming that certain ones of us *are already* like the Pharisees. That is generalizing specific statements about certain people and applying them to fundamentally different situations.

A similar case is found in Matthew, where Jesus says, "An evil and adulterous generation seeks for a sign, but no sign will be given to it except the sign of Jonah" (Matt. 16:4). Time and again I have heard this verse quoted (even by some very reputable Bible scholars) as a means of rebuking people for seeking signs and miracles in the work of the church today. But these writers have failed to observe the context of this verse, where we find that Jesus directed this rebuke against "the Pharisees and Sadducees" who came to him, "and to test him they asked him to show them a sign from heaven" (Matt. 16:1). Nowhere did Jesus ever rebuke someone who came to him in genuine need and asked to be healed or asked for some other miracle. Nowhere is there a hint that it was wrong for the early disciples to pray that God would give "signs and wonders" in connection with the proclamation of the gospel (Acts 4:30). So using Matthew 16:4 against genuine believers who sincerely ask God to perform miracles is wrongly applying the text to a fundamentally different situation from that of "evil and adulterous" opponents of Jesus who were simply seeking to test him and find some way to criticize his ministry.

9) *It is possible to do a short or long study of any passage. Do what you can with the time you have, and don't be discouraged about all that you cannot do.* Imagine that you are a young seminary student and need to prepare a short devotional talk on Psalm 1—with only ten minutes to prepare! I think you could do it. Take two minutes to calm your heart and pray for the Lord's guidance (eight minutes to go). Then take about two minutes to find out something about the structure of the passage and get a brief outline (six to go). Then take two minutes to think about how this psalm will be fulfilled in Christ and then ultimately in the age to come (four to go). Then take the remaining three or four minutes to jot some notes on application. Then give the talk! Life in the ministry includes some situations like that where you have to do the best you can with the time involved.

Please do not misunderstand me: I am not saying that it's a *good idea* to give a devotional talk that you have only spent ten minutes preparing. But I am saying that sometimes unexpected situations come up, and through some emergency that is no fault of your own, your preparation time is taken away, and you still have to give a short talk. I think it's possible. And I say this only to illustrate the point that it is possible to work within the time allowed and still do a reasonably good job of interpreting the text of Scripture for a specific need or circumstance.

Or you could work twenty hours preparing a good sermon for Sunday morning on Psalm 1. Or some scholar could work two hundred or three hundred hours and write an academic article on Psalm 1. Or a PhD student might take an entire year to write a dissertation about Psalm 1 and its place in the book of Psalms. He might eventually publish a commentary on the book of Psalms.

All of these exercises have their place. If we have more time, there is always something more that can be done to give more depth, more certainty, more insight, more accuracy to our interpretation. But it is good to be able to tailor your work to the time you have available for it, and then ask the Lord to bless what you have done.

10) *Pray regularly for the Holy Spirit's help in the whole process of interpreting the Bible.* Even the author of Psalm 119 prayed for help in understanding the Word of God, for he said, "Open my eyes, that I may behold wondrous things out of your law" (Ps. 119:18). If even he needed to pray for help and understanding, then so do we. In fact, there is a strong moral and spiritual component involved in proper understanding of Scripture. Paul says, "The natural person does not accept the things of the Spirit of God, for they are folly to him, and *he is not able to understand them* because they are spiritually discerned" (1 Cor. 2:14; compare Heb. 5:14).

This means that regular prayer needs to be part of our interpretative process. In fact, in my own life, time and again, when I have been puzzled about the meaning of a verse, I have stopped and prayed, asking the Lord to help me understand. And time and again, after praying, I have suddenly seen something I had overlooked that was there in the text all along. I wouldn't say that the Holy Spirit *told me* the meaning of the text. Rather, I think the Holy Spirit enabled me to see more information that I had not yet taken into account, information that was already there but that I had overlooked or not understood.

If "solid food is for the mature" (Heb. 5:14), then personal holiness of life and the maintenance of strong personal faith and a vital relationship with the Lord are all important in right interpretation of Scripture. Paul told the Corinthians, "Among the mature we do impart wisdom, although it is not a wisdom of this age or of the rulers of this age," (1 Cor. 2:6), but then he told them that he could not give them that kind of wisdom, because of their immaturity: "But I, brothers, could not address you as spiritual people, but as people of the flesh, as infants in Christ. . . . For while there is jealousy and strife among you, are you not of the flesh and behaving only in a human way?" (1 Cor. 3:1–3). Their disobedience became a barrier to proper understanding of the wisdom that Paul would have taught them.

Keeping the "Big Picture" in Mind: Some Observations about the Whole of Scripture

A final comment on right interpretation has to do with keeping the "big picture" in mind. After he had graduated, an excellent seminary student told me that the one thing he missed in his seminary training was a class on "how the whole Bible fits together." He had learned thousands of details, but what was "the big picture"? The classes were all on such specialized topics that no class seemed geared to address that question.

So here are some comments on "the big picture." These are general characteristics of Scripture to keep in mind. Interpreters who understand these "big pictures" will be much better at understanding individual verses.

Big Picture 1

The Bible is a historical document. Therefore, always ask, "What did the author want the original readers to understand by this statement?"

When we read Scripture, we are reading a historical document written at specific times and places long ago. Yes, it does speak to today, but sound interpretation requires that we first think about what the text was doing in its original setting. What did the original (human) author want his original readers to understand?

This approach will help us avoid bizarre errors in interpretation, such as the classic story about the man who prayed for guidance and then opened his Bible and stuck his finger on Matthew 27:5, where it says that Judas "went and hanged himself." Not seeing much benefit in that, he prayed again, then turned over to another gospel and blindly stuck his finger on another verse, only to read Luke 10:37, "You go, and do likewise." Surely the original authors did not intend for people to take that kind of guidance from either statement!

By contrast, asking what the original author intended the original readers to understand will help the interpreter avoid fanciful allegories that improperly interpret the text. For instance, an interpreter who doesn't follow this procedure might find all sorts of fanciful interpretations of the "five smooth stones" that David took to fight Goliath (1 Sam. 17:40). A modern charismatic interpreter, given to allegorizing, might say that these five smooth stones are the fivefold manifestations of the Holy Spirit in Ephesians 4:11. "But no," a Calvinistic interpreter might answer. He would say that it's obvious that the "five smooth stones" represent the famous "five points of Calvinism." Then a third allegorical interpreter, an ethics professor, might say that they were both wrong because David is going forth to war against Goliath, and therefore the "five smooth stones" obviously represent the five sides of the Pentagon building in Washington, DC, and they therefore give support to the "just war" theory!

Unless we first anchor our interpretation in what the original author wanted the original readers to understand, there will be no limit to the variety of such incorrect interpretations that have nothing to do with the actual meaning of the text. What then is the correct meaning of David's "five smooth stones" in 1 Samuel 17:40? The correct meaning is that "the five smooth stones" tell us that David took five smooth stones from the brook when he went to fight Goliath. The meaning is no more, no less than that. How do I know that? Because that's what it would have meant to the original author and the original readers as they read this historical narrative.

Big Picture 2

The original authors wanted the original readers to respond in some way. Therefore always ask, "What application did the original author want the readers to make to their lives?"

Just as we want readers to respond in some way to what we write, so the original authors of Scripture had a *purpose* in what they wrote. They wanted to get a response of some kind from the readers. Perhaps they wanted the readers to believe that certain things were true about God; or perhaps they wanted them to obey God's commands, or fear judgment if they disobeyed, or take courage against their enemies, or treat their neighbors with justice and kindness, and so forth. Perhaps the authors wanted the readers to praise God for his excellent character and his wonderful deeds. Perhaps he wanted the readers to avoid the mistakes of people in the past or look forward to a Messiah who was to come.

If we ask, "What application did the *original* (human) author want the *original* readers to make to their lives?" that will be an excellent first step in avoiding wrong applications and finding proper applications to our lives today as well. For example, before David went out to fight Goliath he said, "The LORD who delivered me from the paw of the lion and the paw of the bear will deliver me from the hand of this Philistine" (1 Sam. 17:37). Here the historical narrative in 1 Samuel tells us *David trusted in the Lord* to give him victory, and that God did give him victory over Goliath. In addition, David refused to wear Saul's armor (1 Sam. 17:38–39) but took the weapons with which he was familiar, and God gave him victory with those (vv. 40, 45–49). Just so we don't miss it, the text emphasizes again and again that David trusted in the Lord and the Lord gave him the victory (see vv. 36–37, 45–47).

It is not hard to see that the *original author* wanted the *original readers* to make application to their lives as well. They should be like David and trust in the Lord to protect them, and to work through the "weapons" and abilities God gives them, and to give them victory in the trials of life. As for application to our lives today, we too should trust in the Lord to protect us and work through the tools and abilities that God has given us, and hope that he will give us victory in the tasks he calls us to. But there are some differences: in the New Testament our "weapons" in the ministry of the gospel are the spiritual weapons of the Word of God and prayer (see 2 Cor. 10:3–4).

Related to this question is another: When we read about historical events in the Bible, we should also ask, what was God showing the original readers through this event? Why did he want it recorded for subsequent generations?

Big Picture 3

The whole Bible is about God! Therefore we should always ask, "What does this text tell us about God?"

With respect to the story of David and Goliath, it would be totally foreign to the whole message of the Bible to take the story of David and Goliath as merely an example of human courage: David had courage and therefore we should have courage as well. This is man-centered moralism that misses the God-centered emphasis of the entire Bible. Rather, the text tells us that David trusted in *God*, and *God* gave him courage, and *God* gave him victory over Goliath. In fact, the emphasis on God's work in this story is repeatedly found in the text itself (see 1 Sam. 16:13; 17:26, 37, 45, 49–51).

There is so much more in the story of David and Goliath than a morality tale of a mere human being who had courage against insurmountable odds. The story tells us (1) that *God* has chosen "a man after his own heart" (1 Sam. 13:14) to be king of Israel, and David is going to replace Saul as that king. (2) It tells us that *God* anointed and protected and empowered David to defeat Goliath, the most powerful enemy of God's people. (3) It tells us that no earthly power could stand against the Lord (note the emphasis on the Goliath's size and armor in 1 Samuel 17:4–7). It was *God* who protected and saved his people. (4) It tells us that David was zealous to defend God's honor (1 Sam. 17:26, 45–46). David trusted in God to the point of putting his own life on the line, and God rewarded David's faithfulness and obedience—obedience even to the point of risking death. (5) It tells us that after the battle, God gave great honor to his anointed king and brought the people of God into a time of great harmony, peace, and blessing under the leadership of King David (see James 1:12 for a parallel in the New Testament).

So this text, like the rest of the Bible, has *an emphasis on God* and his excellent character and his wonderful works. A similar emphasis can be found throughout Scripture, and we will do well not to miss it.

Big Picture 4

The center of the whole Bible is Jesus Christ. The entire Old Testament leads up to him and points to him, and the entire New Testament flows from him. Therefore, we should always ask, "What does this text tells us about the greatness of Christ?"

After Jesus' resurrection, he taught his disciples more fully how the whole Old Testament points to him. We read, "And beginning with Moses and *all the Prophets*, he interpreted to them *in all the Scriptures* the things concerning himself" (Luke 24:27). In this verse, "Moses" means the first five books of the Bible, Genesis to Deuteronomy, and "all the Prophets" most likely refers to the rest of the Bible, the "early" prophets who wrote the historical literature and the "later" writing prophets, who wrote the prophetic books and wrote or assembled the wisdom literature as well. Luke seems to be telling us that Jesus saw "things concerning himself" in "all the Scriptures," that is, in the entire Old Testament.

To return to the story of David and Goliath, *does it tell us anything about the Messiah to come?* Is there any way in which God was preparing his people for the Messiah by teaching them what the Messiah would be like through the lives of various historical figures? Yes, this text tells us much about things yet to come. From the perspective of the fulfillment that comes in the New Testament, we now can realize that a number of things are foreshadowed in the story of David and Goliath. These five points follow closely the five points about what God was doing that I mentioned in the previous section:

- God is someday going to choose someone yet greater than David, someone who is truly "a man after his own heart" (1 Sam. 13:14), and this coming one will be King of Israel forever (see 2 Sam. 7:12–16; John 12:13).

- God is going to anoint and protect and empower this coming Messiah, and he will defeat the most powerful enemy of God's people, that is, Satan himself. This was predicted as far back as Genesis 3:15 (see the partial fulfillment in Rom. 16:20) and began to be fulfilled when Jesus came and bound "the strong man" and began to "plunder his house" (Matt. 12:29). This prediction found its culmination in the cross, where God "disarmed the rulers and authorities and put them to open shame, by triumphing over them in him" (Col. 2:15; see Heb. 2:14–15), and it will be more completely fulfilled when Satan is cast into the lake of fire at the final judgment (Rev. 20:10).

- Just as Goliath was not able to stand before David, so no earthly power will be able to stand against the coming Messiah. He will come in the strength and power of the Lord, and will defeat all his enemies and reign as King of kings and Lord of lords (see Rev. 17:14; 19:16).

- David's zeal for God's honor reminds us that there is a Messiah coming who will be zealous to defend God's honor. He will trust in God even to the point of laying down his own life. After he is obedient unto death, God will highly exalt him (see Phil. 2:8–11).

- Just as God brought his people into a time of great peace and harmony after David defeated Goliath, so after the coming Messiah defeats all his enemies, God will empower him to bring his people into a time of great harmony, peace, and blessing under the leadership of Jesus Christ, their eternal king (see Rev. 11:15–17).

Although Jesus in his first coming fulfilled many of these expectations, there will be a yet greater fulfillment at his second coming.

Now it may not be possible to develop all of these points and all of these parallels in any one message. But the Old Testament is filled with many examples of righteous leaders who in their good conduct foreshadowed the greater Messiah yet to come. And, by contrast, the many shortcomings and failures of the leaders (such as Abraham, Moses, and David, all of whom sinned) remind us that Abraham is not the Messiah to come, nor is Moses, nor is David. Someone greater than these is yet to come.

I do not think it is foreign to the text and the flow of all of Scripture to see the Old Testament in this light. It is all leading up to Jesus Christ, and it is all a kind of preparation for him. When we understand that and point it out, we are not imposing something on the text, but we are in fact being faithful to the text as it appears in the larger context of the entire flow of biblical history.

Big Picture 5

All history can be divided into several major "ages" or "epochs" in salvation history. Therefore, we should read every passage of the Bible with a salvation history timeline in our minds and constantly remember where every passage fits on the timeline.

The Bible's perspective on the history of the world is different from the perspective of secular historians of the world. The Bible's focus is not military history or political history or economic history. The Bible's focus is not the history of science or the history of art or the history of the development of various cultures. Rather, the Bible's emphasis is on "salvation history," that is, the study of how God himself was relating to mankind at various periods in history.

So it is good to begin to read the Bible with at least a rudimentary timeline in mind and then to seek to grow in understanding of how God related to his people in a somewhat unique way in each period on that timeline.

Figure 4.1 contains a very simple timeline with which I advise students to begin. It is easy to memorize, it includes only five dates plus the present year, and it helps readers keep the whole Bible in proper

FIGURE 4.1:

Premillennial Timeline

```
                   OT                      NT   †        Second coming
|---------|------|--------|--------|-----|-----------||---------|-------------|------------------>
 Creation Fall Abr   Moses  David  Exile         Christ church age   Millennium Final Judgment
              BC 2000  1440   1000   586      AD   30       2007      New heavens/ new earth
```

historical perspective. (This is a "premillennial" timeline, according to my own convictions. Amillennialists and postmillennialists may adjust the last part as they see fit.)

Now, on that timeline, the old covenant, or the Mosaic covenant, begins with Moses and continues until the death of Christ. Then the new covenant age begins, and the Holy Spirit is poured out in a new fullness and new power that is appropriate to the new covenant on the day of Pentecost (Acts 2).

Such a timeline provides a great help in keeping many interpretation questions in right perspective. Why don't we follow the dietary laws given in the Old Testament? Why can we eat ham and bacon, contrary to Leviticus 11:7, which says "the pig" is one of the unclean animals that should not be eaten? It is because we are no longer under the Mosaic covenant or the old covenant, and so we do not need to be subject to those dietary laws that were particular to that covenant.

But what shall we say then about Genesis 9:6, "whoever sheds the blood of man, by man shall his blood be shed, for God made man in his own image"? Many have argued (and I think rightly) that this provides a fundamental basis for human government to inflict punishments up to and including capital punishment on people who do evil. But is this applicable today, or is it just part of the Old Testament that we no longer need to follow?

I think it is applicable today because it is not part of the Mosaic covenant that was given on Mount Sinai in Exodus 20. These commands to Noah in Genesis 9 are commands that seem to apply to the entire human race that descended from Noah and his wife and children. When this salvation history timeline is in my mind, it helps me to understand that this command is not part of the temporary provisions that were only for the Jewish people in the time of the Mosaic covenant.

But what about the moral commands in the New Testament? What about, "Therefore, having put away falsehood, let each one of you speak the truth with his neighbor" (Eph. 4:25)? Is this a command that we need to follow today, or is it just something that was written 2000 years ago that belongs to another place and another time? Here the salvation-history timeline shows me that the "church age" began in A.D. 30 when the Holy Spirit was poured out at Pentecost, and the "church age" continues until the time Christ returns.

This means that *we are at the same point in salvation history* as were the people in the early church. In terms of the way God acts with people over time, we are closer to Paul's readers in Ephesus in the first century than they were to the Jewish people in Jesus' ministry just a few years earlier, because those people were still under the old covenant. Therefore, these moral commands such as Ephesians 4:25 should be seen as applying directly to us and requiring our obedience as well.

Now the situation is a bit more complex than that. I am not saying that nothing from Exodus 20 to Malachi has any value for us! "All Scripture" is "profitable for teaching" and "for training in righteousness" (see 2 Tim. 3:16), so even the moral standards in the Mosaic covenant can be helpful to us in letting us know, in general, about the kinds of actions that God approves of and the kind of actions that displease him. That is a more complex subject than I can treat here. But the point remains that the salvation history timeline helps us keep the big picture of the flow of biblical history in our minds and helps significantly in the task of right interpretation.

Big Picture 6

Themes: Because the Bible is a unity (it has one divine Author though many human authors), there are many themes that develop and grow from Genesis to Revelation. Therefore, for each significant element in any text, it is helpful to ask, (a) Where did this theme start in the Bible? (b) How did this theme develop through the Bible? and (c) Where is this theme going to end in the Bible?

There are actually hundreds of themes that flow through the tapestry of biblical history like threads that appear again and again. It is rewarding to trace these themes from Genesis to Revelation and see how they develop, and I have found that when this perspective on a text is included in a Bible study, it encourages people's hearts because they can see repeatedly how the entire Bible fits together and forms a consistent pattern in which God has been working through all history to bring about his plans for his glory and for the good of his people.

For example, the story of the Wise Men (the Magi) coming to visit baby Jesus is a familiar one to many people (see Matt. 2:1–12). This is not an isolated event in the Bible, however, but picks up on a number of themes that were present in the Old Testament and will be fulfilled in the age to come. For example, these Wise Men bring gifts from the wealth of the nations to offer in worship to the future King of Israel. These gifts are part of the abundant resources that God has put in the earth for us to develop and use for his glory (see Gen. 1:28, "be fruitful and multiply and fill the earth and subdue it"). All of the wealth that is found in the earth was created by God, and it ultimately belongs to him (see Hag. 2:8: "the silver is mine, and the gold is mine, declares the LORD of hosts"), and so these Wise Men who bring gifts to the Lord are only offering back what belongs to him, and he is worthy to receive all honor and glory from it.

In fact, the Old Testament historical narrative foreshadowed a time when the wealth of the nations would be brought to the king of Israel who reigns in Jerusalem, as happened during the glorious period of Solomon's kingdom (see 2 Chron. 9:22–23). And now when the Magi come to bring their gifts to Jesus, they are simply the first of the leaders of the nations who will ultimately come and bow before Jesus, who will reign as King of kings and Lord of lords. They foreshadow all the rulers of the world bowing before their true King.

In the future, this theme of the wealth of the nations flowing to Jerusalem in the worship of God will be fulfilled in the New Jerusalem, for we read, "By its light will the nations walk, and the kings of the earth will bring their glory into it" (Rev. 21:24). All the glory and wealth of the earth will be devoted to the worship of the King, and when the Wise Men open their treasures and present them to Jesus, it is a foreshadowing of that continual offering in the Jerusalem that is to come.

These Wise Men are also Gentiles, not from Israel but from another nation. But God had predicted as early as Genesis 12 that in Abraham (and, by implication, in his descendants), "all the families of the earth shall be blessed" (Gen.12:3). There are various historical events that anticipated this throughout the history of the Old Testament, as when Gentiles such as Rahab and Ruth became part of God's people. But when we come to the New Testament, these "wise men from the east" (Matt. 2:1) are the first of a long stream of Gentiles who will become part of God's people and worship the Lord Jesus Christ.

This theme finds further development when Jesus commands his disciples to "make disciples of all nations" (Matt. 28:19), and to be his witnesses "in Jerusalem and in all Judea and Samaria, and to the end of the earth" (Acts 1:8). It finds further development when the Gentiles who were not God's people, who were "alienated from the commonwealth of Israel and strangers to the covenant of promise," who had "no hope" and were "without God in the world" (Eph. 2:12), have become part of the church and become "fellow citizens with the saints and members of the household of God" (Eph. 2:19).

But the visit of the (Gentile) Wise Men to baby Jesus finds even greater fulfillment in the age to come when John's vision shows that around God's throne is "a great multitude that no one could number, from every nation, from all tribes and peoples and languages, standing before the throne and before the Lamb . . . crying out with a loud voice, 'Salvation belongs to our God who sits on the throne, and to the Lamb!'" (Rev. 7:9–10). All nations will join in the worship of Jesus

Christ, and the "wise men from the east" are the forerunners of that wonderful theme in Scripture.

If we keep this "big picture" of developing themes in mind in our interpretation, it will help our people understand the Bible not as a series of isolated verses, but as a unified whole that develops as an outworking of God's eternal and wise plans.

Conclusion

No doubt much more can be said about how to interpret the Bible rightly. But I hope that these brief comments might serve as a help and encouragement to many younger seminary students, pastors, and Bible teachers so that they, in imitation of the faithful ministry of Kent Hughes over so many years, might be wise and faithful interpreters of the biblical text, so that they might strengthen the faith and knowledge of their hearers, and so that they might bring glory to God in all that they teach from his Word throughout all their days.

5

Rightly Dividing the Word of Truth: A Study Method for Faithful Preaching

John MacArthur

The apostle Paul was about to die. Incarcerated in one of Rome's most dreadful dungeons, the faithful apostle knew that his execution was imminent. "I am already being poured out as a drink offering, and the time of my departure has come," he wrote to Timothy in his final letter. From an earthly standpoint, Paul's situation was bleak. His coworker Demas had betrayed him; others had abandoned him; he was cold and forsaken in prison. He had been alone at his trial, falsely accused of insurrection by his enemies, and subsequently sentenced to death.

But the apostle was not disheartened. "The Lord stood by me and strengthened me," he wrote. In the face of death, Paul was triumphant: "The Lord will rescue me from every evil deed and bring me safely into his heavenly kingdom."

Faced with the abandonment of his friends, the accusations of his enemies, and the anguish of an impending death sentence, Paul remained unflappable. From an earthly perspective, it seemed as though his life would end in failure. But Paul knew differently: "I have fought the good fight, I have finished the race, I have kept the faith. Henceforth there is laid up for me the crown of righteousness, which the Lord, the righteous judge, will award to me on that Day."

His life was not one of popularity, prosperity, prestige, or social power. It had not been successful by the usual measures of earthly success. *But he had been faithful.* And from God's perspective, *faithfulness is success.* He could look forward to death with confident expectation because he knew the Savior was waiting for him. After a life of faithfulness, he could rightly anticipate hearing the Lord say, "Well done."

The Call to Expository Faithfulness

Significantly, it is in this context that Paul charged Timothy, his son in the faith, with this straightforward command: "Preach the Word!" Earlier in the letter, the apostle had similarly exhorted his apprentice, "Do your best to present yourself to God as one approved, a worker who has no need to be ashamed, rightly handling the word of truth" (2 Tim. 2:15).

As a workman Paul was not ashamed, because he had been faithful to his ministry. First and foremost this meant that he had been faithful to the *message* God had given him (cf. Titus 1:3). He had *kept the faith,* guarding "that which was entrusted to him" (cf. 1 Tim. 6:20). Now he was exhorting Timothy to do the same.

The church was not yet one hundred years old. Yet there were already plenty of lazy, unfaithful, hypocritical preachers to be found. Some were in it for the money (1 Tim. 6:3–10), others for the popularity (2 Tim. 4:3–4). As a result, the truth was being watered-down, twisted, and forsaken. In their pursuit of worldly success, these false teachers continually demonstrated their spiritual unfaithfulness.

Timothy was to be different. He was to handle the Word with precision, from pure motives, for the glory of his Lord. To restate Paul's words, he was to present himself to God as an unashamed worker who interpreted the Word of truth accurately.

Paul's charge to Timothy rings as true today as it did in the first century. Those ministers who long for true success, meaning the Lord's approval, must work hard to handle his Word with precision. They must give maximum effort in the study and imparting of God's truth—so that their sermons will present the Word of the Lord as accurately, articulately, and authentically as possible.

The aim of their ministry will be to present themselves to God as those who are approved. Their congregation may number in the thousands. Their messages may air on radio and television. Their books may top bestseller lists. But unless their preaching is approved by God, they are failures in the only sense that matters. True success is faithfulness, not popularity. And faithfulness in the pulpit demands diligence in the study.

Those who are lazy in their study, undisciplined in preparation, and careless in proclamation will one day be ashamed. But not faithful workmen. Like Paul, they will one day stand with joyful confidence before their gracious Master.

The Mark of a Faithful Teacher

The faithful workman must *divide* the word of truth *rightly*. The Greek term Paul used literally means "to cut straight." It referred to a craftsman cutting a straight line, a mason setting a straight line of bricks, a farmer plowing a straight furrow, or a workman building a straight road. Metaphorically, it was used of carefully performing any task. Because he was a tentmaker by trade (Acts 18:3), Paul could have had in mind the careful, straight cutting and sewing of the many pieces of leather or cloth necessary to make a tent.

The careful exegete and expositor of God's word of truth must be meticulous in the way he interprets and pieces together the many individual truths found in Scripture. His love and reverence for the Author of Scripture demands it. No faithful ambassador wishes to misrepresent the wishes of his King.

Thankfully, the message of the gospel is abundantly clear in God's Word. The student of Scripture need not fear that its message is unknowable. Rather, he can rejoice in knowing that God revealed himself and his plan of salvation in a way that men can understand. Not only does the Scripture repeatedly claim that God revealed what is written within its pages (over 2,000 times in fact), it also describes itself as that which gives light (Ps. 119:105; 2 Pet. 1:19a), is profitable (2 Tim. 3:16–17), explains salvation (2 Tim. 3:15b), addresses common people (cf. Deut. 6:4; Mark 12:37; Eph. 1:1; 1 Cor. 1:2), can be understood by children (Deut. 6:6–7; Eph. 6:4; 2 Tim. 3:14–15), and should be used to test the validity of religious ideas (Acts 17:11; cf. 2 Cor. 10:5; 1 Thess. 5:21–22). It is the truth (John 17:17) that sets men free (John 8:31–36). Thus, to deny the clarity of Scripture is to call into question not only the Bible's own self-claims, but also God's ability to communicate clearly.

It is because "the words of Scripture are objectively God's revelation [that] one person can point to the content of the Bible in seeking to demonstrate to another what the correct understanding is."[1] Moreover, because God's revelation is clear:

> Scripture can be and is read with profit, with appreciation and with transformative results. It is open and transparent to earnest readers; it is intelligible and comprehensible to attentive readers. Scripture itself is coherent and obvious. It is direct and unambiguous as written; what is written is sufficient. Scripture's concern or focal point is readily presented as the redemptive story of God. It displays a progressively more specific identification of that story, culminating in the gospel of Jesus Christ. All this is to say: Scripture is clear about what it is about.[2]

Because God has revealed himself in an understandable, clear way, in keeping with the normal means of human language and communication, the student of Scripture can rightly interpret God's message in the *normal* sense in which human language and communication is interpreted. Whether preaching poetry, prophecy, or Paul's epistles, the student of Scripture is correct if he approaches Scripture with the confidence that God revealed it clearly, and he did so using the normal features of language.

But the clarity of Scripture does not mean that diligent study is unnecessary or unwarranted. In fact, just the opposite is true. Rightly dividing the Word of truth demands great effort. This is true for several reasons. First, because its author is God (2 Pet. 1:21), the message of Scripture is as infinitely profound as it is simple and straightforward. As Thomas Scott explained, "The things that are absolutely necessary to salvation, are few, simple, and obvious to the meanest capacity, provided it be attended by a humble teachable disposition: but the most learned, acute, and diligent student cannot, in the longest life, obtain an entire knowledge of this one volume."[3] Thus, diligent study is needed to draw out the deep truths of God's Word.

Second, because it was originally written many years ago in very different contexts, today's exegete has to work hard to bridge the gaps of language, culture, geography, and history. He must also do his best to understand the flow of the argument, as it would have been understood by its original readers, and as it would have been intended by its original human author. Few ills have done more damage to the contemporary church than the proliferation of sermons that base misguided applica-

---

1. Millard J. Erickson, *Christian Theology* (Grand Rapids, MI: Baker, 2001), 279.

2. James Patrick Callahan, *The Clarity of Scripture* (Downers Grove, IL: InterVarsity, 2001), 9.

3. Thomas Scott, "Preface to *Thomas Scott's Commentary on the Bible.*" This preface, first published in 1804, was often placed in the front of Bibles as an introduction to the text.

tion on misinterpreted or spiritualized texts. The faithful workman will be careful to keep context in view.

Third, because error is so plentiful in the church today, the diligent expositor must approach the text carefully, testing all things to see whether or not they measure up to the truth (cf. Acts 17:11; 1 Thess. 5:21–22; Jude 3–4). Doctrinal error is an eternally serious matter, and no faithful minister would ever knowingly invite it into his ministry. Sound doctrine, on the other hand, is to be guarded and taught (2 Tim. 1:14). The faithful workman, then, studies diligently, "holding fast the faithful word as he has been taught, that he may be able, by sound doctrine, both to exhort and convict those who contradict" (Titus 1:9 NKJV).

Since nothing is as important as the Word, no energy expended by anyone in any field should surpass the effort of an expositor seeking to "rightly divide the Word." Yet this is too seldom the case. As Jay Adams correctly observes:

> I have had the opportunity to hear much preaching over the last few years, some very good, some mediocre, most very bad. What is the problem with preaching? There is no *one* problem, of course. . . . But if there is one thing that stands out most, perhaps it is the problem I mention today.
>
> What I am about to say may not strike you as being as specific as other things I have written, yet I believe it is at the bottom of a number of other difficulties. My point is that good preaching demands hard work. From listening to sermons and from talking to hundreds of preachers about preaching, I am convinced that the basic reason for poor preaching is the failure to spend adequate time and energy in preparation. Many preachers—perhaps most—simply don't work long enough on their sermons.[4]

If one truly believes God inspired every word of Scripture, how can he justify treating it with any degree of triteness or superficiality? And if the Word is the sword of the Spirit (Eph. 6:17; Heb. 4:12) and the power of God for salvation (Rom. 1:16) and sanctification (John 17:17), how can anyone invest more trust in stories and clever insights than in Scripture? A man once said to the Puritan preacher Richard Rogers, "Mr. Rogers, I like you and your company very well, only you are too precise." "Oh sir," replied Rogers, "I serve a precise God."[5] And God

---

4. Jay E. Adams, "Editorial: Good Preaching Is Hard Work," *The Journal of Pastoral Practice* 4, no. 2 (1980): 1 (italics in original).

5. Peter Lewis, "The Genius of Puritanism" (Haywards Heath, Sussex: Carey, 1979), 17 (caption to illustration on opposite page).

has not lowered his standard of precision to accommodate a dumbed-down society.

The Basics of Bible Study

At the foundational level, there are three familiar basics for Bible study: observation, interpretation, and application. The exegete must familiarize himself with the text (observation), identify the intended meaning of the text (interpretation), and determine how to appropriately respond (application).

Observation

Observation is the initial step in Bible study. The interpreter must avoid jumping to conclusions before first familiarizing himself with the content and context of the passage. He must resist the temptation to plunge immediately into commentaries and other study helps before living in the passage himself. Nothing can replace firsthand observation. And thus he should devote extended time to this crucial practice. Robert A. Traina defines observation as "essentially *awareness . . .* the general function of observation is to enable one to become *saturated* with the particulars of a passage so that one is thoroughly conscious of their existence and of the need for their explanation. Observation is the means by which the data of a passage becomes part of the mentality of the student. It supplies the raw materials upon which the mind may operate in the interpretive process."[6]

It includes a broad awareness of the terms, structure, and literary form of the passage. It should be careful, systematic, and persistent. Martin Luther likened his Bible study to gathering apples: "First I shake the whole tree, that the ripest may fall. Then I climb the tree and shake each limb, and then each branch and then each twig, and then I look under each leaf."[7]

Observation begins by reading and rereading the passage until the exegete is saturated with its content; it allows the Bible student to answer the questions *Who? What? Where? When? Why?* and *How?* The interpreter should also note the significance of certain textual markers, such as verbs, connecting words, repeated terms, comparisons and contrasts,

---

6. Robert A. Traina, *Methodical Bible Study* (New York: Biblical Seminary, 1952), 31–32 (italics in original).

7. Cited in Richard Mayhue, *How to Interpret the Bible for Yourself* (Chicago: Moody Press, 1986), 49.

commands and exhortations, or words and phrases the biblical author has used elsewhere. By observing what the text itself says, the preacher has an objective basis upon which to propositionally state the truths of God's Word—rather than just subjectively asserting that "this is what *such and such* means to me."

After making general observations regarding the structure and flow of the passage, the exegete should identify key words and phrases within the passage—noting their lexical and syntactical relationships to one another. Since God chose to communicate using human language, the preacher can best understand the meaning of a passage by identifying the key words and phrases therein.

William D. Barrick notes seven aspects involved in this identification process:

1) Ask, "To what is each word, phrase, clause, sentence, and paragraph related? In what way? For what purpose?"

2) Ask, "Where is the prominence or emphasis?" Pay attention to word order and the employment of emphatic words.

3) Determine what idioms are being employed in the passage.

4) Determine the literary form (genre) of the passage. Is the text narrative, poetry, prophecy, or something else?

5) Determine what literary devices (chiasms, repetition, inclusion, assonance, parallelism, etc.) are being employed.

6) Perform a word study for each key word in the text. Keep in mind that many words have no great "golden nugget" of expositional truth outside of their usage within the text's proposition.

7) State the argument and/or the development of the theme succinctly and in your own words.[8]

Interpretation

As the exegete familiarizes himself with a given text, he should always keep in mind one simple question: "What does this mean?" It is irresponsible to read the text and jump directly to some application; the essential issue for the expositor is to discern the meaning, so that no application is illegitimate.

After this exercise, the exegete should turn to the available resources, such as commentaries, lexicons, Bible dictionaries, theologies, histories, and concordances. In this process new observations may surface, and

---

8. Adapted from Bill Barrick, "Expository Preaching—Exegetical Preparation," Shepherds' Conference seminar (March 2003).

most of the exegete's original questions should be answered and observations expanded. Granted, the interpreter should emphasize research on interpretation in conservative commentaries, while recognizing that liberal commentaries may provide insight related to technical matters in regard to the original language and its usage.

GAPS TO BRIDGE

As briefly noted earlier, there are four gaps that the contemporary student of Scripture must bridge in order to rightly understand what it means. First, the expositor must be equipped to bridge *the language gap*. Since the Bible was originally written in Greek, Hebrew, and Aramaic, the meaning of a word or phrase in the original language is often the key to correctly interpreting a passage of Scripture. Even if a pastor is not fluent in the biblical languages, he should draw from trustworthy sources to aid him in interacting with the original text.

Second, the preacher must overcome *the culture gap*. The Bible must first be viewed in the context of the time and place in which it was written. For instance, without an understanding of first-century Jewish culture, it is difficult to understand the Gospels. Similarly, Acts and the Epistles must be read in light of the Greek and Roman cultures and history.

A third gap that needs to be closed is *the geography gap*. Biblical geography makes the Bible come alive. A good Bible atlas is an invaluable reference tool that can help you comprehend the geography of the Holy Land. Of course, nothing does this more than visiting the land firsthand. But even those who have never been to Israel should do their best to familiarize themselves with it as much as possible.

Finally, students of Scripture must also bridge *the history gap*. Unlike the scriptures of most other world religions, the Bible contains the records of actual historical persons and events. An understanding of Bible history will help the expositor place the people and events in it in their proper historical perspective. A good Bible dictionary or Bible encyclopedia is useful here, as are basic historical studies.

PRINCIPLES TO UNDERSTAND

In addition to the gaps that must be bridged, exegetes should allow four principles to guide their biblical interpretation: literal, historical, grammatical, and syntactical. These principles have already been briefly mentioned. But they bear reiterating here since they are absolutely foundational to the exegete's task.

The literal principle asserts that Scripture should be understood in its normal and natural sense. This is not to say that Scripture contains no figures of speech or symbols. Certainly it does, and they should be interpreted as such, in keeping with the normal rules of language. The faithful interpreter must allow it to speak for itself, without inventing allegorical, spiritualized, or fanciful interpretations.

The historical principle compels the student of Scripture to interpret God's Word in its ancient context. As those who will explain God's truth to a current generation, expositors must first ask what the text meant to the people to whom it was originally written. In this way the interpreter can develop a proper contextual understanding of the original intent of the passage.

The grammatical principle requires that exegetes understand the basic grammatical structure of each sentence in the original language. What are the action and the tense of the main verb? To whom do the pronouns refer? How do the various elements of the sentence relate to one another? Often by asking some simple questions like those, along with diagramming the sentence, the meaning of the text quickly becomes clear.

The syntactical principle is what the Reformers called the *analogia scriptura*. It means that the Bible cannot contradict itself, based on the fact that its Author cannot contradict himself. If the student arrives at an interpretation of a passage that contradicts or opposes a truth taught elsewhere in the Scriptures, the student's interpretation cannot be correct. The right interpretation will always be consistent with the rest of God's revealed truth.

Application

Having read and interpreted the passage, the expositor should have a basic understanding of what it means by what it says. But examining the Scriptures does not stop there. The exegete's ultimate goal is to release the meaning of the Word so as to convict and encourage his own heart, enabling him to grow spiritually by personal application.

From the expositor's personal application flows corporate application. Having embraced the truth in his own heart, the expositor is now ready to preach it to his congregation. In general, it is usually best to emphasize the meaning of the text, then the theological truth it teaches with general application, allowing the Holy Spirit to fill in the specifics for individuals. Though there is only one meaning in each text, there are many applications. The specific nature of those applications depends on the individual circumstances of each member of the congregation.

Application answers the question, "How does this text impact me?" The following questions will help apply the truths discovered in Bible study:[9]

1) Are there *examples* to follow?
2) Are there *commands* to obey?
3) Are there *errors* to avoid?
4) Are there *sins* to forsake?
5) Are there *promises* to claim?
6) Are there *new thoughts* about God?
7) Are there *truths or doctrines* to further explore?
8) Are there *convictions* to live by?

Meditation is also an important part of the application process, since God's people are called to think upon his truth and its implication in their own lives. Meditation entails focusing the mind on one subject, involving reason, imagination, and emotions. It is a natural overflow of the discovery process in Bible study. Concentrated meditation on the truths of God's Word weaves those truths into the fabric of life. Perhaps Paul had this meditative process in view when he told Timothy to be "constantly nourished on the words of the faith and of the sound doctrine" (1 Tim. 4:6 NASB).

Careful Bible study skills are the foundation upon which all good expository sermons are built. The expository preacher is, by definition, a skilled handler of Scripture. He interprets it accurately, applies it personally, and then proclaims it to his congregation so that they can understand and act upon God's Word, as well as instruct others with what they have learned.

A Personal Word on the Study Process

Every expositor should have a careful and deliberate plan for putting these principles to work routinely in preparation. Such will increase both confidence in his study and consistency in his preaching. The following method is the one I usually follow in my own study. It is included here in the hope that it will be helpful to others in their own exegetical preparation.[10]

---

9. Adapted from Mayhue, *How to Interpret*, 64.

10. The following section is adapted from chapter 11 of *Preaching: How to Preach Biblically* (Nashville: Thomas Nelson, 2005), 179–82.

Read the Book

Because I generally preach through entire books of the New Testament, I always begin by reading the whole book. It is imperative for the expositor to be familiar with the overall message and flow of the book before he begins preaching any passages from it. As I have grown in my own preaching ministry, I have come to realize how important this step is. When I was less experienced, I sometimes found myself assuming an interpretation was correct because I lacked familiarity with all that would come later in the book, leading to serious difficulties later. For example, in 1 Thessalonians, God's eschatological wrath is mentioned in 1:10 and again in 5:9. The expositor should make sure that his interpretation of wrath in both of those passages is consistent.

Context is the most important hermeneutical principle. By reading and familiarizing himself with the entire book, the expositor can relate each passage to the overall context of the book. Putting together a general outline of the book and identifying key verses is also helpful in grasping the overall flow.

At this point I also read the introductory sections in several good commentaries. Through this I become familiar with the author of the book, the addressees, the book's theme or purpose, the date of its writing, and other important background material. General introductions for New Testament books along with Bible encyclopedias are also useful sources for finding background material.

Read the Passage

I read whatever passage I am working through repeatedly in my English Bible until it is pretty well fixed in my memory. I try to do that early in my preparation process so I will have plenty of time to meditate on it before I begin my exegesis. Once I begin concentrating on my sermon text, it dominates my thinking, conversation, and reading during my time of preparation. This is a foundational part of becoming familiar with the text. I rarely consciously memorize Scripture, but by the time I finish preparing the sermon, I usually have the text pretty well memorized.

Find the Main Point

In approaching the text, my primary interpretive goal is to find and articulate the main point the passage is teaching. This "big idea" (also known as the *thesis* or *proposition*) is very often connected with the main verb in the passage, though not necessarily so, especially in a parable or narrative passage. I ask myself questions like, "What is the primary message of this passage? What is the central truth? What is the main expositional idea?" Once I have found it, I write it out in a complete sentence because it is crucial that the main idea of the passage be clear in my own mind. Subsequent development of the text hinges on it.

Clearly explaining the main point of the passage is the target I aim for in my preaching. It is the primary message I want my people to retain after they hear the sermon. So it is crucial that the proposition be articulated carefully and clearly. Everything else in the sermon serves to help, impress, convict, and confront the hearer with the main truth. From the introduction to the conclusion, it all connects to the main truth.

Organize the Passage

After I find the main point, I begin to look for the subordinate points that support it. They will often be connected with the subordinate verbs, participles, or infinitives. This is the first step in outlining the passage. It also provides a confirmation of the main point. If the main thought I have determined for a passage is not broad enough to include all the other thoughts or is not fully supported by them, I need to rework it.

Let me illustrate the process of finding the main and subordinate points by looking at Matthew 28:19–20. The main verb is "make disciples," while "go," "baptizing," and "teaching" are all participles modifying the main verb. The main point, then, might be "how to make disciples." The subpoints would be "going," "baptizing," and "teaching." The sermon explains how to make disciples by fulfilling those three duties.

Analyze the Structure

After reading the passage and discovering the main and subordinate points, the next step is a detailed analysis of its words and grammar. I work through the passage in detail in the Greek text, taking notes on a legal-sized note pad. I look first for any problems in the passage, such as an important textual variant, an unusual word, or a difficult grammatical construction. At this point, I begin to use study tools such as linguistic keys, lexicons, concordances, word studies, and exegetical commentaries.

I also find it helpful to diagram the passage. I no longer write out the diagram since I can usually visualize it mentally. Diagramming each sentence helps make me aware of the grammatical structure and the relationships between different words and phrases within each sentence. When studying the grammar of a passage, I pay special attention to prepositions and the case of the nouns. After all, rightly understanding the passage may hinge on correctly identifying the direct object, the indirect object, and whether something is in apposition to something else. A working knowledge of English grammar is essential for this process.

At this point I also read as many good commentaries as I can to assist in the interpretation and to garner cross-references and theological insights.

Put Together an Exegetical Outline

As the final step in the study process, I put together a preliminary outline. It is not the outline I will preach from but is rather an exegetical outline drawn directly from my study of the text. It is not alliterated, and I may write down several different ways of stating each point. I purposely place this step toward the end of the study process. Doing even a preliminary outline before the detailed study of the passage increases the danger of forcing the text to fit our preconceived ideas. We must be careful to let the text speak for itself, rather than trying to bend it to fit an outline of our own creation. Placing the other steps first in the study process helps avoid this tendency.

Add Illustrations

After the outline is refined, I search for the best illustrations. I prefer biblical illustrations because they teach the Word while they illustrate, because they are God's choice of illustrative material, because Scripture interprets itself best, and because they have divine authority to go with human interest. Other illustrations can be added to these. Finally, I write the introduction and conclusion. I wait until the end to do this, so that I know exactly what I am introducing and concluding.

Careful Preparation Produces Confident Preaching

By studying diligently, thoroughly, and precisely, the expositor can be confident that he is rightly dividing the Word of truth. Having prepared properly, he can enter the pulpit with confidence—not only before his people, but also before his Lord—knowing that faithfulness to the message brings honor to the Master.

Rightly dividing the Word of truth, then, is the central mark of a truly successful preacher. In the end, when he stands before the Chief Shepherd, only one factor about his ministry will ultimately matter: *Was he faithful?* He may have been a dynamic orator, a master storyteller, and a winsome communicator. His church might have been large and his ministry well known. But if his own faithfulness is absent, all of those externals are merely wood, hay, and straw (cf. 1 Cor. 3:10–15). Only that which is done out of loyalty to Christ will be rewarded.

True success, then, is found in pleasing him. For pastors and teachers, this begins with guarding the truth by interpreting it accurately and proclaiming it articulately to the flock. Though it ends in the pulpit, such a stewardship begins in the study, as the man of God illumined by the Spirit of God studies the Word of God for the glory of God.

May we therefore approach our privileged task with sobriety and reverence, knowing that as teachers we shall receive a stricter judgment (James 3:1).

PART TWO

BIBLICAL
AND HISTORICAL
PARADIGMS

6

Paul's Paradigm for Preachers

Bruce Winter

This essay contends that preaching that "simply exegetes" the biblical text is not sufficient to secure God's intention of personal transformation through the Word of God. Evangelists, pastors, and teachers need to be able to understand how the secular culture has already programmed, and will continue to program, the mind-set of non-Christians as well as that of Christians on individual issues.

To use contemporary terminology, a mental software package called "the spirit of this age" and another called "the will of God" or "the knowledge of God" cannot operate in the same mind (Rom. 12:2). Paul sees these two programs as incompatible and therefore unable to be stored in the same databank. Our situation is no less comparable to that of the Corinthians. There were, and still are, powerful, culturally shaped citadels that have become entrenched in the mind. The secular world's programming not only hinders the entrance of the gospel for the unbeliever, but it also presents a difficulty for Christians, because conversion to Christ does not automatically deprogram the ways of thinking and acting that have been driven by "the spirit of this age." If the argument and human arrogance mounted by the secular world, which are contrary to the will of God, are not exposed for what they are and subsequently demolished, then transformation by the renewing of the Christian mind will not occur.

Paul's Strategy for Spiritual Warfare (2 Cor. 10:3–5)

Paul's detractors had maliciously put it around the Corinthian church that he had been acting in a worldly fashion (2 Cor. 10:2), by which they meant that his actions were shaped not by the mind of Christ as he had claimed (1 Cor. 2:16) but by contemporary norms. This allegation was made in much the same manner that (sadly) some members of our congregations rumor today about their pastors and teachers. In 2 Corinthians 10–13, Paul demonstrates to the church that this allegation against him was patently untrue, and he contends that any charge made would have to be substantiated upon his return on the same basis as it was done in the Old Testament. Only on the evidence of two or three witnesses can charges be sustained (2 Cor. 13:1).

In the meantime, Paul discloses to the Corinthians how he responds to the charge that he is driven by culture instead of by Christ, and he engages in what the church there might wrongly interpret as his "defense." What Paul has done was done to "build up" the church in Corinth, as he later discloses (2 Cor. 12:19). However, to "build up" means that there has to first be demolition—in this case, the programming of the present age that has been the grid through which some of the Corinthian Christians have evaluated Paul and his motives, they themselves having been shaped on this issue by the world and not by the Word.

To understand this issue in the last four chapters in Paul's second letter to the Corinthians, we need to cast our minds back to a critical discussion in 1 Corinthians 1–4, where Christians themselves had wheeled into the midst of their church in Corinth a Trojan horse that was the cult of secular leadership. There Paul traced its destructive effects of strife, jealousy, and divisions that were manifested at every point of the church's corporate life, namely, the division of the body of Christ into competing parties (1 Cor. 1–4; 11:18; 12:25). Whenever they met together, they engaged in what were culturally acceptable ways of behaving, replicating in the gathering of God (1 Cor. 1:2) the way members operated in the secular, official "gathering of Corinth" in this Roman colony to undertake official business. It is what some today might comfortably call ecclesiastical "politics," as one example of secular programming.

Paul's opponents had not surrendered after his first assault on their entrenched secular thinking (1 Corinthians 1–4). So in 2 Corinthians 10–13, Paul was compelled to deal further with the effects on the ministry of a new movement that trained young people to speak in secular gatherings using all tricks of the grand style of oratory learned in the Corinthian academy (1 Cor. 2:1). Paul was forced to resume addressing this culturally engrained and seemingly intractable problem. As he does so, he discloses a very important paradigm that he developed to counter not only this but any other cultural programming both outside and inside the church. The secular programming of the Corinthian Christians was powerful, and unless Paul could deconstruct it, then culture, and not Christ, would win the battle going on in their minds.

Paul approaches this issue (1) by using an important analogy to describe his approach to disarm the ideas and behavior patterns that are contrary to obedience to Christ; (2) by employing it in his evangelistic speech in the presence of members of the Council of the Areopagus in Athens, which had been programmed to see the world through two major philosophical schools of their day; and (3) by demolishing the secular arguments adopted by some young Christian men to defend conduct that was clearly contrary to God's will for them.

Paul shows not only what has to be done, but also how it is to be done. This self-disclosure is extremely significant in our day and generation for evangelists, pastors, and teachers because it provides a pastoral paradigm for all three aspects of ministry. It is appropriate to explore this issue in a volume that honors a Christian preacher and friend who epitomized so effectively this Pauline paradigm in his long, distinguished, and productive ministry for the kingdom of God.

Roman Warfare and Pauline "Warfare"

Rome's naval strategies had been developed from the Greeks, but it had shaped its own mighty and highly trained military machine. It did so by using standing armies that moved around the vast Roman empire whenever trouble broke out. One of the Roman techniques was that of siege warfare, which was used to conquer a city.[1] Seemingly impenetrable citadels had been built on hills or rocky outcrops overlooking cities in the classical Greek and Hellenistic eras before the Roman conquest of the East began. Thick walls surrounding these citadels were constructed of large stones that were the final defense for inhabitants as well as combatants facing adversaries in an armed invasion.

Once a city was surrounded, the Roman troops built towers as many as three stories high from which weapons such as arrows could be used to great effect against those holed up behind the fortification of the city. The Romans also developed the battering ram, which was highly effective through persistent use in ultimately loosening the large stones that constituted the wall of defense. The stronghold would collapse, and the

---

1. A. Goldsworthy, *The Roman Army at War* (Oxford: Clarendon Press, 1996).

troops inside were then forced to surrender and kneel before the conquering general as a sign of their defeat, or face being massacred.[2]

Corinthian Christians would have clearly understood Paul's uses of this imagery. Their walls had been destroyed in 146 B.C. when the Romans defeated and sacked the city. The Acrocorinth also overshadowed their city. The walls of that stronghold had been there for centuries. Today it is clear that the towering outer wall and two other interior walls on the Acrocorinth constituted lines of defense that still look impenetrable today, although they were breached in previous eras. The city and acropolis walls provide a poignant analogy for what needed to be done to bring down both the ideological and the cultural citadels of the Corinthians' mind-set.

Paul begins by indicating that he, too, has "weapons" to deal with this intransigent problem, but his were not of the worldly type. Paul was not borrowing rhetorical techniques and argumentation taught in the schools of oratory that thrived in the first century and that saw the rise of what is called "the Second Sophistic."[3] Paul reported that there were some who suspect us of walking in a worldly fashion (2 Cor. 10:2). Elsewhere he used the same verb with a synonymous term, that of literally walking "according to man," i.e., in a secular fashion, and behaving just as other Corinthians did (1 Cor. 3:3–4). So the charge made against him seems to be that in spite of his response to those who examine him concerning his *modus operandi* of not exercising his rights as an apostle to carry about a wife nor being supported by the gospel (1 Cor. 9), the reality was altogether different.

Paul refutes such a suggestion in 2 Corinthians 10, explaining that "though we live in the world"—literally "in the flesh"—we do not engage in warfare "according to the flesh" (10:3). The reason Paul gives for not doing this is that the weapons he uses are not "worldly" ones (10:4a NIV). On the contrary, he asserts they are powerful weapons "for God to use" (10:4b).[4] Presumably this weapon is God's Word, for Paul declares later in 2 Corinthians that "we have been speaking in Christ" (12:19; cf. 1 Cor. 2:16).

There are three aspects to his *modus operandi*. First, God's weapons are used to bring down entrenched strongholds that he refers to as

---

2. A. Goldsworthy, *Roman Warfare* (London: Casswell, 2000).

3. See my "Revelation *v.* Rhetoric: Paul and the First-century Corinthian Fad," in *Translating Truth: the Case for an Essentially Literal Bible Translation* (Wheaton, IL: Crossway, 2005), chap. 5, that refutes the recent trend that says Paul used the rhetoric he denounced in 1 Cor. 2:1–5. He declared in 2 Cor. 1:13–14 that he has adopted "plain style" so the recipients could read and understand.

4. The construction according to Blass-Debrunner-Funk, *A Greek Grammar of the New Testament and Other Early Christian Literature*, is the dative of advantage, 188.2.

"arguments." It is a battle for the citadel of the mind that has been programmed by that which is false, even though it has wide currency in the secular world and is regarded as *ipso facto* true. Paul sees it as his task to subject ideas and ideologies that have wide currency in "this age" to scrutiny and to examine the premise upon which they have been erected.

Second, Paul uses the analogy of the destruction of all "exalted obstacles" that rebels would erect as a defense. He explains that these are entrenched intellectual positions in contradistinction to the truth and that actually stand in the way of the knowledge of God. He has already stated in 2 Corinthians that it was God who "through us . . . spread the knowledge of him," i.e., God (2:14), and that the knowledge of the glory of God is to be seen in the person of Christ (4:6).[5] The knowledge of God is given through his Word, for God, like humans, cannot be understood apart from a willingness to engage in self-disclosure.

However, barriers to the knowledge of God had been erected in the culture. For example, Rome had not only brought the benefits of technology to its great empire but had also promoted the concept of "the eternity" of Rome and its empire. This would come with the emperor as a "messianic" savior who had brought the *pax romana* to the inhabited world.[6] Paul had to combat the effects not only of the skillful propaganda of the Romans when it stood in contradiction to the truth, but he also had to deal with the academy of his day and with its philosophical *a priori* assumptions that contradicted it. These had invaded the psyche of the inhabitants of this greatest empire on earth.

Third, Paul's aim was to capture their thoughts. A conquering army brought those in rebellion before their general once the enemy fortress had been sacked. The prisoners knelt before the general to acknowledge their defeat, as well as the general's superior power. The conquered soldiers were now subject to the general. So, too, Paul's strategy, as he indicates by way of this analogy, was to "take every thought captive to obey Christ" (10:5). It was a case of surrendering not only one's life but also one's way of looking at life and death and the ways of the world.

How Paul worked out this paradigm will now be examined in two case studies independent of 2 Corinthians 10–13. One is in evangelism and the other an issue that was widely endorsed in the culture but was unacceptable to Christ. It is important to note that Paul does not demolish people, but rather he addresses their arguments and thoughts

---

5. The word that is literally rendered as "face" refers not to the actual face of Christ, for which we have no first-century portraits, but to its Latin equivalent, *persona*, i.e., the person of Christ.

6. Klaus Wengst, *Pax Romana and the Peace of Christ* (London: SCM, 1987).

that are contrary to the Word of God—a point that has not always been followed in some of the great debates over issues in the church both in past eras and also in our contemporary Christian scene.

Paul's "Warfare" with the Intelligentsia in Athens (Acts 17:16–34)

Much has been written on Paul's famous speech in Athens, the substance of which has been recorded by Luke. For our purposes it provides an excellent paradigm of Paul engaging the mind-set of an audience for an evangelistic outcome. It did result in the conversion of Dionysius, a member of this distinguished council, and also Damarus—both people of rank and status, along with "others with them," presumably their clients (Acts 17:34).[7] What can be deduced from Acts 17 as to how Paul approached the mindset of his audience?

We must ask the important question of how the Athenians "read" Paul before we explore how Paul read the Athenians. Opinions were divided among those in the Greek agora where Paul was arguing with those present. Some dismissed him as having nothing to say because he was engaged in speaking "nonsense." Others thought that he appeared to be the herald of foreign *daimonia* (Acts 17:18). The Greek term was used of the gods or divine spirits in men, including the emperor, who was described in the East as "god, son of god."[8] It was the role of the Council of the Areopagus, exercised for centuries, to admit foreign divinities into Athens, a right they continued to exercise under the Romans (they diplomatically admitted emperors and sometimes their family members as "gods").[9]

The task of the herald of a new god was to prove that his god or goddess existed. This was the first tenet in the traditional philosophi-

---

7. Although detailed discussion of Acts 17 cannot be undertaken within the parameters of this essay, there are five aspects that are essential for those to follow who seek to engage the mind-set of our generation with the gospel. It is being suggested that these are programmatic to such an endeavor to penetrate the minds of the citizens of this world in order for them to become citizens of heaven. Elsewhere I have examined in detail the five aspects to Paul's apologetic over against the mind-set of first-century Stoics and Epicureans who were present. See "Introducing the Athenians to God: Paul's Failed Apologetic in Acts 17?" in R. Chia and M. Chan, eds., *A Graced Horizon: Essays in Gospel, Culture and Church in Honor of the Rev. Dr. Choong Chee Pang* (Singapore: Genesis, 2005), 65–84; and for a less technical version see *Themelios* 31.1 (2005), 38–59.

8. See my *Sharing the Throne of God: the Imperial Cults and the First Christians* (Grand Rapids, MI: Eerdmans, forthcoming).

9. R. Garland, *Introducing New Gods to Athens: The Politics of Athenian Religion* (London: Duckworth, 1992).

cal discussion of the "nature of the gods" (*de natura deorum*), i.e., proof that God or gods existed. Second, it was expected that if the gods were admitted to Athens when this first requirement had been satisfied, a temple would need to be erected by the herald because gods lived in temples. Provision also had to be made to meet the costs of an annual feast or feasts for the divinity. This was attended by the officials and the upper class in the city that was known to be "dear to the gods."[10]

It becomes clear that Paul first of all establishes contact with the audience by drawing attention to the altar on which was an inscription indicating that it was dedicated to "an unknown god." Paul addresses the council's expectations of him by stating that he would disclose the identity of this "unknown god" whom they acknowledged existed, for otherwise they would not have permitted this altar to be built in Athens. He did not have to begin by proving his existence. This was an appropriate opening that satisfied the first of their demands for any herald of foreign divinities.

Secondly, Paul goes on to correct any misconceptions on their part. If he had not done this it would be an obstacle to his ongoing engagement with the minds of his audience. He declared that this God who made the world and everything in it does not live in temples made with hands. This is because he is the Lord, not only of the heavens, but also of the whole earth (Acts 17:24). There will, then, be no need for Paul to erect a temple to him in Athens. He also clarifies that this God does not need a feast day on which food and sacrifices are offered to him, as it is he who gives life and breath and all things to all of his creation (Acts 17:25). God does not need the Athenians, but the Athenians are totally dependent on this God for their life and all sustenance.

Third, Paul is able to converse with the theology of his hearers who held the Stoic and Epicurean views of the world. On the basis of these two ancient philosophical schools, the former of which had originated in Athens, the traditional approach had to be argued, i.e., that god or gods existed, that God made the world, and that he cares not only for the whole of the creation but also for individuals.[11]

Fourth, Paul examines their compromise with their own beliefs. The basis of their own poets is that "in him we live and move and have our being" and "for we are indeed his offspring" (Acts 17:28). Paul argues as a logical consequence of this that "being then God's offspring, we ought not to think that the divine being is like gold or

---

10. Aeschylus, *Eumenides*, 869.
11. Cicero, *De natura deorum*, II.3.

silver or stone" carved by men (Acts 17:29). Some Athenians would have asserted "here dwells Athena," pointing to the statue, but Paul's implication is that metal or stone produces no human offspring. In the first century both philosophical schools had warned their adherents not to become "superstitious," even though previously they had been discouraged from entering temples.[12] Given the coming of the Roman imperial cult, it would be neither diplomatic nor advisable to forbid their following to enter temples dedicated to the imperial gods. However, they reached a compromise so that when they did so on imperial and other high and holy days, they were not to take the activity seriously and thereby act superstitiously but to participate in the cult with tongue in cheek.

Fifth, given the compromises with their beliefs about a "living" God, Paul confronts them, calling on them to repent. It was on the grounds of general revelation that he based this call to them to admit the error of their ways. He announced that God has appointed a day of judgment as well as the standard by which they would be judged. God had given proof to the world that this is his clear intention. For the Athenian audience this represented a window of opportunity to repent now because they would be unable to pass the judgment, given the compromises with what they knew and taught. Here was a time of clemency in which they could repent (Acts 17:30).

The fact that some mocked when they heard of the resurrection of God's appointed judge is explicable. When the ancient Council of the Aeropagus had been established centuries before, it was founded on the premise that "when a man dies, the earth drinks up his blood. There is no resurrection."[13] Their judicial role as a criminal court was no longer theirs. With the coming of the Romans, the exercise of this *imperium* was devolved by the emperor on the Roman governor, as was the case in all the Roman provinces. Furthermore, after Paul's speech, their role in standing in judgment on the official admission of Paul's God to Athens was no longer relevant. They were not making the judgment about God. They now stood under his judgment because of their failures, hence the need of immediate repentance.

Paul clearly engages both their minds and those of the Epicureans in his Athenian audience, demolishing their false understanding about the nature of God by those whose intellectual history and superiority remained legendary even in Roman times.

---

12. *P. Oxy.* 215.
13. Aeschylus, *Eumenides*, 647.

Paul connects with their world, corrects their misunderstanding as to what he is doing, converses with their world of beliefs that resonated with the Old Testament, convicts them of their compromises, and finally confronts the Athenians with the future reality, calling on them to respond to the generous clemency God was offering, giving clear proof of future judgment through the resurrection of Jesus.

Paul does not "pull down" his audience, engaging in some rhetorical *argumentum ad hominem.* He demolished the citadels that stood in the way of the gospel's gaining entry into their hearts and minds. His *modus operandi* achieved his purpose of bringing every thought captive in obedience to Christ for the first time in the lives of at least two leading Athenians along with their unnumbered retinues.

This program was not only for Paul, but also for those engaged in dealing with generally accepted views about the reality of our world, views that have to be examined and overthrown because they are false, in order to clear the decks so that hearers may hear and embrace the gospel.

Paul's "Warfare" with Christian Young Men (1 Cor. 6:9–20)

Young Christian men received the *toga virilis* as a sign of their entry into adulthood. After this rite into maturity, they often had sexual intercourse with high-class call girls brought in for their dinner parties. Ancient historians have dubbed this "the unholy trinity of eating, drinking, and sex." The last was euphemistically referred to as "after dinners," an activity graphically portrayed by first-century pictures still found on walls of some ancient houses. These young men justified doing "it" by citing a culturally endorsed aphorism that was widely used in the Paul's day: "Everything is permissible for me" (6:12 NIV).[14]

Cicero clearly agreed with the Christian young men of Corinth when he powerfully put the case in favor of what they were doing:

> If there is anyone who thinks that youth should be forbidden affairs with courtesans, he is doubtless eminently austere, but his view is contrary not only to the licence of this age, but also to the custom and concession of our ancestors. For when was this not a common practice? When was it blamed? When was it forbidden? When, in fact, was it that what is allowed not allowed? [*quod licet, non liceret*].[15]

---

14. The Greek verb for "it is permitted" that the young men in Roman Corinth used is rendered in Latin as *licitum est.*

15. Cicero, *pro Caelio,* 20.48.

Cicero's argument was based on the "the licence of this age," "the customs and concessions of our ancestors," and "common practice." Every young man in the past did it, they were still doing it, and when was this ever forbidden, for it never had been contrary to Roman conventions and therefore was not wrong.

If the Corinthians had a culturally accepted aphorism to justify their conduct, Paul had a set of powerful, alternative arguments that would demolish this citadel. It was not the ineffectual one that has become popular in recent times in some Christian circles that "true love waits." That would never have been sufficient to dissuade young Christian men in Corinth from their activity. Paul's pastoral sensitivity in dealing with this issue provides us with a powerful paradigm, for he does not say that because they did not wait, they could never subsequently experience true love, as is implied by some contemporary Christians.

Paul draws attention to a momentous event that had occurred in the lives of these young Christian men that declared the status that they had achieved "in the name of the Lord Jesus Christ and by the Spirit of our God" (1 Cor. 6:11). He then provides eight compelling reasons why only extremely foolish Christians would continue to fornicate, giving in the midst of these arguments three binding apostolic commands: "do not be deceived," "flee from sexual immorality," and "glorify God in your body" (1 Cor. 6:9, 18, 20).

Paul's response to this situation commences with a strong wakeup command to the young men: "You must not be deceived," even if everybody else is doing "it" as their "after dinners" activity. This is an activity that excludes from the kingdom of God. You cannot have both. Paul cites fornication as the first of ten activities that exclude one from the kingdom, regardless of popular aphorisms and arguments mounted to the contrary in Roman society.

In passing, we might note that it is something of an enigma that six of these activities tend to be ignored by contemporary preachers. At least one other finds little pulpit time—adultery, including its consequences that can end in divorce. Fornication seems also to have slipped off many preachers' programs. Homosexual activity has somehow become the intense focus, given much of the present-day discussion of this matter (6:9–10). But omission does not provide permission then or now.

The young men received a stark warning that they must not be deceived. At heaven's gates fornicators will not be provided with access. The message is clear. That is how it will be, as it will be for all the other activities cited (6:9–10). It will not be negotiable, and arguments coined by secular society, then and now, that abstinence was contrary to the "spirit of the age," will never change God's mind.

When Paul declared that "such were some of you," his immediate next step was to remind them of the great reversal in which three great things had occurred. Three times Paul used the stronger of the Greek adversatives, "but." He wrote, "*But* you were washed, *but* you were sanctified, *but* you were justified" (6:11 NKJV). The great cleansing from the filth of sin, the great transformation of their soiled lives, and the great acquittal had done this for each one of the young Christian men to whom he was writing. Second, he reminded them that two persons of the Trinity had done this in their lives—it had been achieved "in the name of the Lord Jesus Christ and by the Spirit of our God" (6:11), thereby opening the kingdom to those who had rightly been excluded from it because of their previous willful conduct.

The young men of Corinth would have happily recalled the great event of becoming Christians and no doubt remembered this at the Lord's Supper. However, Paul's pastoral strategy does not leave it there. He cannot do so if he really cares for their spiritual well-being. He provides eight reasons in 6:12–20, adding two further commands based on these arguments.

Fornication is against their well-being (v. 12a). The young men said "everything is permitted." Paul strongly refutes this using the strong "but," declaring not everything is "helpful," i.e., for the well-being of the person. The portrayal of the male genitalia in Pompeii with the words underneath that "here resides happiness" (*hic habitat felicitas*) was and is simply not true. Like all sin, it never delivers long term on its promises.

Second, fornication is harmful because it becomes addictive (v. 12b). Whereas they said "everything is permitted," Paul confronts them with fornication as slavery. While perhaps during the first experience the young men felt they were in control, fornication went on to control them in their thoughts and actions, so that they could not do without it. It was not love but lust. Long-term joy did not dwell there. It is interesting to note that in Roman marriage men continued this addiction outside the marriage bed, and the Roman society that endorsed fornication had traditionally been indifferent to men's adultery provided it was with a social inferior.

Third, fornication is against the Creator's intention (v. 13). The young men said that food is for the body and the body was designed to consume food. That was obvious. But Paul declares the Designer's intention was never that the body would be used for immoral purposes. The body was intended to achieve the Lord's purposes, and the Lord clearly has a purpose in giving us "the body."

Fourth, this sin contradicts the body's future (v. 14). The body is not "the prison house of the soul," to cite Plato's known and memorable analogy, which in the first century had become "the house of the soul" as a justification for self-indulgence among Epicureans and contemporary Platonists. The Christian's mortal body will be raised just as God raised the Lord at his resurrection.

Paul's next argument is that illicit sexual indulgence was totally inappropriate because a Christian is a member of Christ's body (v. 15a). In his opening greeting, Paul had described Christians as "sanctified in Christ Jesus" (1:2), which they are because they have been joined to Christ ontologically as members of his body. The participants in the immoral activities clearly had not registered the implications of this fact.

Paul goes on to declare that in spite of the popular belief, there is no such thing as casual sex (vv. 15b–17). Young men saw this as simply a fun evening with a casual partner. But even a one-night stand with a high-class prostitute created a "one flesh" relationship, another fact they had not taken into account. Paul's reason for stating this is Genesis 2:24. He affirms that the Christian is joined to the Lord and therefore is one spirit with him.

Contrary to the spirit of the age, Paul declares that fornication is a unique sin (6:18). All other sins are "outside" the body, but their sexual activity is the one sin that damages the intrinsic nature of who the person is. Harm is done to the person himself.

Finally, the Christian does not have ownership of his body because its title deeds have been transferred (v. 19). The young Christian men no longer owned their bodies to use them as their passions dictated and society endorsed. They were not only indwelt by the Holy Spirit whom they have from God by reason of the work of "the Spirit of our God," but Christ had purchased them body and soul at enormous cost to himself as the Lamb of God. He is the one who now has the title deeds of their bodies, so it is no longer theirs to do with it as they wished.

In the context of dealing with this issue, Paul has issued three nonnegotiable, binding commands that will solve what might be seen as an impasse because they had "permanently damaged" their purity—true love had not waited. From now on these commands provided the way forward for them. "You must not be self-deceived" (v. 9). "Fornicators will not enter the kingdom," as this sin is contrary to the maker's manual and a rebellious act. You must flee immorality (v. 18). No longer are they to attend the "unholy trinity" evening with other young men, for they are to "glorify God in your body" (v. 20). Immorality is not the appropriate way of doing this.

Later Paul extends this discussion, using his own struggles as a paradigm for the young men of Corinth. He did not preach down to them from the high moral ground. He disclosed that he had to bring his own body under control after a Sunday in the pulpit (9:27); he had to die daily to sexual passion and fight against the metaphorical "beast" (15:31). He also addresses the issue further by commanding them again not to be deceived because "bad company corrupts good morals" and therefore they must wake out of drunkenness and stop sinning (15:33–34).

In conclusion, it is important to note there was a significant difference between Roman warfare and Pauline warfare. The former was used against people literally in battle and metaphorically in vexatious litigation. Paul battles against ideas or ideologies that were held by people. In our generation it is sometimes the case that Christians use *argumentum ad hominem* against their fellow Christians or others to the detriment of fellowship and the quality of our witness in our world. The *modus operandi* must be appropriate to, and enhance the message of, the Word of God.

The brother to whom I have dedicated this essay has not demolished people in his preaching or engaged in cheap polemics. He has been an astute observer of the cultural programming that has been a danger to the church and has therefore been a careful assessor of this present age. In his long ministry, Kent Hughes has addressed the "arguments" and removed the "obstacles" that would preclude the Word of God taking root in the lives of his hearers. He has also been a skilled expositor of the Word of God, as his commentaries clearly demonstrate. He has been scrupulous not to operate as the secular world has done, even if others have chosen so to do in the church and in their ministry. For this we thank God, that he, like Paul, has provided a paradigm for the rising generation of evangelists, pastors, and teachers he has influenced.

7

Swallowing Our Pride: An Essay on the Foolishness of Preaching

Duane Litfin

For since, in the wisdom of God, the world did not know God through wisdom, it pleased God through the folly of what we preach to save those who believe.

—1 Corinthians 1:21

rom time to time there appear in every discipline books whose effects echo for decades. C. H. Dodd's *The Apostolic Preaching and Its Developments*, published in 1936, was one of those books. In this seminal work Dodd stressed the New Testament distinction between *didache* and *kerygma*, that is, between teaching and preaching, and then attempted to distill from the New Testament documents the core content of that preaching. In doing so Dodd almost single-handedly raised the word *kerygma* to the status of technical term and prompted a discussion that continues to this day.

The scholarly response to Dodd's work was at first largely positive. With time, however, a reaction set in as researchers began to question whether Dodd's strong distinction between *kerygma* and *didache* was warranted by the evidence. More enduring was Dodd's outline of the content of the *kerygma,* but even that came under fire, with other scholars wading in with this or that addition, deletion, or substitution.

These responses inevitably moved the debate beyond Dodd's handling of the issues. Such is the life of the scholar. But Dodd performed the important service of initiating the discussion. Moreover, much of his work remains relevant today. It is probably fair to say, for example, that while the dichotomy may not be as stark as Dodd would have us believe, there remains in the New Testament a useful distinction to be made between teaching and preaching. And Dodd's distillation of the content of that apostolic preaching continues to serve as the base from which contemporary scholars advance.

What seems to have endured from Dodd's work untouched, however, is the use of the term *kerygma* as a technical term, or what William G. Doty calls the "theologians' shorthand for merely 'the central message of the New Testament.'"[1] Scholars continue to speak as freely of the *kerygma* today as they did decades ago. We may doubt that the word was ever a technical term during the first century, since, after all, *kerygma* occurs only eight times in the New Testament, and six of those are from a single source, the apostle Paul. Moreover, as Margaret Mitchell has demonstrated, *kerygma* is only one of several shorthand terms even Paul used for the gospel.[2] Yet there is no reason the term *kerygma* cannot continue to serve usefully out into the future, provided, that is, that we get it right. And by "get it right" I mean, provided *we understand the term accurately, as it is used in the New Testament.*

When we coin our own terms we are free to define them however we like, and scholars do this all the time. But when we merely *transliterate* an ancient term, things are not so simple. By conjuring up the ancient term we are offering the impression that we want to borrow something useful from another time and place. We transliterate their term and then work to define it for our audience, because we think the original users were saying something significant, something our own terms appear to lack. In doing so, we thereby incur an obligation to the term's original users. It is their term, so to speak, and we must let them have the first crack at setting its semantic boundaries.

Which brings us to our subject. It is my rather bold thesis that C. H. Dodd, and a host of others following him, may have gotten this critical term *kerygma* wrong, or at least, that their grasp of it was partial enough

---

1. William G. Doty, *Contemporary New Testament Interpretation* (Englewood Cliffs, NJ: Prentice-Hall, 1972), 168. Oscar Cullmann, following Bultmann, calls the term a "kerygmatic summary of the faith" ("'Kyrios' As Designation for the Oral Tradition Concerning Jesus," *Scottish Journal of Theology* 3 [1950]: 186).

2. Margaret Mitchell, "Rhetorical Shorthand in Pauline Argumentation: The Functions of 'The Gospel' in the Corinthian Correspondence," in *Gospel in Paul*, ed. L. Ann Jervis and Peter Richardson, JSNT Supplement Series, 108 (England: Sheffield Academic Press, 1994): 63–88.

to be seriously deficient. This may be an impertinent claim, but I hope nonetheless to show that it is a claim worth considering.

The Problem

The essential question I wish to raise is this: Does the term *kerygma*, as it was used in the New Testament, refer to the *content* or the *form* of the apostolic preaching? But immediately upon posing this question we face a problem. To answer it we must first refine it. If we are asking of *kerygma* how it was used in the New Testament, we are for all practical purposes asking, how did *the apostle Paul* use the term? For, as we have already noted, *kerygma* is essentially in the New Testament a Pauline term. Matthew and Luke both place the word in the mouth of Jesus, but both writers are citing the same sentence: "The men of Nineveh," Jesus says in both Gospels, "will stand up at the judgment with this generation and condemn it; for they repented at the *kerygma* of Jonah, and now one greater than Jonah is here" (Matt. 12:41; Luke 11:32 NIV). These two references are jot-and-tittle duplicates of one another. So, as it turns out, there is really only one non-Pauline use of *kerygma* in the New Testament, occurring twice. In the end this single dominical reference will emerge as simply another instance of the fully nuanced meaning we will find in Paul. But first we must pick up our account with C. H. Dodd.

Dodd answered the form versus content question in the very first paragraph of his book. Quoting what is no doubt the *locus classicus* for determining the meaning of *kerygma*, 1 Corinthians 1:21, Dodd began his book this way:

> It pleased God, says Paul, by the foolishness of the Preaching to save them that believe. The word here translated preaching, *kerygma*, signifies not the action of the preacher, but that which he preaches, his message, as we sometimes say.[3]

End of paragraph. And more importantly, end of argument. With no discussion whatsoever, much less any evidence, Dodd simply assumes what will form the working definition of *kerygma* throughout his influential work, namely, that the term *kerygma* refers only to the *content* of the preaching.

Dodd was not the first modern scholar to make this assumption. Long before Dodd, for example, J. B. Lightfoot had claimed that in 1 Corinthians 1:21 the foolishness of preaching refers "to the subject, not

---

3. C. H. Dodd, *The Apostolic Preaching and Its Developments* (New York: Harper, 1936), 7.

to the manner of the preaching."[4] Similarly, Robertson and Plummer had also limited the term to content, though they acknowledged a slight emphasis upon the presentation.[5] But Dodd's work, focusing as it did entirely on delineating the content of the *kerygma,* solidified the trend, and there has followed ever since a train of commentators who without exploration or argumentation have simply assumed that *kerygma* in 1 Corinthians 1:21 refers to content. Let us consider a few examples so we can see the dimensions of the problem. In his commentary on 1 Corinthians, Moffatt says, "It is the content rather than the form of utterance that engages [Paul's] . . . attention [in 1 Cor. 1:21]."[6] G. G. Findlay, in *The Expositor's Greek Testament,* put it this way: "The term *kerygma* "signifies not the act of proclamation . . . , but *the message proclaimed* by God's herald."[7] In 1944 A. M. Hunter, though he acknowledged that *kerygma* may signify either the act of proclamation or the thing proclaimed—indeed, he even conceded that in 1 Corinthians 2:4 the *act* of preaching lies in the foreground—nevertheless asserts that for the most part in Paul, and in 1 Corinthians 1:21 in particular, "the emphasis falls on the *content* of the *kerygma.*"[8] F. W. Grosheide later concurred, claiming that "the *foolishness of the preaching* represents the content of the preaching which God has commanded."[9] In 1968 C. K. Barrett added his considerable weight to the discussion, asserting that *kerygma* "means not the act but the content of *preaching.*"[10] The following year, Hans Conzelmann made the point even more emphatically: "The folly," he said, "lies exclusively in the content of the preaching."[11] More recently still, Gordon Fee has written, "The word *kêrygma* . . . here means not the act of preaching

4. J. B. Lightfoot, *Notes on the Epistles of St. Paul* (London: MacMillan, 1895), 161; cf. also H. A. W. Meyer, *Kritisch exegetisches Handbuch über den ersten Brief an die Korinther,* 5th ed., (Gottingen: Vandenhoeck & Ruprecht, 1888), 40.

5. Archibald Robertson and Alfred Plummer, *A Critical Commentary and Exegetical Commentary on the First Epistle of St. Paul to the Corinthians* (New York: Charles Scribner's Sons, 1911), 21.

6. James Moffatt, *The First Epistle of Paul to the Corinthians* (London: Hodder & Stroughton, 1947), 14; cf. 15–16.

7. G. G. Findlay, *St. Paul's First Epistle to the Corinthians,* in *The Expositor's Greek Testament,* ed. W. Robertson Nicoll, vol. 2, sec. 3 (Grand Rapids, MI: Eerdmans, 1983), 769.

8. Archibald M. Hunter, *The Message of the New Testament* (Philadelphia: The Westminster Press, 1944), 25; cf. *idem, The Unity of the New Testament* (London: Student Christian Movement Press, 1943), 21.

9. F. W. Grosheide, *Commentary on the First Epistle to the Corinthians* (Grand Rapids, MI: Eerdmans, 1953), 47.

10. C. K. Barrett, *A Commentary on the First Epistle to the Corinthians* (New York: Harper & Row, 1968), 54.

11. Hans Conzelmann, *An Outline of the Theology of the New Testament,* trans. J. Bowden (London: SCM Press, 1969), 241; cf. also *I Corinthians: A Commentary on the First Epistle to the Corinthians* (Philadelphia: Fortress Press, 1975), 45.

itself, but the content of that proclamation."[12] And with this Anthony Thistleton agrees. He states flatly that in 1 Corinthians 1:21 *kerygma* refers to *"the substance of the preaching"* and has nothing to do with "the mode of communication."[13] So well entrenched has this assumption become, that William F. Orr and James A. Walther claim in their commentary on 1 Corinthians that in the old King James translation "preaching" has been "superseded in almost all modern versions to indicate the content of the message."[14] And apparently this trend is to continue. In the United Bible Society's *Translator's Handbook*, Paul Ellingworth and Howard Hatton instruct future translators of 1 Corinthians 1:21 that "the word which Paul uses here for 'preaching' means, not the act of preaching, but its content."[15]

This is a very impressive lineup. Yet it is my contention that such views, common though they may be, represent a serious truncating of the meaning of the term *kerygma*. I will argue that, while *kerygma* certainly does refer to the content of Paul's preaching, it also delineates something important about its form, about its mode of communication. In fact, I will argue that this term was specifically *chosen* by the apostle to keep *both* content and form before his readers, stressing not only *what* Paul proclaims (i.e., his message), but also what he simply *proclaims* (i.e., its form).

But now, supposing this argument is correct—a conclusion which, of course, remains to be demonstrated—that would mean that this litany of experts who limit *kerygma* to content alone must be mistaken. How could so many eminent scholars have cut the term *kerygma* short? And does it really matter?

Importance of the Issue

The latter question is easier to answer than the first. This issue matters a great deal, for several important reasons: First, if the term *kerygma* has any usefulness at all, it is useful as shorthand for ideas that lie at the core of the Christian faith. If we have left out significant elements of its meaning we are not merely truncating an important term; we are likely

---

12. Gordon C. Fee, *The First Epistle to the Corinthians*, in *The New International Commentary on the New Testament* (Grand Rapids, MI: Eerdmans, 1987), 73.

13. Anthony C. Thistleton, *The First Epistle to the Corinthians: A Commentary on the Greek Text* (Grand Rapids, MI: Eerdmans, 2000), 167.

14. William F. Orr and James Arthur Walther, *I Corinthians*, in *The Anchor Bible* (Garden City, NY: Doubleday, 1976), 155.

15. Paul Ellingworth and Howard Hatton, *A Translator's Handbook on Paul's First Letter to the Corinthians* (London: United Bible Societies, 1985), 27.

truncating our understanding of what that term represents. Second, and more particularly, this term also stands at the center of—and in fact, serves essentially as a distillation of—Paul's argument in 1 Corinthians 1:17–2:16, a passage that Gordon Fee describes as nothing less than "the key theological passage to the whole of the Corinthian correspondence, arguably to the whole of the Pauline corpus."[16] If we cannot get this term right, it will likely mean that we will not have gotten this passage right either. And those are high stakes indeed.

What's more, this issue also carries some large theoretical implications, implications that have the power to shape our entire understanding of how we do ministry. Paul is working from some theological presuppositions that he here applies to his preaching. But those same presuppositions, once surfaced and understood, may prove to have implications for other forms of ministry as well. It is not too much to say that an entire philosophy of ministry is at stake here. Seeker strategies and church growth theories come into question. Are we to function as persuaders or heralds, and what's the difference? All of these issues and more are involved in this question of *form* versus *content* in the term *kerygma*.

The issue we are raising here is therefore not a minor word game, and missing out on a key dimension of *kerygma*'s meaning is not a minor loss. It is my contention that scholars who stress *kerygma* as content alone have bypassed a significant aspect of the apostle's thought, and it is my rather ambitious goal to set the record straight. In the end the reader will be the judge of whether the exercise has succeeded.

Reasons for the Problem

As to the question of how so many first-rate scholars could be mistaken regarding this important aspect of Paul's thought, I would offer two related explanations. The first is a grammatical one. I want to suggest that the nature of this primitive verbal substantive, *kerygma*, may have been misjudged.

Word Formation

Examining the technical details of Greek word formation is a bit like going to the dentist; it's unpleasant but necessary. So we will attempt to keep the procedure as brief and painless as possible.

---

16. Gordon D. Fee, "Another Gospel Which You Did Not Embrace," in *Gospel in Paul*, ed. L. Ann Jervis and Peter Richardson, JSNT Supplement Series, 108 (England: Sheffield Academic Press, 1994): 122.

Greek primary substantives are nouns comprised of a verbal *root* in combination with a formative *suffix*. Actually, there are two such substantives that concern us here. The first is our term *kerygma*; the second is a related word, *keryksis*. The root for both of these words is *keryk-*, which stems from the verb *keryssein*, which means "to proclaim as a *keryx* (herald)."

While sharing the same root, *kerygma* and *keryksis* obviously sport different suffixes, the one a *-ma* suffix, the other a *-sis* suffix. Of these two suffixes Blass and Debrunner say: "Derivatives in [*-ma*] . . . specify the result of the action for the most part. . . . Abstracts are formed with [the *-sis* ending]."[17] Thus *kerygma* stresses the "result of the action" of the verb *keryssein*, while *keryksis* serves as an abstract of the verb, similar to what in Latin or English we call a gerund. For instance, "running" is a gerund from the verb "to run." Like the Greek nouns ending in *-sis*, gerunds serve to abstract the verb, as in the sentence, "Running is my favorite exercise." Similarly, *keryksis* gives us the abstract of *keryssein*, which is to say, "proclaiming." Thus, for example, Dio Cassius can use the term to speak of Nero crossing over into Greece, where he spent his time (translating very literally) with "playings of the lyre, proclaimings (*keryksei*), and actings in tragedies."[18]

Here is how this technical material is sometimes used. Though I know of no example of the evidence being argued at any length, the grammatical case for the "content alone" view, to the extent it is mentioned at all, seems to run like this: The *-ma* suffix on the word *kerygma* means that term is referring to the "result" of the verb "to proclaim." This is therefore a reference to the *content* of the preaching. Had Paul wanted to stress the *act* of preaching, he would have used the verbal abstract *keryksis*, or "proclaiming."[19]

This argument, however, fails at two points. On the one hand, the mention of *keryksis* is misleading. The word never occurs in the New Testament and is rare even in the nonbiblical literature. We have no way of knowing whether it was even part of Paul's vocabulary. In any case, *keryksis* would have been unusable to Paul in this context because as a verbal abstract it would have focused too *exclusively* on the act of preaching. In speaking of the "foolishness of the preaching" Paul required a term that would allow both the content *and* the form of the preaching

---

17. F. Blass and A. Debrunner, *A Greek Grammar of the New Testament and Other Early Christian Literature,* trans. and rev., Robert W. Funk, (Chicago: The University of Chicago Press, 1961), 59.

18. Cassius Dio Cocceianus, *Dio's Roman History,* in *The Loeb Classical Library,* Vol. 8 (London: William Heineman, 1925), 62.8.2., 149.

19. E.g., see Findlay, *The First Epistle of Paul to the Corinthians,* 769.

to remain in the frame. Thus, the term *keryksis*, being merely an abstract of the verb *keryssein*, would not do.

On the other hand, what also will not do is to conclude that the "result" of the verb *keryssein* is merely "content." As A. T. Robertson long ago warned, when dealing with Greek verbal substantives it is important to keep in mind the influence of both the suffix and the root.[20] But this is just what the "content alone" approach fails to do. If we are careful to maintain the balance between the meaning of the verb ("to proclaim as a herald") and the significance of the -*ma* suffix ("result"), we discover that the "result" of this particular verb is not merely content, but content in a particular *form*, namely, "proclamation" or "heralding." This is why a lexicographer such as Gustav Friedrich, in his article on *kerygma* in the *Theological Dictionary of the New Testament* (*TDNT*), concludes that the word "has a twofold sense . . . , signifying both the result of proclamation (what is proclaimed) and the actual proclaiming. In other words, it denotes both the act and the content. In many cases it is hard to say where the emphasis falls."[21]

It is mistaken, then, to claim that *kerygma* inherently refers to content alone. The combination of the root and the -*ma* suffix provides a balance to the term, so much so that if the apostle wished to keep both the form and the content of his preaching before his readers, *kerygma* was the only term available to him. It is the context that must determine which of the two emphases, if either, predominates in any given passage. Better yet, it is probably more accurate to say that when *kerygma* is used *neither* emphasis ever completely disappears from the picture.

Blind Spot toward Greco-Roman Rhetoric

Most New Testament scholars understand these technicalities, we may presume, and so we must ask why, given these options, so many still come down on the side of "content alone" in 1 Corinthians 1:21. Even Friedrich, after acknowledging the dual possibilities inherent in the term *kerygma*, along with the difficulty of deciding in any particular case which one predominates, concludes that in 1 Corinthians 2:4 *kerygma* refers to the *act* of preaching, while in our passage, just thirteen verses back, the focus is on the *content* of preaching.[22] Why would so many

---

20. A. T. Robertson, *A Grammar of the Greek New Testament in the Light of Historical Research,* 4th ed., (Nashville: Broadman Press, 1934), 150–51.

21. "κήρυγμα," Gerhard Kittel, ed., *Theological Dictionary of the New Testament* (Grand Rapids, MI: Eerdmans, 1965), 3:714.

22. Ibid., 716, n. 15.

call the issue in this way? To answer this question we must turn to the second and more important reason why, in my view, scholars have left *kerygma* short.

Elsewhere I have documented the blind spot that has existed within modern New Testament scholarship regarding the subject of classical rhetoric.[23] This problem is a modern one because for most of the church's history, students of the Scriptures, steeped as they were in classical studies, were fully aware of the Greco-Roman backgrounds of the New Testament. They were typically trained in classical rhetoric and tended to think within its categories. But over the last century or so, as modern education broke free from its classicism and thus fewer and fewer scholars arrived at the New Testament with classical training, these backgrounds were eclipsed, especially in the exegesis of 1 Corinthians, by more fashionable interests such as gnosticism, the mystery religions, or the syncretistic influences of the Hellenistic synagogue. The result was that for years the subject of Greco-Roman rhetoric not only fell into disuse but was actively avoided by New Testament scholars.

Part of the problem, of course, lies in what was happening within the field of rhetoric itself during this period. At its best during the ancient period, rhetoric was about both thinking well and communicating effectively. But periodically, political and social developments would shear away its substance and leave rhetoric to deal only with issues of style and ornamentation, thus vindicating many of Plato's otherwise misguided criticisms. Unfortunately it was this diminished version of rhetoric, with its penchant for flowery elocution and its arid obsession with classification, that tended to dominate nineteenth-century teaching. One need only conjure up the name E. W. Bullinger to catch the point. In his 1898 book of endless classifications of figures of speech from the ancient period (actually there are only five hundred or so, but they just *seem* endless), Bullinger epitomizes the limited definition of rhetoric with which he begins his work: "Rhetoric," he says, "is an adaptation of Figurative Language for the purposes of elocution."[24] This is a far cry from the way Isocrates or Cicero or Quintilian defined the art they taught, but it was just this cramped sort of thing against which many moderns were reacting. Hence we may be sympathetic to the demise of interest in rhetoric we have witnessed during modern times.

Today, of course, this problem seems to have turned itself around. For a variety of reasons rhetorical studies have become ubiquitous in

---

23. Duane Litfin, *St. Paul's Theology of Proclamation: 1 Corinthians 1–4 and Greco-Roman Rhetoric*, SNTS Monograph Series, 79 (Cambridge: Cambridge University Press, 1994), 4–18.

24. E. W. Bullinger, *Figures of Speech Used in the Bible* (London: Eyre & Spottiswoode, 1898), ix.

New Testament circles, so much so that one can scarcely open a scholarly journal in New Testament studies without stumbling upon another one. Yet ironically, in some ways we do not seem to have risen very far beyond the old stereotypes of rhetoric. A passion for classification worthy of Bullinger himself remains heavy upon the field. Hundreds of rhetorical studies have appeared, but most of them seem bogged down in the task of trying to demonstrate this or that rhetorical pattern in the text. When done carefully these studies can offer insight, but they are in danger of prolonging the stereotype of rhetoric as concerned only with the externals of discourse. Instead of viewing classical rhetoric as ancient persuasion theory and seeking to understand something about its unchanging core, New Testament scholars have too often settled for hauling out its extensive classificatory systems and then foisting them on unsuspecting texts. Relatively few of these studies seem inclined to cut through to the essence of ancient (or modern) rhetorical theory and contend with the deeper and more interesting ideas we discover there.

It is my thesis that this avoidance may have cost us something in our understanding of the verb *keryssein*, "to proclaim as a herald." A jeweler understands that her customer is much more likely to appreciate the exquisite features of a string of pearls if she sets them against a backdrop of dark velvet rather than laying them on a glass counter. Similarly, we moderns may have missed some of *keryssein*'s underlying nuances—or at least, failed to appreciate their significance—because we have not seen clearly enough what *keryssein* is semantically designed to stand over *against*. And if this be so, then we should not be surprised to discover that when we come to *keryssein*'s verbal substantive, the word *kerygma*, we may have missed some of its nuances as well.

The Remedy

The remedy for this situation lies, I think, not in the discovery of new facts about the role of the herald, but rather in a fuller appreciation of the significance of the facts we already know. For that we require an appropriate background. All are agreed that *keryssein* means "to proclaim," and none disputes that the verb describes the behavior of the *keryx*, the herald. But what specifically does this mean? What is *peculiar* about the role of the herald?

To answer this question, let us begin by examining the essential role of the herald's counterpart: the orator, or the persuader. Then we shall be in a better position to understand (1) the herald himself, (2) Paul's argument in 1 Corinthians 1 and 2 in particular, and finally, (3) the full significance of the term *kerygma* as Paul uses it in 1:21.

The Orator

Training in Greco-Roman rhetoric formed the crown of a liberal education in the ancient world, and the orators it produced became the celebrities of their day. The people of the first century loved eloquence and lionized those who could produce it. Eloquence was perhaps their primary entertainment, and it was ubiquitous throughout the Roman Empire. Audiences consisted of avid and sophisticated listeners who knew what they liked and what they disliked. But the orators were willing to risk their displeasure for the sake of gaining audience approval and the rewards that accompanied it.

The training of an orator was a marvelously complex thing. (For an indication of just how complex, see first-century Quintilian's twelve-volume *Institutes of Oratory* on the training of the orator from birth up.) But when all else is pared away and we lay bare the essence of Greco-Roman rhetorical theory, we discover that ancient rhetorical education was designed to train an orator in the art of persuasion. At its best the study of rhetoric was not about how to compose purple prose, much less how to manipulate an audience. It was about the discovery and delivery of ideas and arguments that would engender belief in one's listeners. Given *this* audience, and *this* subject matter, how can I achieve the desired result? This was the question the persuader was trained to ask and answer, and the measure of his skill was the degree to which he could do so successfully, in whatever rhetorical situation he might be facing.

The persuader was always working with what I will call the Grand Equation of Rhetoric. This equation encompassed three primary parts: the audience, the desired results, and the speaker's efforts.[25] It can be laid out as follows:

FIGURE 7.1:

Grand Equation of Rhetoric

The Audience + The Speaker's Efforts = The Results

The audience for the orator was a *given*. Usually the orator could do little to choose his auditors. The point, instead, was to adapt to what he was given in order to achieve his goals, which sends us to the opposite

25. By contrast, modern rhetorical theory tends to be much more complex. See, for example, C. Perelmann and L. Olbrechts-Tyteca, *The New Rhetoric: A Treatise on Argumentation*, trans. J. Wilkinson and P. Weaver (Notre Dame, IN: Notre Dame University Press, 1971).

end of the equation: the results. These constituted the *independent vari-able*, i.e., that which once set determines the remainder of the equation. What was it the persuader wanted to accomplish with his audience? It was the answer to this question, the desired results, that determined the *dependent variable*, the speaker's efforts. The persuader had to be able to adapt his efforts in whatever way possible to accomplish *this* result with *this* audience, and all of his rhetorical education was designed to train him in how to do so. It was his skill in successfully adapting himself and his efforts to this particular situation and this particular audience that made the rhetorical equation work.

So, for the persuader the Grand Equation looked like this:

FIGURE 7.2

Persuader's Grand Equation

	The Audience	+ *The Speaker's Efforts* →	*The Results*
The Persuader	A Given	Dependent Variable	Independent Variable

We should note that the persuader's role was both audience- and results-driven. Once set, the desired results govern the equation. That is why so much attention is paid in the ancient rhetorical literature to the psychology of the audience, to their belief systems, to their likes and dislikes, and to what is required to win specific responses from them. To be successful in achieving his intended result the persuader was required to adapt himself and his message to his audience in every possible way: content, organization, wording, and delivery. In fact, the ability to do so constituted the genius of classical rhetoric. Without this ability one could not design an effective strategy for achieving the desired goal. With this ability, however, the persuader could strategize effectively to achieve what he was after—or to credit Aristotle's famous qualification, to come as close as was humanly possible.[26] Since he was not methodologically obligated or constricted, the persuader was free—within the bounds of honesty, generally—to choose from his full repertory of technique whatever would most likely achieve his purposes. The message was the persuader's to design, and he it was who would be given credit or blame for whether or not it achieved its intended effect.

It is unfortunate that today we can scarcely use the term "rhetoric" without the word "mere" attached to it. We tend to think of "rhetoric" as empty verbiage at best or shameful tricksterism at worst. Often the word is used as a virtual synonym for bombast or the proverbial purple prose.

---

26. Aristotle, *Rhetoric* 1.1.1.

But in the classical world this was not so. For the ancients rhetoric was something powerful, and at its best, even noble. It was that art which replaced violence and coercion in free societies, the art of persuasion through discourse. And at its core lay the kaleidoscopic ability of the persuader to mold all of his efforts, form, and content, to the demands of the given situation, with a view to winning a particular result from a particular audience. This was what classical rhetoric was designed to teach.

The Herald

With this backdrop in mind, let us now turn to the ancient figure of the herald. We can do this more quickly because, as I have said, the role of the herald in the classical world is widely understood, and we need only cite some standard observations to make our point. In fact, though we could turn to any number of sources, let us settle for the summary by Gustav Friedrich in his widely cited *TDNT* article on the *keryx*. It was demanded of heralds, says Friedrich, that they:

> deliver their message as it is given to them. The essential point about the report which they give is that it does not originate with them. Behind it stands a higher power. The herald does not express his own views. He is the spokesman for his master. . . . Heralds adopt the mind of those who commission them, and act with the plenipotentiary authority of their masters. . . . Yet there is a distinction between the herald and the envoy. In general one may say that the latter acts more independently and that he is furnished with greater authority. It is unusual for a herald to act on his own initiative and without explicit instructions. In the main the herald simply gives short messages, puts questions, and brings answers. . . . He is bound by the precise instructions of the one who commissions him. . . . The good herald does not become involved in lengthy negotiations [*sic*] but returns at once when he has delivered his message. . . . [I]n general he is simply an executive instrument. Being only the mouth of his master, he must not falsify the message entrusted to him by additions of his own. He must deliver it exactly as given to him. . . . [H]e must keep strictly to the words and orders of his master.[27]

If we return to what I have called the Grand Equation of Rhetoric, now with the herald in mind, we discover a striking contrast. For the herald the audience was also a given. He could not dictate who would make up his audience; like the persuader he had to work with what he received. But beyond that the equation is a study in contrasts. Far from being an ever-malleable *dependent variable*, the herald's message was set

---

27. "κήρυγμα," 687–88.

for him by another. It was required to be not a *variable* at all, but rather a constant—he had been given a message by the one he represented and it was his assignment to deliver it accurately and clearly to the designated audiences. And the results? Instead of an *independent variable*, set by the herald, the results turn out to be the equation's *dependent variable*. The herald could not maneuver rhetorically to achieve some particular effect. It was his fate to deliver his message and then watch the chips fall where they may. Upon completion of his assignment the herald might discover a variety of responses from or within his audience, but these were not his affair. Whatever the herald might desire for the audience, he had to remain mindful that the responses of the audience were not in the end responses to himself but to the one he represented. It was not the herald's task to modulate his efforts so as to win this response or that, to negotiate the message with his audience, so to speak, in order to construct a word they might find maximally palatable, or better yet, wonderfully convincing, or best of all, simply irresistible. Unlike the orator, the herald was not results-driven; he was obedience-driven. He was a man under assignment, methodologically obligated, so to speak, restricted to the task of announcing. Instead of offering impressive arguments, he was an announcer. His role was to declare, to notify, to report. This is what it meant to be a *keryx*. For the herald the Grand Equation, therefore, looked like this:

FIGURE 7.3
Herald's Grand Equation

	The Audience	+ The Speaker's Efforts →	The Results
The Persuader:	A Given	Dependent Variable	Independent Variable
The Herald:	A Given	Constant	Dependent Variable

The Apostle Paul

With this contrast in mind, we are now in a position to appreciate more fully the dilemma Paul faced in Corinth, along with his response to it in 1 Corinthians 1 and 2. And this in turn will lead us to the fuller significance of our term *kerygma*.

The Corinthian Situation

The difficulties Paul faced in Corinth were multifaceted, but beneath them all lay the problem of his preaching. When the apostle originally proclaimed the gospel in the city of Corinth, a sizeable group of Corinthians responded in faith. To be sure, they responded not because they found Paul to be such a persuasive preacher—at least, not by the standards of eloquence to which they were accustomed—but because they recognized, through the inner confirmation of the Spirit, that the gospel Paul preached was true. So they embraced this gospel, became followers of Jesus, and eventfully under the tutelage of Paul formed a church.

With the subsequent departure of the apostle and the advent of Apollos, however, the attitude toward Paul of some within the congregation began not so much to change as to solidify. The reservations they had harbored about Paul from the beginning—reservations about him personally, despite the fact that they found the gospel he preached worthy of acceptance—became in Paul's absence more pronounced. What had been before merely nagging embarrassments, perhaps kept to oneself, now crept to the surface and became the object of more or less open discussion.

These embarrassments centered upon Paul's public speaking. The apostle had sustained a relatively visible profile during this stay in Corinth, but it was scarcely an impressive profile. Both his physical appearance and his speaking itself were deficient, even contemptible, by the sophisticated standards of Greek rhetoric (2 Cor. 10:10). Paul was simply out of his league. These people were accustomed to the *euglottia* ("beautiful speech") of orators of the caliber of Favorinus, that paragon of Greek culture whose eloquence was both *sophos* ("wise") and *potimos* ("sweet, pleasant").[28] According to Philostratus, "Even those in [Favorinus's] audience who did not understand the Greek language shared in the pleasure that he gave; for he fascinated even them by the tones of his voice, by his expressive glance and the rhythm of his speech."[29] Such a one as this could impress the Corinthians. But by this standard the apostle was an embarrassing figure. Whatever else one could say for him, he was woefully short by the stringent criteria of genuine Greek eloquence. He was simply a layman (*idiotes*, 2 Cor. 11:6) as a speaker. He appeared to lack the high-octane ability to discover convincing arguments and then sculpt them at will into irresistible phrases. He came far short of the polish and sophistication in word choice, in diction, in voice, in physical charm and self-possession that was indispensable to impress and move a Greco-Roman crowd. By contrast, Apollos proved to be an eloquent man (*aner logias*, Acts 18:24) and through this some-

---

28. Philostratus, *Lives of the Sophists* (Cambridge, MA: Harvard University Press, 1998), 489, 491.

29. Ibid., 491.

thing of a champion in Corinth; he was no embarrassment. But Paul was a different story.

Yet the difficulty was that these Corinthian Christians were inevitably associated with Paul, stuck with him, so to speak. In fact, he was, in a sense, perceived as their leader, their teacher. Hence their embarrassment. Like so many of their Greco-Roman neighbors, connoisseurs of eloquence and wisdom and acutely conscious of related matters of status and esteem, some of the Corinthians found Paul's all-too-public deficiencies a painful liability. After all, they supposed, and with ample justification, it was difficult enough to attain distinction in Corinth without being burdened with someone so culturally lacking as Paul.

These status-conscious Corinthians apparently harbored few reservations about rendering a negative judgment of Paul's abilities as a speaker. They perceived the wandering Jewish apostle in this respect in much the same light as they perceived other itinerant speakers—as fair game for their evaluations. How could they embrace the gospel Paul preached while yet remaining critical of Paul's lack of eloquence? The inconsistency seems in retrospect odd, and so it was. In fact it is precisely this inconsistency and the misplaced values that allowed it to exist that Paul addresses in 1 Corinthians 1 to 4.

Paul's Response

Upon coming to understand these Corinthian complaints, the apostle faced a dilemma. The Corinthians were critical of Paul because he did not look or sound or behave like the orators they so revered. But Paul considered himself to be commissioned by Christ as a herald, not a persuader, and he understood enough about Greco-Roman rhetorical eloquence to know the difference. Thus, he wrote the early chapters of 1 Corinthians to explain to the Corinthians why their criticisms were misplaced, and why, for theological reasons, the more limited role of the herald was his only methodological option.

It is important to observe that whenever Paul spoke of his own ministry, he consistently used the language of the herald. But only here, in 1 Corinthians 1 to 4, does Paul *explain* this *modus operandi* and spell out its theological rationale. Thus, these early chapters of 1 Corinthians become a uniquely important passage in understanding why Paul attempted to function as he did.

As with both the orator and the herald, the audience was, for Paul, a given; he had to work with whatever he received. But beyond this the remainder of the equation directly parallels the herald. Instead of an ever-changing *dependent variable*, Paul viewed his proclamation as a never-changing *constant*: "I decided to know nothing among you except Jesus Christ and him crucified (1 Cor. 2:2)." And the results? Instead of an *independent variable*, set by Paul, they turn out to be Paul's *dependent variable*. To his announcing of the gospel Paul discovers a variety of responses: to the Jew his message appears as a scandal; to the Greek his message is ridiculous; but to those "who are being saved" (*oi sozomenoi*, 1 Cor. 1:18), that is, to "the called ones" (*oi kletoi*, 1 Cor. 1:24) whether Jew or Greek, this same message turns out to be the wisdom and power of God (1 Cor. 1:24). What did Paul believe determined the difference? Not the rhetorical skills of the speaker, but something outside the equation altogether—the work of the Spirit. And this, of course, was just as Paul would have it. He was determined to depend on the Spirit's working through the simple heralding of the "word of the cross," rather than on the human psychological dynamic of the persuader. While this might mean that his preaching would remain unimpressive to the world, this was a consequence Paul was willing to accept, for he considered his approach to be required by a fundamental insight into how God operates in the world: "God chose what is foolish in the world to shame the wise; God chose what is weak in the world to shame the strong; God chose what is low and despised in the world, even things that are not, to bring to nothing things that are, so that no human being might boast in the presence of God" (1 Cor. 1:27–29).

Paul may have at times been tempted to lapse into the persuader's role (especially, some have argued, during his unhappy experience in Athens), but if so he resisted the impulse because he was concerned about the possibility of emptying the cross of its power by preempting it with false human-centered results (1 Cor. 1:17). As elsewhere, Paul focused his preaching in Corinth on the straightforward proclamation of a herald, so that the Corinthians' faith "might not rest on men's wisdom, but on God's power" (1 Cor. 2:5 NIV).[30]

---

30. One might be tempted at this point to raise an objection, citing 2 Cor. 5:11, where Paul says, "Since, then, we know what it is to fear the Lord, we try to persuade men" (NIV). Didn't Paul himself practice "persuasion"? This is a more complicated question than it might seem on the surface, and it would take us far afield "into the lexical work on the verb *peitho* and into theoretical definitions of persuasion" to answer it in full. Suffice it to say that this single nontechnical use of the verb *peitho* by Paul serves to prove the rule. In the dozens of places in Paul's writings where he refers to his own preaching, he scrupulously uses the language of the herald (*kerusso, parakaleo, martureo, euangelizo*), language which plays little part in the rhetorical literature because it describes non-rhetorical behavior. 2 Cor. 5:11 is the only instance where Paul uses a verb that could also be used by the rhetoricians, and the context there makes it plain that Paul is not introducing an exception. In fact, the entire section (2 Cor. 4–5) is one of the locations in the Corinthian epistles which most strongly echoes the anti-rhetorical concerns of 1 Cor. 1–4. Paul was careful to portray his ministry as

We may note, then, how the language of 1 Corinthians 1–2 radically challenges the orator's stance. In contrast to the persuader, Paul enters the equation by asking, not, What do I want to accomplish?, but, What is it God has called me to be and to do? Then he sets out to be that and do that (1 Cor. 1:13–17). As a herald, his efforts are neither results-driven nor audience-driven; they are assignment-driven, obedience-driven (1 Cor. 4:2). And Paul is radically willing to let the results fall where they may.[31] If this meant that those who measured his efforts by the world's standards remained unimpressed, so be it; it is God's way to use what the world considers unimpressive to accomplish his purposes, so that no mortal may boast. If it meant that Paul would not achieve the response he would like to see, then he would have to accept that; his part was to fulfill his calling and leave the results to God. Paul was determined to limit himself to his assigned role in the transaction, lest by stepping in and applying his own strategies he engender false results. His role was simply to "placard"[32] the gospel of Christ crucified, a message which he considered to be "the power of God for the salvation of everyone who believes" (Rom. 1:16). It is the Spirit of God who must be responsible for the results.

Implications for *Kerygma*

With this in mind, then, let us focus on our central passage, 1 Corinthians 1:21. Paul's assumption throughout this passage—indeed, throughout all of his writings—is that the human race is lost in its sin, and that it desperately needs to be saved from the condemnation of the Creator against whom it has mutinied. But human pride is the great barrier. Humans are convinced that if only they apply themselves, they can solve this dilemma. But this was just the notion Paul sought to put to rest. "Where is the wise man," he asks, "Where is the scholar? Where is the philosopher of this age" (v. 20, NIV) when it comes to solving this most pressing of all human problems? Whatever else their vaunted wisdom might accomplish, has not God made foolish all of their feeble attempts to solve *this* problem on their own? The world may be impressed by the prideful efforts of its best and brightest to scale the heights and achieve for themselves eternal life—indeed, to come to know God. But God himself will have none of it. In his divine wisdom he has cut off

---

that of a herald rather than a persuader, and his single use of the elastic term *peitho* in 2 Cor. 5:11 constitutes no exception.

31. Cf. Jesus also, in passages such as Mark 10:17–22 or John 6:22–69.

32. C. K. Barrett, *A Commentary on the First Epistle to the Corinthians*, 51. See John 12:32.

this approach. Humans simply cannot and will not solve this dilemma in their own strength. If they are to come to God at all, says Paul, they must do so on God's terms.

And his terms are these: God will provide the race with an avenue of salvation, but it will be available only through a means which runs profoundly *contrary* to human pride. To discover this salvation men and women will need to renounce their pretensions to self-sufficiency, acknowledge their helplessness, and give up striving to save themselves. Instead, they must humble themselves before God by acknowledging a crucified Jewish peasant to be Lord of the universe and his death on a Roman cross as their only hope of salvation. They must trust him, and him alone, as their only means of salvation.

What's more, the medicine becomes more bitter still. God will not tolerate any lingering pride. Humans must be willing to place their faith in Christ solely on the basis of hearing and accepting God's *announced* word[33] on the subject, the gospel. He will not satisfy their pride in other ways. If in order to respond positively they demand miraculous signs to authenticate the announcement, God will not provide them. If they insist on something more along the lines of what the Greeks required to be impressed—that is, "wisdom" in the form of convincing arguments designed to satisfy self-sufficient minds, all dressed in winsomely impressive language—he will not provide this either. All they will receive is the simple declaration of the gospel by God's designated herald proclaiming, "Jesus Christ and him crucified." As Jesus himself often put it, "He who has ears to hear, let him hear."

No doubt Paul understood that many in his audience, to the extent they were unwilling to renounce their pride, would find this announcement absurdly unsatisfying. The typical Jew, he says, will be scandalized by it, while the typical Greek will merely disdain it as ridiculous. In their vanity neither will be willing to identify themselves with such a low-status salvation because neither will be willing to accept the premise that they should be reduced to such a humble estate. But God knew from the beginning what he was doing. He could have come to the race through their own striving, but he knew that in the end they would as a result pridefully claim credit for their own salvation. Instead, God intentionally chose to make himself available through means the proud would find unacceptable—that is, through a means that put aside all human pretensions and allowed only the humble acceptance of a simply-announced, crucified Christ—so that in the

---

33. Cf. how the only other use of *kerygma* in the New Testament, Christ's reference to Jonah in Matt. 12:41 and Luke 11:32, fits this pattern.

end it would be clear that God alone was responsible for their salvation. No mortal could boast.

This is the argument that forms the context for Paul's use of *kerygma* in our central passage, 1 Corinthians 1:21. It should not be difficult, therefore, to see that when Paul speaks of "the foolishness of the *kerygma*" he intends his reader to understand more than "content alone." To be sure, the term *kerygma* refers here to the content of Paul's preaching. By the standards of the world, the gospel of "Christ crucified" is indeed a supremely foolish message. But it is important to see that this content is not the only thing that lacks standing in the eyes of the world. When an audience wants and expects to hear the persuasive argumentation and formal eloquence of the orator—in fact, *demands* them if they are expected to be impressed—the simple heralding of a declarative message will be greeted by derision. Along with the content, this form too will appear paltry and foolish by comparison, so much so that it will insult them. It will offend the worldling's pride and seem demeaning to him that he should be expected simply to *accept* the message as announced, on the mere say-so of its source.

It is just this point that we may find most difficult to appreciate. As today, first-century audiences expected to be gratified by taking part in a transaction in which they held the upper hand. It was a buyer's market, so to speak, and they were in the happy position of being the buyers. Their role was to sit in judgment on the speakers who came before them and to decide whether they should be convinced. The occasion of listening to a speaker thus provided audiences not only amusement and entertainment but also immense ego satisfaction. Paul Corcoran captures this dimension of the ancient rhetorical transaction as follows:

> To be addressed by a speaker who wins you over, persuading you clearly of the good and the true position, is in itself gratifying. Doubt, hesitation, ignorance or ill-confidence are happily laid to rest. To fall under the sway of a learned and convincing orator is gratifying simply because of the coincidence of interest between oneself and the speaker, who manifestly desires what you have to give: your attention and applause. The distance between oneself and the enlightened orator is no cause for pain, because in the very act of listening this gap is narrowed, and a community of interest expanded. It is gratifying, moreover, just to be the object of concern for the superior intellect, especially when one stands only to gain by it. Finally, it is highly rewarding to be, as an audience, with the strength of numbers and in a position to judge and evaluate the man of learning. It is not humiliating to fall under

the sway of the orator, precisely because of the element of choice. If he were unconvincing, he could be ignored.[34]

This prideful stance, Paul argues, is what makes not only the *content* of the *kerygma* unpalatable but also its *form*. In hearing the message of God's herald, the audience is dethroned from its proud role as judge. Indeed, far from gratifying their pride, the audience is being called simply to accept "the word of the cross" as proffered. But this the prideful will be unwilling to do. If the content of the gospel, Christ crucified, will be considered scandalous or foolish by the world's standards, so will be its mere heralding. But this is very much by God's design. It pleased God, says Paul, through the foolishness of both the *content* and the *form* of the heralding to save (*tous pisteuontous*) those who simply believe. This humble response is all God asks—indeed, all he will accept. But any such kneeling in repentance and submission is a tall order for the proud.

Conclusion

When the apostle referred to his own preaching as the *kerygma* he was identifying his ministry explicitly with the figure of the *keryx*, the herald, with all that term implies. The verb *keryssein* was not merely a generic term for public speaking; it carried a distinctive meaning, a meaning that can only be fully appreciated against the backdrop of the splendidly felicitous eloquence of the persuader.

It was Paul's argument that God is not in the business of gratifying prideful hearts and minds with convincing content and irresistible forms. "Faith," if we are thinking in biblical terms, means taking God at his word, and when it comes to the gospel, that word is all he is inclined to give us. It is in this sense that the "foolishness" of the *kerygma* applies to both its *content* and its *form*.

---

34. Paul E. Corcoran, *Political Language and Rhetoric* (St. Lucia, Queensland: University of Queensland Press, 1979), 46.

8

Preaching with a Pastor's Heart: Richard Baxter's
The Reformed Pastor

Wallace Benn

Some books mark you deeply and change your life, although there are not many that you want to read over and over again. Richard Baxter's *The Reformed Pastor,* first published in 1656, is one of those rare life-changing books. In the thirty-five years that I have been in the ministry, I have tried to read this great work on pastoral ministry every five years. I need to, lest I forget what being an under-shepherd of the flock of God is really all about.

As a primer, I offer the following passage to provide a preliminary taste of the passion and power of Baxter:

> The first and greatest work of ministers of Christ is acquainting men with the God who made them; He is the source of their blessing. We should open up the treasures of His goodness for them and tell them of the glory that is in His presence, a glory that His chosen people shall enjoy. By showing men the certainty and excellence of the promised joy, and by making them aware of the perfect blessedness in the life to come in comparison with the vanities of the present life, we may direct their understanding and affections toward heaven. We shall bring them to the point of due contempt of this world and fasten their hearts on a more durable treasure. This is the work we should be busy with both night and day. For when we have affixed their hearts

unfeignedly on God and heaven, the major part of the ministry is accomplished. All the rest will follow naturally. (p. 108)[1]

It is small wonder that Jim Packer describes *The Reformed Pastor* as "another all-time classic, admonishing, motivating, and instructing the clergy."[2]

The Man behind the Book

Baxter was a salaried preacher at Kidderminster, England, from 1641 to 1642, and then vicar of the same town from 1647 to 1661. More than any other English preacher, he has been the model parochial minister. His was "a ministry during which he just about converted the whole town."[3] The effect of Baxter's ministry at Kidderminster was extraordinary. Packer writes that "Kidderminster was a town of some 2,000 adults, and most of them, it seems, were converted under his ministry. He found them, he tells us, 'an ignorant, rude and revelling people, for the most part . . . they had hardly ever had any lively serious preaching among them.' But his ministry was wonderfully blessed."[4]

Baxter was a powerful gospel preacher and teacher of Scripture with a real heart to see people won for Christ. His ministry had such an effect on the town that, two hundred years later, a statue was erected to his memory by town officials. He believed that "there is no better way to make a good cause prevail than to make it plain," and he preached with a clarity, power, and straightness that were compelling. He spoke so as to be understood, and he expected as well as longed for people to come to Christ. His pastoral care and instruction were second to none and he remains, even in a different age, a good role model in many ways.

The Reformed Pastor: The Biblical Point of Departure

Baxter's magnificent book *The Reformed Pastor* is a heartfelt appeal to other Puritan ministers for good pastoral practice and is an extended

---

1. All the quotations from Richard Baxter have been taken from Richard Baxter, *Watch Your Walk: Ministering from a Heart of Integrity*, ed. James M. Houston (East Sussex: Victor, 2004). Baxter is wonderful but wordy, and I think this is the most accessible edition to whet your appetite to read him yourself. But there is an older and somewhat fuller abridgement published by Banner of Truth, reprinted in 1974 from the 1862 edition and currently in print.

2. J. I. Packer, *A Man for All Ministries*, St. Antholin's/Bishopsgate Lecture 1991 (London: St. Antholin Trust, 1991), 3.

3. J. I. Packer, *A Man for All Ministries*, 3.

4. J. I. Packer, *Among God's Giants* (Eastbourne: Kingsway, 1991), 53–54.

discussion based on Acts 20:28, which reads, "Pay careful attention to yourselves and to all the flock, in which the Holy Spirit has made you overseers." Before we look at what Baxter has to say that is relevant to our subject, let us take a tour of what Paul says in this magnificent chapter.

Paul is on his way to Jerusalem, and he is in a hurry to get there (v. 16). So he sends for the elders of the church in Ephesus to come some thirty miles and meet him in Miletus. This is the church that Paul has spent the most time with—nearly three years of his life—and they are clearly very dear to him. The particular reason he wants to see the elders is that he does not think that he will have an opportunity ever to see them again, and he has some very important things to say to them (v. 25).

The poignancy of this chapter, then, is clear, as final conversations with loved ones, or those which we believe to be our last, are times for expressions of love as well as a reminder of things that are important to keep in mind. So it is here, and if I could go back to New Testament times, other than hearing Jesus teach or seeing him perform a miracle or being there on resurrection morning, this is the scene for which I would most like to have been a fly on the wall!

We should note that there is an "I know /you know" structure to the passage (see vv. 18, 22, 25, 29, 34). Within this format, Paul makes five key points. First, Paul appeals to the elders on the basis of their knowledge of him (vv. 18*ff.*, 34). His life backed up his proclamation, and his lifestyle did not jar with it either. Despite trials and problems, he didn't shrink from declaring "anything that was profitable" (v. 20). Nothing put him off or hindered his testifying "to the gospel of the grace of God" (v. 24). Nor was he a drain on those amongst whom he worked, seeking, in this situation at this time, to support himself and his team financially (v. 34). Paul knew that a minister's life must back up what he preaches and that much pastoral damage is done by inconsistency in this area.

Second, Paul was much more than a pulpiteer. He proclaimed the gospel not only in public, but from house to house (v. 20). In other words, he was a man of the Word who took every opportunity to share it, in large situations as well as in small groups or with individuals.

Third, Paul's gospel is very clear. It is his testimony to "the gospel of the grace of God" (v. 24) that drives him. It is a gospel that calls for "repentance toward God and . . . faith in our Lord Jesus Christ" (v. 21). It is the revealed good news of God's love to repentant sinners in and through his beloved Son Jesus. It is God's gospel and is not to be altered or adjusted to suit politically correct ideas but rather to be proclaimed and testified to. Interestingly, Paul sees no difference between "the gospel of the grace of God" (v. 24), and "proclaiming the kingdom" (v. 25), but rather they are different ways of saying the same thing! How different that is from some liberal critics who want to see a difference between the gospel of the kingdom as proclaimed by Jesus in the gospels and the gospel of justification by faith as proclaimed by Paul. Paul would have had none of it.

Fourth, Paul didn't just preach to the Ephesians evangelistically but also shared with them "the whole counsel of God" (v. 27). He would have shared with them the Old Testament Scriptures as well as the apostolic testimony to the life, teaching, death, and resurrection of the Lord Jesus. In our terms, he expounded all of Holy Scripture to them. He didn't just share his favorite bits but "anything that was profitable" (v. 20).

Fifth, personal profit or ease was not Paul's overarching motivation, but rather it was being faithful "to testify to the gospel of the grace of God" (v. 24) and finishing his God-given "course and the ministry" (v. 24) that he had received from the Lord Jesus.

His dear friends would need to remember his priorities and example if the church was to be preserved from the damaging effect of false teaching, even from some of their own number who were more concerned with building their own reputations and empires than with the good of the kingdom of heaven (vv. 29, 30). So the elders must be alert (v. 31). The faithfully taught and believed gospel of grace is that which alone builds the church and causes it to grow (v. 32).

Paul's advice is summed up in the key verse of the chapter (in Baxter's view)—verse 28. Two very important things ought to be noticed about this verse, which Baxter (we shall see) emphasized.

First, the order of the first part of the verse is significant. We cannot watch over or "pay careful attention to . . . all the flock" if we are not watching over ourselves first. We cannot lead others where we have not gone ourselves. Keeping a guard over our spiritual lives is critical in the ministry, as is taking care of our responsibilities as husbands and fathers. We must preach to ourselves first what we would preach to others.

The other key thing to notice, which is not obvious until we see it and then wonder why we missed it, is the Trinitarian nature of the verse. If you exercise an ordained ministry it is because, I trust, you know that behind the promptings, advice, and encouragements to seek ordination is no one other than the Holy Spirit who both calls you and equips you for ministry (v. 28b).

The high calling you have been given is to care for the church of God. It is not your work, but God's work, that you are privileged to be involved in. So it is not about your success, nor is it about building your own empire. "Unless the LORD builds the house, those who build it labor in vain" (Ps.

127:1). Acts 20:28 is the verse that most helps me, as a senior church leader, to sleep at night! Sometimes there are real problems and difficulties in church congregations and between Christians that look too difficult for human wisdom to sort out. But God cares for his church much more than we can ever do, and ultimately the church's health and well-being depend on him and, thankfully, not on us. It is his work and his church.

Furthermore, the church of Christ has been bought at great cost: "which he obtained with his own blood." This is a *hapax legomenon* (a unique phrase) in Scripture. Normally it is "the blood of his beloved Son" or something similar. This is what it means here, too (it can be read as "with the blood of his own"; see F. F. Bruce on Acts), but the more natural reading of the Greek is that it is the blood of God, stated as starkly as that. When Jesus voluntarily and willingly went to the cross, he did so in love and in obedience to the will of his Father. Oh, how much our redemption cost not only the sinless Son but the whole Trinity.

As we turn now to see the emphasis in the *Reformed Pastor* that relates to the thrust of this chapter, I hope that it will be obvious how Baxter picks out and expresses truths enshrined here, and elsewhere, which, according to the great apostle, are so important for a healthy preaching ministry. In particular I want to draw attention to three things emphasized by the good Puritan.

The Preacher's Spiritual Walk

Recently a fairly well-known evangelical minister came to see me (one not working in my area). He told me that his preaching was valued by his congregation and that he had a reputation as a good Bible teacher whose ministry was much appreciated. He was clearly upset, so I asked him why he had come to see me. His answer was that although he produced skilled and appreciated sermons for others to believe, he had no personal walk with Jesus Christ. He said, "I have become a sermon factory for others to take to heart, but I am spiritually nowhere myself!" He asked for advice.

I told him that in my opinion he should take a sabbatical and spend a lot of time at the foot of the cross until his heart was warmed again by the love of Christ,[5] for he dare not preach to others what is unreal to him or what he is unwilling to take on board personally. I also encouraged him to read Baxter in that time off. He did what I suggested and

---

5. "The cross is the blazing fire at which the flame of our love is kindled. But we have to get near enough to it for its sparks to fall on us." Quoted in John Cheeseman, *The Priority of Preaching* (Edinburgh: Banner of Truth, 2006).

thankfully has been helped and blessed. His story underlines the fact that it is dangerously possible to be simply "professional" in the job of ministry and forget or neglect our own walk with God. We must never forget the words of our Savior, "Apart from me you can do nothing" (John 15:5), and, "Out of the abundance of the heart the mouth speaks. The good person out of his good treasure brings forth good" (Matt. 12:34–35). Otherwise, preaching is not done "in the presence of God and of Christ Jesus" (2 Tim. 4:1), before them to please them (which is awesome but also liberating), but before people for the praise of men. It defies Paul's advice to Timothy, "Set the believers an example in speech, in conduct, in love, in faith, in purity . . . practice these things, devote yourself to them . . . keep a close watch on yourself and on the teaching. Persist in this, for by so doing you will save both yourself and your hearers" (1 Tim. 4:12, 15–16).

As a fine and faithful preacher and pastor himself, Baxter understood only too well the dangers that must be avoided in ministry. Here is great practical wisdom from Baxter:

> My second exhortation is preach to yourself the sermon that you propose before you preach it to others. When your mind is enjoying heavenly things, others will enjoy them, too. Then your prayers, praises, and doctrines will be heavenly and sweet to your people. They will feel when you have been much with God.
>
> Conversely, when I am depressed in soul, my flock will sense my cold preaching. When I am confused, my preaching is, too. Then, the prayers of others will reflect my own state of preaching. If we, therefore, feed on unwholesome food, either of errors or of fruitless controversies, then our hearers will likely fare the worse for it, whereas if we abound in faith, love, and zeal, how it will overflow to the refreshing of our congregations and to the increases in the same graces in others
>
> So, brethren, watch over your own heart. Keep out sinful passions and worldly inclinations. Keep up the life of faith and love. Be much at home with God. Let it be your daily, serious business to study your own heart, to subdue corruptions, and to live dependent on God. If not, then all your work that you constantly attend to will go amiss, and you will starve your hearers. If you only have an artificial fervency, then you cannot expect attendant blessings. Above all, be much in secret prayer and meditation.
>
> For your people's sake, then, look into your own hearts. If spiritual pride overtakes you, and you develop any dangerous ideas of schisms, and you try through your overvalued intentions to draw away disciples after you, how you wound the Christian body! Therefore, take heed to your judgments and affections. Error and vanity

insinuate slyly. Apostasies usually have small beginnings. How easily also will bad spirits creep into our affections, and our first love for the Lord cools.

A minister should take special care of his own heart before he goes before his congregation. If it is cold, how is it likely to crown the hearts of the hearers? Go then especially to God for life, and read some rousing, challenging books. Meditate on the theme and thirst for the subject that you are about to speak on. Carry the burden of your people's souls on you before you go the house of the Lord.[6]

We might add that a pastor needs to take relationships at home very seriously. I will never forget the teenage son of a well-known evangelist saying to me at a conference, "The trouble with my dad is that he is a street saint and a house devil!" It is at home that we are seen at our best and worst, and so much damage is done to young hearts if the preacher is inconsistent at home (bearing in mind none of us is as good as we might be). There needs to be a transparency and reality about our spiritual life that backs up our preaching. Otherwise how dare we expect others to travel where we have not and to expect God's blessing on our preaching? We need to read the Bible and pray, not just to produce sermons for others but for our own spiritual well-being too. It is a great privilege to have to engage with Scripture every week to preach properly and in an expository manner, but our engagement with Scripture must first be to speak to ourselves. We need to use our responsibility to preach God's Word as an opportunity for a regular health check. Baxter as ever is a wonderful soul friend.

Two comments of Baxter's that I particularly treasure and that sum up my point are the following: "Be much at home with God" and "When our mind is enjoying heavenly things, others will enjoy them too." (See also a key passage about Old Testament leadership in Malachi 2:5–7, which is applicable to presbyters in the New Testament.)

The Preacher's Pastoral Involvement

We have already noticed that the apostle Paul was more than a pulpiteer and that he took every opportunity to share the truth of the gospel. Baxter was assiduous in his pastoral care, spending two days a week in a hectic life to see families and catechize each one for an hour. He worked his way through all his parishioners every year with the help of

---

6. Richard Baxter, *Watch Your Walk: Ministering from a Heart of Integrity*, 139–40.

two assistants, believing that this one-to-one work was at the very heart of the success of the ministry in Kidderminster.

Despite his high regard for preaching, Baxter was concerned that some of his colleagues spent too many hours each day in the study, with the result that they had little pastoral contact with people. Baxter saw that as bad for the people under a pastor's care, but he knew that it was bad for preachers also. How would preachers understand their congregants' questions and needs if they did not know their flock? How would they be prayerfully guided in the selection of a book of the Bible to preach through if they did not have the information as to which book of the Bible would be most relevant to their people at that point in their spiritual lives?

Today there is an urgency for pastors to apply Baxter's advice in a modern context where daytime visiting might find both mom and dad at work. If one parent is at home, it is likely to be the wife, and in today's world how appropriate is one-to-one, male-to-female pastoring? Evening visiting finds commuters exhausted and distracted with television, and children needing help with their homework. How helpful and serious can a spiritual conversation be in that context? However, I am convinced that with adaptation and imagination Baxter's model of pastoral care can be used effectively and helpfully today.[7]

My concern is that preachers have little pastoral contact with ordinary people except in emergencies, and this is not good for their preaching. Indeed, we must honestly admit that some preachers appear not to like people much, withdrawing from contact with them and sometimes justifying it by saying they believe in the priority of preaching. With Baxter, I believe passionately in the priority of preaching, but this must not be used to distance us from involvement with people. It is a question of balance. The problem that Baxter was addressing is especially a problem for a senior pastor in a large church, where, by the nature of the job, pastoral involvement with people becomes harder; the more senior the leader, the more isolated you can become.

Baxter would have agreed that much counseling and pastoral care are done through good preaching, and indeed where the Bible is faithfully and powerfully taught and applied, many counseling problems will disappear. But Baxter's point for preachers is that we will not preach powerfully to people if we don't really know them or understand the challenges they face. He is also crystal clear that the teaching of the

---

7. See my Orthos 13 booklet, *The Baxter Model: Guidelines for Pastoring Today* (Fellowship of Word and Spirit, 1993), where a suggested and practiced way of using Baxter's insights are developed. An online version is also available at www.fows.org/html/baxter_model. html.

Word of God publicly must be reinforced by teaching in a smaller group context where individual questions can be addressed. Here are three passages in which Baxter addresses the issue:

> I know that public preaching of the Gospel is the most excellent means of ministry because we speak to so many at once. Other than that single advantage, it is usually far more effective to preach the Bible's message privately to a particular sinner. In public we may not use the more homely expressions, and our speeches are so long that we overrun our hearer's understanding and memory. Thus they are not able to follow us. But in private we can take them at their own pace of understanding and keep their attention by argument, answers, and objections as they raise them. I conclude, therefore, that public preaching is not enough. You may study long but preach to little purpose unless you have a pastoral ministry.
>
> Like the apostle John, we should not count our lives dear to us, so that we may find our crown of rejoicing by doing the work of God for their salvation. When the people see, then, that you love them unfeignedly, they will hear what you say—they will bear whatever you ask—and they will follow you more readily. And when a wound is given in love, it will be more readily accepted than when one issues a foul word that is merely given in malice or anger.[8]
>
> Moreover, we have the best opportunity to imprint the truth upon the hearts of men when we can speak to each one's personal needs. If you have the compassion of Christ, you will exercise this ministry. If you are coworkers with Christ, you will not neglect the souls for whom he died. . . .
>
> Such personal teaching will make our public preaching so much better understood and regarded. When you have acquainted the people with the principles, they will better understand all that you say. They will better perceive your intent when you have prepared their hearts and minds beforehand. So you will not lose in public service if you have been fruitful in this private ministry.[9]

In large church situations, this work needs to be delegated to a good pastoral team that reports to the senior pastor. Baxter shared the work with others. But he would have cautioned the pastor to be doing some of this himself, lest he remain aloof and fail to understand his peoples' needs personally. There is wisdom here for effectiveness in our preaching, for clearly pastors need to pastor in more ways than in the pulpit. They also need to be people (as they encourage their congregations to

---

8. Richard Baxter, *Watch Your Walk: Ministering from a Heart of Integrity*, 53.
9. Ibid., 150.

be) who are on the cutting edge of mission and evangelism in seeking to win individuals they know personally for Christ. Such involvement will make our preaching so much sharper and on the ball. Edward Donnelly's comment is apt: "This perhaps is where Baxter may prove most serviceable to the ministers of today—in the forging of a strong link between pulpit and pastorate."[10]

The Preacher's Application in Sermons

The greatest need of the church today is powerful expository preaching. There is a lamentable lack of it even in evangelical churches. John Stott in a marvelous chapter on "the paradoxes of preaching" reminds us of the following:

> Our understanding of preaching is that it is essentially, in its very essence, an exposition of the Word of God. In that sense all Christian preaching is expository preaching—not in the narrow sense of that term, meaning a running commentary on a long passage of Scripture—but in the broad sense that it opens up the biblical text. Preachers are trustees of God's revelation, stewards of the Word of God; and we must be determined, above all else, to be faithful in our stewardship.

But Stott goes on to say:

> Yet at the same time, authentic Christian preaching is also *contemporary,* or should be. It resonates with the modern world; it wrestles with the realities of our hearers' situation. In our resolve to be biblical we must refuse to lapse into irrelevance. Instead, we should seek to relate the ancient text to the modern context. True biblical exposition goes beyond exegesis, which simply explains the *meaning* of the passage, to application—grasping the heart of the *message.*[11]

In England we have not only a lack of good expository preaching, but also many complaints about some otherwise good young ministers. I speak of preachers who see the vital importance of understanding the text of Scripture and getting it right but fail to see that is only half the job done. A vital half for sure, but devoid of application. Too much sound preaching is unnecessarily dull. We dare not forget what Mar-

---

10. Edward Donnelly, introduction to *Dying Thoughts*, by Richard Baxter (Edinburgh: Banner of Truth, 2004).

11. Greg Haslam, ed., *"Preach the Word!"* (Lancaster: Sovereign Word, 2006), 43–44.

tyn Lloyd-Jones said in his great book *Preaching and Preachers*: "What is preaching? Logic on fire! Eloquent reason. . . . Preaching is theology coming through a man who is on fire."[12]

Wilbur Ellsworth also reminds us in a timely fashion that "in fact, our increasing technology seems to create an even greater need for human touch and the human voice speaking to the human heart."[13] Considered application as well as a heart moved by what we are preaching is essential for powerful biblical preaching. "In all cases preaching will employ you in teaching, plus application, for the purpose of persuasion."[14]

As my old professor and friend J. I. Packer used to tell his students, "Preaching is teaching, first and foremost. It is more than teaching; it is teaching plus application . . . but it is never less than teaching. It is a kind of speaking aimed at both mind and heart, and seeking unashamedly to change the way people think and live. So it is always an attempt at persuasion."[15]

So, then, application is essential to good biblical preaching. In fact, we could say with the wonderful Bible expositor J. A. Motyer, "The art of preaching is application." Of course there are different ways to do that, and the place to start is by laying the meaning of the text of Scripture bare and thinking in applicatory ways of how to teach the text, so that the message of Scripture comes home forcibly to us. But without limiting the application of Scripture to a congregation, I am persuaded that modern people need examples of how Scripture can apply. Here is John Cheeseman on the subject:

> Application is absolutely crucial. This is what really makes the message come home with force and penetration to the congregation. People want to hear something that is relevant to them in their daily lives. We must spare no effort in making our application as real and down-to-earth as we can. But do not always keep the application to the same part of your sermon. For example, some preachers save it all up to the end. This is not a good idea on every occasion. If you inject your sermons with applications all the way through, it will help your people stay alert and awake [16]

---

12. Martyn Lloyd-Jones, *Preaching and Preachers* (Hodder & Stoughton, 1971), 97.

13. Wilbur Ellsworth, *How to Preach Memorable Sermons* (Ross-shire: Christian Focus, 2000), 30.

14. David Eby, *Power Preaching for Church Growth*, (Ross-shire: Mentor, 1996), 35.

15. J. I. Packer, "Why Preach?" in David Eby, *Power Preaching for Church Growth*, 174.

16. John Cheeseman, *The Priority of Preaching* (Edinburgh: Banner of Truth, 2006), 17.

By now it will not surprise you when I say that Baxter knew this all a long time ago! And in many ways he puts the issues of prayerful application best of all:

> Augustine remarked, "A preacher must labor to be heard with understanding, with willingness, and with obedience. Let him not doubt that he will effect this with fervent prayers more than with all the power of his oratory. By praying for himself and his audiences he will be fit to be a petitioner before he is a teacher. So when he comes and when he goes, let him raise his voice to God, and lift up his soul in fervent desire."
>
> Prayer must carry on our work as well as our preaching. For he who does not pray for his people will not preach powerfully to his people. If we do not prevail with God to give them faith and repentance, then we are unlikely to prevail with them to believe and to repent. Thus Paul gives us frequently his own example, as one who "prays night and day" for his hearers. When our hearts then are out of order, theirs will also be out of order. If we do not prevail with God to help others, then our work will be in vain. . . .
>
> Even in our sermons we are often negligent to study more than gathering a few points of data, and we fail to go deeper, to see how we can set these matters forcibly in the hearts of other people. We ought to study how to convince and how to get inside people and how to learn to bring the truth to the quick—not to leave it in the air. Experience tells us that we cannot be learned or wise without hard study, unwearied labors, and experience.
>
> Moreover, if ministers are to do the work of the Lord, it must be done more vigorously than most of us do it. How few ministers preach with all their might or speak of everlasting joy or torment with conviction. Instead, we speak so drowsily or gently that sleeping sinners cannot hear.
>
> What a tragedy it is, then, to hear a minister expand doctrines and yet let them die in his people's hands for the lack of a relevant and living application. Could we speak coldly of God and of men's salvation? So, in the name of God, brethren, labor to waken your own hearts before you come and are fit to awaken the hearts of sinners.[17]

Richard Baxter has much to teach us today both about good expository preaching that understands the need for good application, as well as the importance of the preachers speaking from a heart that is "enjoying God" and walking prayerfully with him. Here is a powerful reminder that there is more (not less) than an academic engagement with the text which the preacher must do. It will take our best efforts

---

17. Richard Baxter, *Watch Your Walk*, 48, 93–94.

and above all the strength and enabling of the Holy Spirit of God, who not only calls us to ministry but thankfully equips us for it too. Baxter was a magnificent example of a preacher with a pastor's heart. We need to digest his wisdom and make it our own. Our preaching, by the grace of God, will be far more effective if we do. In preaching as in the whole of ministry there is really no substitute for love of God and love of his people.

Edward Donnelly sums up Richard Baxter well as a preacher: "This then is Richard Baxter of Kidderminster. A preacher who labored to make plain the truth of God, who spoke from a burning heart as he pleaded with his people to close with Christ. A pastor who knew his sheep by name, who spoke to them personally about the great concerns of their souls. He is not merely an historical curiosity, a fossil to be marvelled at, but a stimulus, a rebuke, an encouragement."[18]

It has been a great pleasure and joy to be able to commend a few of Richard Baxter's key insights, which have meant so much to me personally. He needs to be widely read by a whole new generation of young pastors as well as again by us oldies! I know of no better example of a modern powerful expository preacher, who preaches with the kind of pastoral heart that Richard Baxter exemplified, than my very dear friend Kent Hughes, to whom this volume is dedicated. To God be the Glory!

---

18. Richard Baxter, *Dying Thoughts*, xix.

9

Expository Preaching:
Charles Simeon and Ourselves[1]

J. I. Packer

harles Simeon (1759–1836) is one of the towering evangelical preachers in the history of Anglican preaching. He stands as an inspiration to many contemporary evangelical preachers first of all because of his exemplary life as a preacher and mentor of preachers. Initially despised by the Anglican elite, his influence eventually became nearly without precedent in the annals of English ecclesiastical history. But Simeon's continuing influence rests even more on his homiletic theory, which is the subject of this essay.

Toward a Definition of Expository Preaching

If we wish to appropriate the wisdom of Charles Simeon as theorist on expository preaching, we must first make clear to ourselves *what we mean when we speak of expository preaching*. This is necessary because the word *expository* has often been used in a restricted sense to denote simply a

---

1. "Expository Preaching: Charles Simeon and Ourselves" is a revised and enlarged version of an address to pastors first published in *Churchman*, LXXIV (1960): 94–100 and reprinted in J. I. Packer, "Honoring the Written Word of God," *Collected Shorter Writings of J. I. Packer* (Carlisle: Paternoster, 1999), 3:269–76.

sermon preached from a long text. Thus, Andrew Blackwood wrote: "An expository sermon here means one that grows out of a Bible passage longer than two or three verses . . . an expository sermon means a textual treatment of a fairly long passage."[2] He went on to suggest that young pastors should preach such sermons "perhaps once a month"[3] and to give hints on the problems of technique they involve.

Without suggesting that Blackwood's usage is inadmissible for any purpose, I must discuss it as too narrow for our present purpose—if only because it would exclude all but a handful of Charles Simeon's sermons (his texts, you see, are far too short!). We shall find it better to define "expository" preaching in terms, not of the length of the text, but of the preacher's approach to it, and to say something like this: expository preaching is the preaching of the man who knows Holy Scripture to be the living Word of the living God, and who desires only that it should be free to speak its own message to sinful men and women; who therefore preaches from a text, and in preaching labors, as the Puritans would say, to "open" it, or, in Simeon's phrase, to "bring out of the text what is there"; whose whole aim in preaching is to show his hearers what the text is saying to them about God and about themselves, and to lead them into what Barth called "the strange new world within the Bible" in order that they may be met by him who is the Lord of that world.

The practice of expository preaching thus presupposes the biblical and evangelical account of the relation of the written words of Scripture to the speaking God with whom we have to do. Defining the concept in this way, we may say that every sermon that Simeon preached was an expository sermon; and, surely, we may add that every sermon that we ourselves preach should be an expository sermon. What other sort of sermons, we may ask, is there room for in Christ's church?

Expository Preaching in Our Contemporary Milieu

Having understood what expository preaching is, we must secondly be clear to ourselves *why we are so interested in expository preaching at the present time.* Professor Blackwood had in view the American scene when he wrote almost sixty years ago: "Pastors everywhere are becoming concerned about expository preaching";[4] but it is no less true of ourselves

---

2. *The Preparation of Sermons* (Nashville: Abingdon, 1948), 69.

3. Ibid., 70.

4. Ibid., 64.

today. And we do well to stop and ask ourselves, Why is this? What lies behind this concern? Why are we all thinking and writing and talking about expository preaching these days? I am sure that we are seeking something more than tips for handling long texts. It is at a deeper level that we want help.

What troubles us, I think, is a sense that the old evangelical tradition of powerful preaching—the tradition, in England, of Whitefield and Wesley and Berridge and Simeon and Haslam and Ryle—has petered out, and we do not know how to revive it. We feel that, for all our efforts, we as preachers are failing to speak adequately to men's souls. In other words, what lies behind our modern interest in expository preaching is a deep dissatisfaction with our own ministry.

There is a delightful seventeenth-century tract by John Owen entitled *The Character of an Old English Puritane* (1646), in which we learn that such a man "esteemed that preaching best wherein was most of God, least of man."[5] Our own constant suspicion, I think, is that our own preaching contains too much of man and not enough of God. We have an uneasy feeling that the hungry sheep who look up are not really being fed. It is not that we are not trying to break the bread of life to them; it is just that, despite ourselves, our sermons turn out dull and flat and trite and tedious and, in the event, not very nourishing. We are tempted (naturally) to soothe ourselves with the thought that the day of preaching is past, or that zealous counseling or organizing or management or fundraising makes sufficient amends for ineffectiveness in the pulpit; but then we reread 1 Corinthians 2:4 (NKJV)—"my speech and my preaching were . . . in demonstration of the Spirit and of power"—and we are made uneasy again, and the conclusion is forced upon us once more that something is missing in our ministry. This, surely, is the real reason why we evangelicals today are so fascinated by the subject of expository preaching: because we want to know how we can regain the lost authority and unction that made evangelical preaching mighty in days past to humble sinners and build up the church.

Charles Simeon: Exemplary Preacher and Homiletician

When we ask, "What is expository preaching?" our question really means: "how can we learn to preach God's Word in demonstration of the Spirit and of power?" What is the secret of the preaching that achieves what

---

5. Op. cit., 2.

our sermons are failing to achieve? To help us address these questions we shall draw on the wisdom of the English clergyman Charles Simeon, fellow of King's College, Cambridge, who was vicar (in America it would be rector) of Holy Trinity parish church in the city for fifty-four years, from 1782 to his death at seventy-seven in 1836, who by common consent excelled as a preacher, and who regarded the mentoring of students and young ministers as central to his life's work.

Simeon, an upper-class English gentleman, son to a wealthy attorney, was an arresting if slightly odd person; fulsomely articulate and courteously forceful, and almost obsessively meticulous over little things (a fusspot, one might say), a sharp dresser with a pointed chin and bodily and facial gestures that were expressive to the point of being grotesque, he was a man easy to make fun of, and many did. His quick temper, heavy humor, and patrician style did not help at this point, and as a lifelong bachelor he had no one to wean him away from his eccentricities.

The significant fact about him, however, is that he was determined and thoroughgoing, clear-headed, warm-hearted and passionate (he sometimes wept in the pulpit, as did George Whitefield before him), a man marked by deep sincerity, sympathy, charity, and humility, and a total commitment to biblical preaching and instruction in order to make Christ and his salvation fully known. For most of his ministry he was in the Holy Trinity pulpit twice each Sunday, and his congregation grew till it averaged 1,100 week by week.

Theologically, Simeon made a point of distancing himself from the evangelical party debates of his day, deprecating systems and declaring that he was Calvinistic one day and Arminian another, just as his text led. In fact, however, he was not doctrinally indifferent or superficial, as those statements made him sound; he was consistently reformed Augustinian according to the Anglican Articles and Prayer Book, and his sermons were always directly biblical. Guided by John Brown's *Self-Interpreting Bible*, a massive study aid from Scotland on which he constantly relied, he read the canonical Scriptures catechetically, as a sustained call from God to repentance and righteousness, faith, hope, and love, all focused on the divine grace and mercy shown in the cross, resurrection, and reign of the Lord Jesus Christ. In his 2,536 outlines, he was exploring these themes all the time, achieving endless freshness by letting each new text shape the material but never shifting from the goal of furthering adult evangelical piety by everything he said.

Mentoring students into the maturity that would make them the next generation of evangelical leaders became more and more a focus of Simeon's ministry as the years went by. In an age when, incredibly, the Church of England provided no preparation for any form of pastoral ministry, leaving it to young clergy to acquire skills on the job, Simeon would hold a class on preaching every second week for would-be ministers, usually with fifteen to twenty in attendance, plus a conversation party weekly that might attract eighty, where aspects of preaching were often discussed in response to students' questions. Simeon's passion to raise standards of preaching among Anglican clergy was brought into focus when he ran across *Essay on the Composition of a Sermon* by the seventeenth-century French Protestant preacher Jean Claude, translated by Robert Robinson, Whitefield convert, nonconformist minister, and author of the hymn "Come, Thou Fount of Every Blessing," who died in 1790.

In 1796 Simeon republished the *Essay*, correcting and improving the translation, removing the rambling and anti-Anglican notes with which Robinson had adorned it, and appending one hundred "skeletons" of sermons on texts. Each "skeleton" consisted of introduction, topical headings marking thematic divisions of what the text contained, expository material for developing each thought, and application to the listeners of, or as he sometimes phrased it, addresses to them about what the text thus opened out had shown. From this grew his *magnus opus*, twenty-one volumes long, the full title of which in its final edition was as follows: *Horae Homileticae or Discourses (Principally in the form of Skeletons) . . . forming a Commentary upon every Book of the Old and New Testament; to which is Annexed an Improved Edition of a Translation of Claude's Essay on the Composition of a Sermon.* This huge effort reached its completion in 1833, when Simeon was seventy-four.

Knowing by now that he was something of a celebrity, one of the best-known clergy in the Church of England, and believing that this work could be epoch-making in raising pulpit standards, Simeon was bold to present a copy of it to King William IV, and one to each of the Archbishops, and one to all the leading libraries in Europe and America, and one to each Cambridge college library.

To call it in effect a commentary on the whole Bible, as Simeon did in his title, was a revealing yet understandable overstatement. Though not a work of professional biblical learning, it offered a full-scale presentation of what Simeon took to be the consistent message of the Bible throughout, namely, a profile, hortatory and doxological, of the inward reality of evangelical religion as men like Richard Baxter, John Wesley, George Whitefield, John Newton, and William Wilberforce understood, expounded, and lived it. Simeon dreamed of clergy, young and old, using his outlines to help them create and preach sermons like his own, smoothly polite in style yet thunderously powerful and searching in substance, sermons that would be delivered with passion on the lips due to unction from the Holy Spirit in the heart. "If it leads the ignorant to preach the truth, and the indolent to exert themselves, and the weak to attain a facility for writing their own [sermons], and the busy and laborians to do more and unto better effect than they otherwise could have done, I shall be richly repaid for my labours," he wrote to a friend. "My prayers for God's blessings on it will, I hope, ascend as long as I am able to pray at all."[6] How far Simeon's dream ever found fulfillment is not known, but the work itself is monumental, both as a vivid profiling of godliness and as a masterful demonstration of the abiding principles of pulpit rhetoric—communication, as we would say. It is natural to suppose that Simeon field-tested most, if not all, of the outlines by preaching them himself before putting them in print.

The essence and genius of Simeon's outlines is that they show the preacher (who, we assume, as he did, will have eyes to see) how he may sustain the sense that the text is doing the talking through what he says, and that what the text is doing throughout the sermon is exhibiting and elaborating and enforcing one key notion. Simeon would have agreed with the late Martyn Lloyd-Jones who observed and enforced the maxim "one sermon, one thought" and who ventured to draw out its corollary: more than one thought from the text in the preacher's heart, more than one sermon on the text from him in the pulpit. The generalizing smoothness of Simeon's language, culturally correct as it was in his day, seems old-fashioned to us, and with reason, but in technique with texts Simeon is far ahead of most of us today, and we would do well to try and catch up with him.

Simeon's Theory of the Sermon

Suppose that we could put the clock back two centuries and set our problem before Charles Simeon at one of his sermon classes or conversation parties—what would he say to us? The records suggest a number of things of which he would wish to remind us.

Being a supremely practical man, he would begin at the beginning and say: *expository sermons are sermons* and must therefore obey the ordinary formal rules of sermon construction. Otherwise, however good their matter, they will fail of their purpose.

"Simeon," wrote Canon Charles Smyth, "was almost the first man . . . to appreciate that it is perfectly possible to teach men how to preach, and

---

6. W. Carus, *Memoirs of the Life of the Rev. Charles Simeon MA*, 3rd ed. (London: Harchard, 1848), 527.

to discover how to do so."[7] In his edition of Claude's *Essay on the Composition of a Sermon*, and in his sessions with students, Simeon tirelessly hammered away at the basic lessons. A sermon is a single utterance; therefore it must have a single subject. Its divisions (which should be clearly marked, to help the listener follow and remember) should act like the joints of a telescope: "each successive division . . . should be as an additional lens to bring the subject to your text nearer, and make it more distinct."[8] In the interests of effective communication, all obscure and artificial forms of expression must be avoided. Of his own 2,536 skeletons, Simeon wrote: "The author has invariably proposed to himself three things as indispensably necessary in every discourse; UNITY in the design, PERSPICUITY in the arrangement, and SIMPLICITY in the diction."[9] Since a sermon is meant to instruct, it must not be above the congregation's heads ("do not preach what you cannot tell, but what your people can receive"[10]). Nor must it be too long, or their concentration will go, and "where weariness or exhaustion comes upon people, there is very little chance of your doing them more good on that occasion."[11]

A sermon, Simeon would further remind us, is as long as it seems, and an unnatural and monotonous way of talking in the pulpit can make it seem very long very quickly. Simeon's own commanding urgency and constant movement in the pulpit (he preached, he said, with his mouth, his eyes, and his hands) would keep people listening for up to an hour, but the sermons he created out of the material in the skeletons would, so he guessed, take not more than half an hour to deliver, and that in his view would be quite long enough for beginners and for many others too. Again, sermons are more than lectures and have a further aim than the mere imparting of information. "The understanding must be informed, but in a manner . . . which *affects the heart*, either to comfort the hearers, or to excite them to acts of piety, repentance, or holiness."[12] Claude elsewhere lays it down that a sermon has a threefold aim—"to instruct, to please and to affect":[13] the introduction being designed chiefly to please, to win the hearers' interest and goodwill; the exposition to instruct, to win their minds and judgments; and the application to affect, to win

---

7. Charles Smyth, *The Art of Preaching* (London: SPCK, 1940), 175.

8. A. W. Brown, *Recollections of the Conversation Parties of the Rev. Chas. Simeon* (London: Hamilton, 1863), 177.

9. *Horae Homileticae*, 21 vols. (London: Holdsworth & Ball, 1832–1833), 1:vi (preface).

10. A. W. Brown, *Recollections of the Conversation Parties of the Rev. Chas. Simeon*, 183.

11. Ibid., 189.

12. Jean Claude, *Essay on the Composition of a Sermon with Notes and Illustrations . . .* (London: Cornish, 1866 ed.), 5.

13. Ibid., 114.

their hearts and wills. Don't cheapen your message, if you can help it, Simeon adds, either by cracking jokes in the pulpit ("a very painful style and manner"[14]), or by saying odd, fantastic things ("the pulpit is the seat of good, natural sense; and the good sense of good men"[15]).

As to the mode of delivering your sermons, speak exactly as you would if you were conversing with an aged and pious superior. This will keep you from undue formality on the one hand, and from improper familiarity on the other.[16]

And so on, down to best method of voice production.

Neglect these rules, Simeon would say, and your sermons will deservedly fail, however good your heart and your material, for communication will not be achieved. Moreover, he would add, there is no excuse for such failure; for anyone can master the art of effective communication from the pulpit if he will only take the trouble. Daniel Wilson, in his memorial essay on Simeon, says the same: "Nor is there anyone destitute of the means of engaging the attention of others, if he will but take pains early, and be persevering in his use of the natural means of acquiring the faculty of teaching with effect. Every man can be plain, and intelligible, and interesting when his own heart is engaged on other subjects, and why not in religion?"[17] Of course, it takes time—Wilson notes in the same paragraph that "few [of Simeon's sermons] cost him less than twelve hours of study—many twice that time." But who are we as ministers of the Word to grudge such as outlay?

Preaching from Biblical Texts

Such would be Simeon's first point to us. Then he would go on to remind us that *expository sermons should be textual in character.* The preacher's task, according to him, was not imposition, giving texts meaning they do not bear; nor was it juxtaposition, using texts merely as pegs on which to hang general reflections imported from elsewhere ("preachments of this kind are extremely disgustful"[18]); it was, precisely, exposition, bringing out of the texts what God had put in them. "I never preach," said Simeon, "unless I feel satisfied that I have the mind of God as regards the sense of the passage."[19] The motive behind his almost obsessive outbursts

---

14. A. W. Brown, *Recollections of the Conversation Parties of the Rev. Chas. Simeon*, 376.

15. Jean Claude, *Essay on the Composition of a Sermon with Notes and Illustrations*, 5.

16. W. Carus, *Memoirs of the Life of the Rev. Charles Simeon MA*, 483ff.

17. Ibid., 591.

18. Jean Claude, *Essay on the Composition of a Sermon with Notes and Illustrations*, 4.

19. A. W. Brown, *Recollections of the Conversation Parties of the Rev. Chas. Simeon*, 177.

against Calvinistic and Arminian "system-Christians," as he called them, was his belief that, through reading Scripture in light of their systems, both sides would be kept from doing justice to all the texts that were there. Be "Bible-Christians" rather than slaves to a system, he argued, and so let the whole Bible have its way with you all the time. Whether or not we agree that such speaking is the wise way to make that point, we must at least endorse Simeon's "invariable rule . . . to endeavour to give to every portion of the word of God its full and proper force."[20]

Sermon texts should be chosen with care, for the sermon should come out of the text whole and rounded, "like the kernel out of a hazel-nut; and not piecemeal . . . like the kernel out of a walnut."[21] Therefore, do not take a text that is too long to manage properly, and, on the other hand, "never choose such texts as have not a complete sense: for only impertinent and foolish people will attempt to preach from one or two words, which signify nothing."[22] The text chosen should so shape the sermon "that no other text in the Bible will suit the discourse,"[23] and nothing foreign to the text must be allowed to intrude. For the prime secret of freedom and authority in preaching, as Simeon was well aware, is the knowledge that what you are saying is *exactly what your text says*, so that your words have a proper claim to be received as the Word of God. In a journal article in 1821, Simeon boiled down sermon preparation to the following: "Reduce your text to a simple proposition, and lay that down as the warp; and then make use of the text itself as the wood; illustrating the main idea by the various terms in which it is contained. Screw the word into the minds of your hearers. A screw is the strongest of all mechanical powers . . . when it has been turned a few times scarcely any power can pull it out."[24]

C. H. Spurgeon mistrusted continuous exposition of whole books of Scripture because it increased the risk of boring the congregation, and Simeon, like Spurgeon, like Claude, and like most revival preachers, past and present, looked instead for single verses carrying specific messages about God and ourselves that, as it were, said to the preacher as he read, thought, and prayed, "Preach me." But all the texts of Simeon's skeletons are put into context sufficiently to ensure that they do not become a pretext for the preacher to say things that they do not say themselves.

---

20. *Horae Homileticae*, I.xxxiii.
21. A. W. Brown, *Recollections of the Conversation Parties of the Rev. Chas. Simeon*, 183.
22. Jean Claude, *Essay on the Composition of a Sermon with Notes and Illustrations*, 1.
23. W. Carus, *Memoirs of the Life of the Rev. Charles Simeon MA*, 505.
24. Hugh Evan Hopkins, *Charles Simeon of Cambridge* (London: Hodder & Stoughton, 1977), 59.

Expository Preaching as Doctrinal

The next thing I think Simeon would tell us is this: *expository sermons must have a doctrinal substructure.* Let me explain, lest this be misunderstood. I do not mean, any more than Simeon would have meant, that expository sermons should take the form of doctrine lectures, nor that they should be weighed down with theological technical terms not used in the text itself—the less of that, we may say, the better. The point is rather this: doctrines are to Scripture as the sciences are to nature. And as the scientist is to nature, so should the expositor be to Scripture.

The scientist, just because he has studied the laws that natural phenomena illustrate and embody, is able to explain these phenomena individually to the non-scientist, who hitherto has observed them without understanding them. Similarly, the expositor who knows his doctrine (the truths and principles exhibited in the acts of God) is able to see and bring out the significance and implications of each particular text in a way that another man is not. And this is what he is called to do: to open up individual texts in the light of the *analogy of faith,* i.e., in terms of the broad framework of doctrinal truth that the Bible embodies.

Simeon did not have to stress this in his own lifetime, for it was everywhere taken for granted. As we saw, the characteristic error of evangelicals then, both Calvinists and Arminians, was, to his mind, not neglect of the analogy of faith in their interpreting, but an over-rigid application of it. But he avowed the principle quite explicitly (in exposition, "I have in mind the analogy of faith,"[25] he wrote), and I think he would emphasize it strongly could he speak to us now. For his own sermons are doctrinal through and through, abounding in clear and exact (though often unobtrusive) formulations of the great foundation truths of Scripture—God, creation, sin, the Trinitarian plan of salvation, the atonement, the work of grace, the means of grace, the church—and one suspects that by comparison he would find our would-be expository sermons distinctly foggy from a doctrinal standpoint.

One suspects too that, whereas he told the evangelicals of his day that their handling of Scripture was cramped and lopsided because of their undue preoccupation with doctrinal issues, he would tell us that ours is cramped and lopsided because of our undue neglect of them; for, he would say, we have our few favorite subjects, which we can see in every text, but we leave great expanses of biblical teaching untouched, as if we were unaware of their existence. The truth seems to be that part, at any rate, of the recipe for maintaining breadth and variety in one's

---

25. Ibid., 376.

regular exposition of particular texts is a thorough acquaintance with the doctrinal contents of the Bible as a whole, and no better proof of this could be given than the remarkable variety of theme and freshness and fullness of matter maintained throughout Simeon's own 2,536 printed sermons.

Evangelical and Theocentric Sermons

Next, Simeon would remind us that *expository sermons will have an evangelical content.* Always in some way they will set forth the gospel in its double aspect as a revelation and a remedy; always in some way they will throw light on the twin themes of sin and grace; for these are things that the whole Bible is about. Always, therefore, their tendency will be threefold—"to humble the sinner; to exalt the Saviour; to promote holiness"[26]—for that is the tendency of the Bible, and of every part of the Bible. Whatever part of the counsel of God they deal with, expository sermons will relate it to "Christ, and him crucified," for the Christ of Calvary is, so to speak, the hub around which the whole biblical revelation revolves. It was in this sense that Simeon, following Paul, insisted that "Christ, and him crucified" was the whole of his message. And the preacher is not handling his texts biblically, Simeon would say, unless he is seeing and setting them in their proper relation to Christ. If the expositor finds himself out of sight of Calvary, that shows he has lost his way. Again, Simeon's own sermons provide the best illustration of his principles here.[27]

The fifth point he would wish to make to us would, I think, be that *expository sermons must have a theocentric perspective.* The key that unlocks the biblical outlook is the perception that the real subject of Holy Scripture is not man and his religion, but God and his glory; from which it follows that God is the real subject of every text, and must therefore be the real subject of every expository sermon, as he is of Simeon's own sermons. This, again, is a point that Simeon could take for granted in his day, but on which he would need to expostulate with us; for we, to a greater extent, perhaps, than we realize, have inherited the later nineteenth-century outlook that sets man at the center of the stage, even in religion, and our thoughts and interests in the spiritual realm have become habitually and oppressively man-centered.

---

26. *Horae Homileticae,* I.xxi.

27. See by all means the seventeen discourses by Simeon reproduced in *Let Wisdom Judge,* ed. Arthur Pollard (London: Inter-Varsity Fellowship, 1959).

What, really, do we preach about? *Man*—man and his religion, his needs, his problems, and his responsibilities—for all the world as if man was the most important being in the universe, and the Father and the Son existed simply for man's sake.

This is an age of great thoughts of man and small, sentimental thoughts of God, within evangelical Christendom hardly less than outside it. Simeon would tell us that we have things topsy-turvy; nor can we expect God to honor our preaching unless we honor him by giving him his rightful place in the center of our message, and by reducing man to what he really is—a helpless, worthless rebel creature, saved only by a miracle of omnipotent, holy love, and saved, not for his own sake, but for the praise of his Savior. He would tell us that we can only expect great blessing on our preaching when our sole concern is to do what he himself was solely concerned to do—to magnify the great God who works all things to his own glory, and to exalt his Son as a great Savior of great sinners.

Power in Preaching

But what about the thing that most concerns us—this question of *power* in preaching? What would Simeon say to help us here? He would tell us that ultimately this was a matter of God's sovereign gift. "It is easy," he once said, "for a minister to prate in a pulpit, and even to speak much good matter; but to preach is not easy—to carry his congregation on his shoulders as it were to heaven; to weep over them, pray for them, deliver the truth with a weeping, praying heart; and if a minister has grace to do so now and then, he ought to be very faithful."[28]

Meanwhile, he would say, we should seek to put ourselves in the way of such an enduement, first, by making it a matter of conscience to observe in all our sermon preparation the five principles set out above, and then by laboring constantly to be compassionate, sincere, and earnest in heart whenever we preach—men possessed by our message, saying what we say as if we meant it. How can we do this? By taking care deeply to digest the bread of life in our own hearts before we set it in the view of others.

"[D]o not seek to preach what you do not feel [Simeon advises]; seek to feel deeply your own sins, and then you will preach earnestly . . . preach . . . as fellow sinners."[29]

---

28. A. W. Brown, *Recollections of the Conversation Parties of the Rev. Chas. Simeon*, 105ff.
29. Ibid., 332.

Simeon himself is our example here. The feature of his preaching that most constantly impressed his hearers was the fact that he was, as they said, "in earnest," and that reflected his own overwhelming sense of sin and of the wonder of the grace that had saved him; and that in turn bore witness to the closeness of his daily fellowship and walk with his God. As he gave time to sermon preparation, so he gave time to seeking God's face.

"The quality of his preaching" [writes a past Archbishop of Canterbury] "was but a reflection of the quality of the man himself. And there can be little doubt that the man himself was largely made in the early morning hours which he devoted to private prayer and devotional study of the Scriptures. It was his custom to rise at 4 a.m., light his own fire, and then devote the first four hours of the day to communion with God. Such costly self-discipline made the preacher. That was primary. The making of the sermon was secondary and derivative."[30]

That was primary. If our question is: Where is the Lord God of Charles Simeon? we now have our answer. As so often with God's answers, it takes the form of a counter-question: Where are the preachers who seek after the Lord God as Simeon did? This, surely, is the final word, if not from Simeon, at least from God through Simeon to us who would preach the gospel of Christ in the power of God's Spirit today. God, help us to hear it, and to heed it.

Appendix

Claude's principles of sermon construction may be summarized as follows:

- *The Aim of Preaching.* "To instruct, solve difficulties, unfold mysteries, penetrate into the ways of the divine wisdom, establish truth, refute error, comfort, correct and censure, fill the hearers with an admiration of the wonderful works and ways of God, inflame their souls with zeal, powerfully incline them to piety and holiness."

- *The Five Parts in a Sermon.* The Exordium or Introduction; The Connection; The Division; The Discussion; The Conclusion or Application.

- *The Choice of Texts.* (1) "Never choose such texts as have not a complete sense"; i.e., do not isolate one or two words from their setting. (2) The words of the exposition must "include the *complete*

---

30. F. D. Coggan, *Stewards of Grace* (London: Hodder and Stoughton, 1958), 32.

sense of the writer: it is his language and they are his sentiments which you explain."

- *General Rules for Sermons:*

  1) A text must be explained *clearly* as most listeners are simple people.

  2) It is essential to give the *entire sense* of the passage.

  3) A sermon must be *wise*, not frivolous; *sober*, not treating of matters beyond our knowledge; *chaste*, not stretching metaphors too far.

  4) A sermon must be *simple*, free from metaphysical speculation; *grave*, presented without abasing oneself to the common expressions of the people.

  5) A sermon must affect the *heart*, comforting the hearer or exciting him to repentance, holiness, or good works.

  6) Avoid all *excess*—of brilliance, of doctrine, or metaphor, or reasoning, of critical points, of quotations.

- *The Introduction.* Intended "to prepare the hearer's mind and insensibly to conduct him to the main subject," which includes stirring up in him "such dispositions as he ought to have, to hear well and to profit much." It must be brief, clear, engaging, simple. "All Exordiums must be condemned which make you, as it were, 'tumble from a precipice' into the theme."

- *The Discussion:*

  1) By *Explication*, "which unfolds the text." Explain its import; vindicate its reasonableness, display its excellency.

  2) By *Observation*, "which draws out its substance in remarks, ranging all the illustrations under a few leading remarks."

  3) By *Propositions*, "which prove the truths in it from other Scriptures."

  4) By *Perpetual Application*, "which makes the statements or examples in the text press constantly upon actions and habits."

- *The Conclusion or Application.* Ought to be lively and animating, aiming to move Christian affections—as the love of God, hope, zeal, repentance, self-condemnation, etc.

- Simeon's own briefer summary, made for his students of Claude's principles, put into practice, amounted to this:

153

1) Take for your subject that which you believe to be the mind of God in the passage before you. (Be careful to understand the passage thoroughly; and regard nothing but the mind of God in it.)

2) Mark the *character* of the passage. (It may be a declaration, a precept, a promise, a threatening, an invitation, an appeal; or more complex, as a cause and effect; a principle and a consequence; an action and a motive to that action.)

3) Mark the *spirit* of the passage. Whatever it be, let that be the spirit of your discourse. The soul should be filled with the subject and breathe out the very spirit of it before the people. God himself should be heard in us and through us.[31]

---

31. Cited from Hugh Evans Hopkins, *Charles Simeon Preacher Extraordinary* (Bramcote, UK: Grove, 1979), 8ff.

PART THREE

CONTEMPORARY CHALLENGES AND AIMS

10

Preaching the Word Today

Phillip Jensen

sking a preacher to write on preaching is a courageous invitation. Some, like Paul, have a reputation for weighty writing combined with weak speech, while with others it is the reverse. Few are, like Kent Hughes, gifted in both. It is in thankfulness to God for the gifts of Kent as both a preacher and a writer, to say nothing of pastor, host, friend, and dearly loved brother in Christ, that I offer this essay.

Forty years ago when I was training for a preaching ministry, two essays made a profound impact on my thinking and on all my preaching since. One was an essay by D. W. B. Robinson, then vice principal of Moore College, entitled "The Theology of the Preached Word." The other was a book by Ed Clowney entitled *Preaching and Biblical Theology*.

I remember reading Ed Clowney's book assuming that I would get all kinds of hints and tips about how to preach. To my amazement I received an account of biblical theology. There was no advice on how to use microphones, notes, and pulpits—no discussion on how long to preach or whether to use illustrations from personal life or from the Bible. I wondered if I had misread the title of the book. Slowly it dawned on me—for it was so foreign an idea—that the theology of the Bible is the most important ingredient in the training of the Christian preacher. Anything else, important in its place, is mere trivia in comparison. Having been helped in this way, I thought it time for me to discuss the theological basis of preaching in this essay.

Preaching the Words of God

In 1 Peter 4:11 Christians speakers are called upon to speak "oracles of God." The apostle Peter warned: "The end of all things is at hand," and so called upon his readers to behave appropriately. We are to "be self-controlled and sober-minded." But that is not the end of the matter. There are other ways to behave, given the end of all things. We are to love one another, show hospitality, and use our gifts to serve each other—especially those who speak are to speak "oracles of God."

This is the Christian preacher's task: to speak God's Word to his people. It is a task that has all the appearance of arrogance and all the reality of humility. For how can a human speak God's oracles? The Bible refers to humans speaking or writing God's words. There is a frequent ascription of dual authorship. God's words may be clothed in our words. The words of men are called the Word of God. The Old Testament prophets, conscious that they were speaking God's Word, commenced their speech with the bold claim "thus says the LORD . . ." The New Testament, when quoting the Old, sometimes jumps between ascribing the same words to men and to God. For example, in Hebrews 3–4 the words of Psalm 95 are said to be spoken sometimes by the Holy Spirit, sometimes by "he," i.e., God, and sometimes by David.

Paul spoke to the Thessalonians his own words. But in those words God spoke. The Thessalonians rightly heard the apostle's word not as the word of men but as it really was: "the word of God which is at work in you believers" (1 Thess. 2:13). Preaching God's Word requires an understanding of the nature of both God's Word and human speech.

The Nature of the Word of God

God's Word is described as living and active—*at work in you believers.* It is powerful and creative, actively fulfilling God's purpose in the world. Like a sword it pierces and divides our very being. For when, and as, we deal with the Word of God, or more accurately when the Word of God deals with us, we deal with God himself: "No creature is hidden from his sight, but all are naked and exposed to the eyes of him to whom we must give account"(Heb. 4:13), for God and his Word are indivisible.

Yet this existentially powerful Word of God has form and content as well as utility. It is expressed in the normal propositions of human language. It is possible to misrepresent God and his Word. There are not many gospels but only one. And that gospel can be distorted, denied, twisted, or contradicted. It is not endlessly malleable. There is a pattern of sound words: a tradition that was received and handed on, a faith expressed in words that was learned, held on to, and fought for. The gospel proclamation falls into the category of true or false, not opinion and interpretation. Our preaching of it is faithful and accurate or faithless and inaccurate. Effectiveness is not the only criterion of judgment—false prophets can be effective. Truthfulness is more important than effectiveness.

Yet this single unchangeable gospel message of God came in a complex history of revelation spanning many centuries. While the Word of God is unitary, it has many writers and books, two testaments, and many ideas and concepts, and it covers a couple of thousand years of known history apart from its descriptions of the beginning and the end of the world. While God spoke at many times in many ways to our fathers, his many words did not give a confused and contradictory message. God was communicating a message to Israel—his plan for the salvation of mankind that always centered on the coming of his Son. All that came before was preparation for this great event. God's fragmentary speech to the fathers was in accordance with, but overwhelmed by, his great proclamation through his Son. For the Son was the full revelation of the Father.

The prophets of old did not always understand what they were prophesying, but the Spirit of Christ was within them predicting the sufferings of the Christ and the subsequent glories. Their prophecies were not their own interpretation of the events that were to unfold but they "spoke from God as they were carried along by the Holy Spirit" (2 Pet. 1:21). For God's Word is his interpretation of the events that he sovereignly planned and executed.

Yet in all this revelation, though some things in them may be hard to understand (2 Pet. 3:16), the words themselves are not difficult. God's Word is expressed in normal human speech. It was written in straightforward common languages. It does not use either mythological or mystical language but the plain statement of the truth to be understood by everyman. Indeed, even the eloquent words of wisdom were eschewed. The words of God were to be taught to children, and all the people were held responsible to obey them.

Preaching God's Word Explicates the Text

The activity of preaching the Word of God requires the faithful exposition of the words that God has given us in the text of Scripture. It is fashionable today to claim to be "an expository preacher"—so fashionable in some circles that the word "expository" has become meaningless.

As an alternative to the word *expound* we could use *exegete* or *explicate*. Behind each of these words is the idea of explaining the meaning of a text. Because it is God's Word to us, explaining the text will involve explaining its implications for us.

Explicate is not a word currently in use and so it is slightly more useful and precise. It means (1) to explain something, especially a literary text, in a detailed and formal way; and (2) to explain and develop an idea or theory and show its implications.[1] Explication is not the work of controlling the text but of being controlled by the text. It is not explaining things about the text but explaining the text itself.

Sometimes the text's meaning is so transparent that there is little more to do than read it and spell out its implications. Sometimes the text requires considerable effort from the preacher to place it in its right context within the theology and narrative of the Bible in order to explain its meaning to the congregation. This differing degree of effort is determined not only by the text but also by the congregation. Preaching to a biblically literate congregation is a very different experience from preaching to a congregation that has never before been taught the Bible and different again from preaching to a congregation that is not yet Christian. But the aim is always the same: to say what the text means.

Preaching God's Word in Human Words

Given the nature of God's special revelation by his Word, preaching God's oracles requires great care. Given also that God's Word came to us in the common grace of human language, we are able to speak God's Word to people. God's oracles are a given deposit that we have received. We must not misrepresent him or them, but faithfully handle the word of truth. It is the task of faithful men to teach others what they have heard: to follow the pattern of sound words and to guard the good deposit. For preaching is not a matter of novelty but contending for the faith once for all delivered to the saints.

Our activity of preaching involves the normal way God has created us to speak, listen, and learn. The New Testament acknowledges the importance of speaking to the hearers' ability to understand. First Corinthians 13 and 14 and Hebrews 5 contrast the talking and thinking of children and adults. Those texts also spell out the importance of speaking in a language that the hearer can understand.

1. *Encarta Dictionary* (Microsoft Corp., 1999).

To understand our hearers is important in preaching the Word of God today, for preaching is not an activity void of hearers. We do not preach to the air. We preach God's words to others. But who are the others and how much do they affect our preaching of God's Word?

Preaching God's Word is Pastoral Preaching

It has long been taught that we must exegete the Scriptures and exegete our audience. Some would even say we need to also exegete our culture. But while this image of exegeting our audience or the world may be right in any exercise of normal communication, it generally fails to appreciate the nature of special revelation that is our work in preaching the Word of God. It is right in the fairly simple areas of making the words simple, the diction clear, the microphones turned on, etc. But it misses the point of how God's Word exegetes people.

It is not the preacher but the Word of God that exegetes our audience. The Word of God is the interpretation of the society to whom we are preaching. That is why we are preaching it and not our own wisdom, learning, or opinions. What enables the Christian preacher to preach Christianly is that he is preaching God's Word, not his own. It is the special revelation of the Word of God that teaches us of people's sinfulness and need to repent, of Christ's sacrifice for our sins, resurrection, and return in judgment. It is this special revelation that explains the nature of our hearers' spiritual state and pilgrimage in life.

It is also the Word of God that tells us about the audiences' reception of the word of our preaching. It warns us of the deceitfulness of sin, the uselessness of controversies over words, and the difficult times in which we live, where people with itching ears choose preachers who tell them what they want to hear.

It is the Word of God that identifies that our problems with hearing are sinful, not intellectual. Those who have been regenerated by the Word of God may eagerly long to hear all that God has said. Yet they still need to be warned daily not to harden their hearts. Those who have not yet been regenerated by the Word of God have a veil over them, for the god of this world has blinded them from seeing the truth. Yet in what we preach, the light of the glory of Christ may break through, bringing them new life.

These are the real truths about our audience that we need to understand. They are not taught to us by observation but by revelation. Yet having once heard these truths, they can be observed daily by our audience as we preach the Word of God. These truths do not lead us to fatalistic indifference to our hearers' reception of the Word. The New

Testament itself shows the apostles passionately reasoning, arguing, pleading, persuading, and appealing to people to be reconciled to God. The letters of Paul are just such pastoral arguments and appeals.

Yet only God can open the eyes of the blind and draw the sinner to himself. Paul's advice to Timothy is undergirded with the knowledge that "God may perhaps grant them repentance leading to a knowledge of the truth" (2 Tim. 2:25).

Preaching God's Word Is Evangelistic Preaching

Because God's Word is unitary, to preach it faithfully will be to preach the whole counsel of God. Because God's Word centers on the person and work of Jesus, to preach the whole counsel of God will be to preach evangelistically.

Preaching the whole counsel of God does not mean preaching detailed exegetical sermons on every verse of all sixty-six books of the Bible. Preaching the whole counsel of God is to declare repentance toward God and faith in our Lord Jesus Christ to one and all. For the whole counsel of God is contained in the gospel of the grace of God—that is, the proclamation of the kingdom. It is the same message to Jew and Greek, to slave and free, to male and female, to old and young.

As we expound the Bible we are to declare this gospel of our Lord Jesus Christ. If we truly explicate the passage before us, we will always be preaching this whole counsel of God. Placing any part of the Bible into its context and explaining what that passage means will always lead to an exposition of the gospel. For the context of the Bible is God's Word to mankind. And each passage of the Bible is part of that Word. We are only preaching each part or passage properly when we do so from the framework of the gospel.

Every sermon should be evangelistic, for every sermon should make the gospel clear. Those who use the gifts God has given to them to speak should speak the oracles of God.

The essence of evangelistic preaching is not the extraverted personality of the preacher. It is not the warmth of his handshake or the humor of the evangelist's jokes. It is not the method of "the appeal" or the existence of "an altar call." These are but the expressions of any good human communication. The essence of evangelistic preaching is the Holy Spirit speaking by humans the sufferings of the Christ and the subsequent glories—the very subjects that the prophets in the Old Testament preached with limited knowledge but which have now been announced to us.

Preaching God's Word Depends on Systematic Theology[2]

Again, because the Word of God is unitary, preaching God's Word will always display our systematic theology. Expository preaching is sometimes put in opposition to systematic theology. This is a sad mistake. Expository preaching in particular will reveal our competence or incompetence as systematic theologians.

The preacher who prides himself on being "a simple Bible man" does not understand himself. He may claim to just "preach the passage" in front of him without being bogged down by theology or doctrine or systems. Yet he rarely preaches the passage in front of him. Rather, he will unconsciously preach the church tradition from which he comes. Or worse, he will preach his own hobbyhorses and ideas. For without a consciously self-aware and well-considered theology that is open to being framed, corrected, and developed by the text of Scripture, the preacher's own frame of reference will overwhelm the text. That frame of reference may be his church's tradition or maybe his own personal experience, but it will not be the Bible.

But the *simple Bible man* is not the only incompetent theologian. The modern liberal who rejects God's inspiration of the Scriptures is committed to the rejection of any systematization of theology. He also fails to understand how much he is preaching his tradition. Being modern and fashionable does not make it any less human tradition. The Bible, with all its diversity, is unitary in its authorship and message; it must be preached as a whole even when it is being preached in its parts. Each part must be considered in the light of the rest. No part is to be preached as being repugnant to another. The failure or capacity to understand the whole is critical to dealing with any part properly. An ill-considered systematic theology will produce ill-considered expository sermons.

Preaching God's Word Depends on Biblical Theology[3]

Similarly, preaching God's Word reveals the preacher's biblical theology or lack of it. If the preacher's systematic theology lacks an overall biblical theology, there will be a failure to place each text within its biblical context. Rather, there will be the temptation to place the text into a doctrinal system without reference to where in the biblical revelation it comes.

---

2. By "systematic theology" I am referring to the systematic study of the knowledge of God. For Christians the primary and normative basis for this knowledge is the Scriptures.

3. By "biblical theology" I am referring to the study of the Bible's unfolding revelation of God in a way that enables us to understand the Bible as a whole.

163

The Word of God comes to us in two testaments. These have a complex but clearly explicated interrelationship. The promise of the Old Testament meets its fulfillment in the New. There is a narrative of revelation that runs right through the whole Bible; it is not a random collection of books, nor a collection of random experiences or inspired insights into the supernatural. God sovereignly organized the affairs of humanity. He spoke by his prophets interpreting these affairs for us in order to prepare us for the coming of his Son. Understanding this narrative as it develops is essential to understanding any text within the Bible. This is particularly apparent when preaching on the Old Testament. The jump from the Old Testament text to the twenty-first century without passing through the New Testament is a common failure of those who lack a biblical theology.

But the failure is also apparent in New Testament preaching. Preachers often ignore the New Testament writers' concerns of the Old Testament being fulfilled. They only think of the twenty-first century exegetical or doctrinal significance of the text, thus unwittingly distorting what God said.

The Problem of Preaching the Word Today

For all of the foregoing importance of preaching God's Word, there is something of a crisis in confidence in preaching today. Preaching is an unattractive activity in the twenty-first century. The very word has negative connotations.[4] The individualism and moral relativism of Western culture make all preaching seem arrogant, self-righteous, opinionated, and oppressive. "Who are you to tell me how to live!"

A society hell-bent in the defiance of God will not want anybody declaring the words of God. Rather than listening to the message, it will ridicule the activity and shoot the messengers. Part of this spiritual resistance to preaching today is the intellectual culture of modern Western society.

Some thinkers question the possibility of conveying meaning with words—not only between author and reader, speaker and listener, but especially between one age or culture and another. Some say that it is an impossible task to explicate a text. Others suggest that it is simplistic to think that you can communicate accurately by words. Still others complain that it is arrogant and power-tripping to think that you can speak

---

4. *Encarta Dictionary* has three entries, the second being "to give people advice on their morals or behavior in an irritatingly tedious or overbearing way."

for God. Add to this the problems that some have expressed about the use of religious language in particular, and the difficulties of preaching seem insurmountable. If we have such trouble talking to each other, how can we ever preach God's Word?

While Christians may not believe the more extravagant forms of these propositions, they still feel the effects of the arguments, and the confidence of the preacher is undermined.

The Triumph of Technology

The dismissal of the Divine in the university departments of divinity has meant the rejection of the Holy Bible. This book is treated like any other book and is no longer considered holy. Its inspiration is like the inspiration of Shakespeare. Its authors are many, not one. It has no single central message but a broadly common ethos or culture or provenance.

Systematic theology is therefore cut off at its roots. Biblical theology is an impossibility. All emphasis is upon the human authors—their differences and developments or the historical background explain their meanings. One can talk of Pauline theology or Petrine or Johannine theology but never the Bible's. The New Testament department does not have to converse with the Old Testament department, except about the trivia of academic standards, appointments, and budgets. The departments need not be in the same faculty: one studies the Hebrew Bible in Semitic studies; the other, the New Testament in Graeco-Roman studies.

The background historical contexts in which the biblical authors wrote become determinative in understanding the texts. Such "scholarship" will understand the New Testament in the context of any contemporary historical background but never allow the Old Testament to play its part. It ignores the New Testament authors' explicit and specific identification of the Old Testament as the proper context in which to understand their writings.

With the discriminating eye of the cynic, the modern scholar can deconstruct the author's writings so as to explain what he "really" meant. Only the expert—never the ploughboy—can know what was meant. The priesthood of all believers is no longer replaced by the sacerdotalism of the sacramentalists but by the arrogance of the academy.

This is the triumph of technology over theology. The highly educated liberal and the uneducated fundamentalist are one and the same. They are not reading the Bible they preach—one out of fear of education, the other out of the pride of education. This triumph of technology over theology is the conquest by the bureaucrat. The rules are kept; the controls are all in place. We are now managing the text. The reader rules the author. We have tamed the living and powerful Word of God. We have tamed God. We can no longer hear God's Word.

It is ironic that within this godless world there is ultimately no place for exegesis. As modernity gives way to postmodernity the very notion that text had a meaning to exegete disappears into the mist.

The Triumph of Meaninglessness

It is because God created humanity in his image that any language and knowledge of God are possible. Without God we cannot know what another person means. In a godless world talk and language are not about meaning but about power and control. So trying to exegete the speaker's words is a failed enterprise. Instead we turn to interpretation and hermeneutics.

Interpretation was once thought to be a noble enterprise. It was the "explanation or establishment of the meaning or significance of something."[5] That assumes that some speech had meaning. But over time and under the growing skeptical relativism of the Western intellectual tradition, interpretation has come to mean "an ascription of a particular meaning or significance to something." As skepticism moves to solipsism, interpretation comes to mean "the way in which an artistic work, for example a play or piece of music, is performed so as to convey a particular understanding of the work."[6] The preacher now dominates the text in the name of interpretation.[7]

Hermeneutics takes the concept of interpretation one step further. Hermeneutics is today defined thus: "(1) the science and methodology of interpreting texts, especially the books of the Bible; (2) the branch of theology that is concerned with explaining or interpreting religious concepts, theories, and principles."[8] Apparently not only the Bible needs to be interpreted but also its own science and methodology of interpretation. This could be because of its uniqueness in being both the Word of God and the word of man, but it tends rather to be because of its antiquity and particularity. The Word spoken in one particular context so long ago needs interpretation for today.

---

5. *Encarta Dictionary.*

6. Ibid.

7. Fortunately the congregation can similarly dominate the preacher. For the congregation can "interpret" the sermon, and they are at liberty to think whatever they wish. They can even claim later that it was what the preacher meant!

8. *Encarta Dictionary.*

If the term *hermeneutics* means simply the study of interpreting texts, there could be little objection to it. It would then be the study of how we read, comprehend, and understand the Scriptures. It would be an unnecessarily technical term about an everyday activity. But the discipline of hermeneutics has been introduced into Christian studies in the context of uncertainty and subjectivity in line with the more recently developed meaning of interpretation.[9] Modern hermeneutics imaginatively connects us in our cultural context with the biblical cultural context, thus bridging the gulf between ancient text and modern reader. For example, by demythologizing the ancient world's miracles, we can preach to the modern world of science and technology. Armed with this new imaginative technology, we are able to revise whatever part of the Bible is uncomfortable for modern belief. For the mid-twentieth century, it was the miraculous; for the twenty-first century it is the ethical, especially sexual and bioethical morality. We end with people speaking of "my hermeneutic" and "your hermeneutic" as if there is no science and methodology but the same subjective relativism of those who speak of "my truth" and "your truth."

The Bible as Interpreter

These modern problems arise because people fail to come to terms with the Bible's description of God, of itself, and of us. They fail to see the Bible as interpreter. They also fail to see the Bible as a contemporary word to us.

The Bible is an interpretation. It does not simply record facts; it interprets them also. For example, in 1 Corinthians 15 the fact of Jesus' death is interpreted for us in the little phrase "for our sins." And the meaning of that interpretation is placed within the qualifying phrase "in accordance with the Scriptures" (1 Cor. 15:3).

The Bible is God's interpretation of God's own sovereign plan for the world and us. It is not the human authors' interpretations but God's interpretation. As the apostle Peter says: "No prophecy of Scripture comes from someone's own interpretation. For no prophecy was ever produced by the will of man, but men spoke from God as they were carried along by the Holy Spirit" (2 Pet. 1:20–21).

Therefore, if it is true at all, it is "the" interpretation. God puts his plans into effect through the Word he speaks. He is good and can be trusted to make himself and his plans clear to those who need to re-

---

9. E.g., see Diogenes Allen, *Philosophy for Understanding Theology* (Louisville, KY: Westminster, 1985), 270–75.

spond. As the Scripture is read or preached, we are guided by its living and powerful message because we are dealing with God—or rather being dealt with by God.

Obsession with how we are to interpret God's interpretation of us will only deflect us from understanding the clear message he has spoken. It is like the person looking at the lenses in their spectacles rather than looking through the lenses at the world that the lenses have now brought into clear perspective.

The Bible is unique and may require a different way of reading than any other literature. But its difference lies neither in its antiquity nor in its particularity. Its uniqueness lies in its divine inspiration and consequent continuous power and authority. This places the readers in an unusual position. We cannot be the controllers or determiners of the text but must be the prayerfully obedient servants of the text. It is important to remember that it is not by our brilliance that we come to understand the Word of God but by the work of the Holy Spirit. The activity of Bible reading and preaching is profoundly spiritual.

Unlike reading a fellow human's writings, we are reading the writings of our Creator, Ruler, Judge, and God. The right framework for Bible reading is obedience. The right posture for Bible reading is on one's knees. The right context for Bible reading is amongst the family of those who live according to its message.

This in no way removes responsibility for intelligent reading of the text. Just the reverse: to fail to read the text intelligently is to fail to love God with all our mind. To distort or ignore his Word—to twist it out of our personal instability so as to make it mean what we want it to mean—is to treat God's Word (and God!) with contempt.

Yet the exercise of reading and comprehension is not different from reading any other text. It requires mastering dead languages to gain greater precision in our reading. It will be helped by knowledge of the background historical setting in which the text was written. But these major intellectual activities of common grace are minor matters in reading the words of God's special revelation. Scholarship may create more doctoral theses in background studies, but greater learning of the Scriptures will not necessarily come from these studies.[10] There are very few changes in our understanding of Scripture since the time of the Reformation, when we were freed from institutional censorship to read the text of Scriptures for ourselves.

---

10. No sooner had Stephen Neill published his Firth Lectures concluding with the twelve "positive achievements of New Testament studies in the century that has elapsed since 1861" than people started to raise doubts about them. Stephen Neill, *The Interpretation of the New Testament 1861–1961* (Oxford: Oxford University Press, 1966), 338–40.

Unlike other areas of empirical scholarship where the community of scholars is increasing the sum total of knowledge by their research, biblical scholarship has a more humble task. For the Bible scholar at the end of his life has no more knowledge than the apostle had two thousand years ago. The biblical scholar is not pursuing "neo-orthodoxy" but "paleo-orthodoxy." A lifetime of working on the text of Scripture is not enough for a sinful person to master the subject. Whatever we discover has been known before. While we can and should build on others' scholarship, we can never move by scholarship into a fuller understanding than the apostles possessed. All biblical scholars are sinners being shaped by what they read, and we are sinners being transformed by what we read.

The preacher must learn to trust the interpretative power of the Bible. We do not need to be clever or scholarly but faithful to what the Bible is saying. God can be trusted to make himself clear to the hearers. His Word will deal more wisely with them than any cleverness we may devise.

Understanding That the Word of God Is Living and Abiding

According to 1 Peter, the imperishable seed by which our regeneration comes is the living and abiding Word of God. Similarly, Isaiah taught that "the Word of the Lord endures for ever." The relationship of the Word of God to time, place, and culture needs to be understood from the teaching of the Word of God itself, not from worldly theories of interpretation and hermeneutics. For though God's Word has the particularity of being spoken or written in a particular context, it comes with a message beyond that context. It is not that we have to bridge a gap between it and ourselves, for God spoke the Word with us in mind.

Hebrews 3 and 4 uses Psalm 95 to show the contemporary nature of the Word of God. The psalm was not written in Moses' day but centuries later, in David's day. The people were already well settled in the Promised Land of rest at the time of the writing of the psalm. Yet the events of the Exodus are recalled to warn people to listen to the Word of God properly lest they fail to enter God's rest. This is because the events of the Exodus were written down not for the sake of the generation who perished in the wilderness but for the sake of the generation upon whom the end of the ages comes—that is, Christians (see 1 Cor. 10:6, 11). Furthermore, God's "rest" that was typified by the Promised Land is the reality into which we enter through Jesus Christ's death and resurrection.

What happened, under God's sovereign control, was written in his Scriptures for Christians' instruction (Rom. 15:4). The Old Testament is the Christian Bible, not the Bible of the Jews. To ignore or reject the New Testament is to reject the Old also. Non-Christian Jews have the veil over their minds and hearts that prevents them from hearing the message of the Old Testament. Even the prophets who prophesied knew that they were not serving themselves but us (1 Pet. 1:12). The great heroes of faith did not receive what was promised for they, too, were waiting for what God has provided for us (Heb. 11:39–40).

Thus the Old Testament, written hundreds of years before the New, and in different cultural settings, is consistently assumed by the New Testament writers to be God's contemporary Word to them. It was not as if the New Testament writers were ignorant of the times and cultures in which the Old Testament was written. The writer of the book of Hebrews understands that David referred to the events of Moses' time, clearly ignoring Joshua's generation entering into the "rest." Yet Hebrews can take David's psalm as the word not just of David but also of God, and not just for David's day but also for today.

Similarly, Jesus warns the Sadducees about ignoring the Word of God: "Have you not read what was said to you by God: 'I am the God of Abraham, and the God of Isaac, and the God of Jacob'? He is not God of the dead, but of the living" (Matt. 22:31–32). Jesus knew that this was spoken to Moses at the burning bush. If it were not spoken later than the patriarchs, the point of the argument would not stand. But for Jesus this saying of God, written in the book of Exodus, was not said just to Moses but also to "you" Sadducees.

Sometimes the human authors knew that their writings were for another day or another audience than the original. For example, Daniel was told that the revelation in Daniel 12 was for later, while Paul was conscious of writing to both Colossae and Laodicea. On other occasions, the writer had his original audience in mind while God had other destinations or generations in view. For example, one wonders if Moses understood that the law against muzzling the ox "was written for our sake" (1 Cor. 9:10).

Whether or not the human author was conscious of writing for another day and another audience, God intended his words for those upon whom the end of the ages has come. For the biblical view of history places much more importance on the distinction between B.C. and A.D. than it does the number of revolutions that the earth has made of the sun.

Consequently, the basic assumption with which we approach the Word of God is that though it was written in a particular context, it was written for the context in which we find ourselves. It is God's Word for "today."

The preacher does not need to "make the Bible relevant." It is always relevant. Preachers need to trust its relevance. It will speak to people today in ways and on topics that preachers would never imagine to raise.

Preaching the Word Today

Hearing and preaching God's Word today is not in the end an intellectual but a spiritual issue. It is the Word by which we are regenerated. It is a word that we need today and every day to warn us to continue in the faith.

Consider the problem of the children of Israel. They were at Mount Sinai with Moses when he received the oracles of God. But they refused to obey him. And their initial rejection of the Word of God was perpetuated in their behavior as they traveled in the wilderness. As Psalm 95 makes clear, the Creator God was their shepherd, but they failed to obey his Word and so perished.

The psalmist's lesson to his hearers is forceful: "Today when you hear his voice do not harden your hearts." Hearing God's Word is an everyday experience. But importantly, hearing God's Word is a spiritual matter of the heart. It requires a soft heart. The challenge that the psalmist brings, and Hebrews reiterates, is to hear God's Word today without hardening your heart.

The most natural place to preach God's Word is in the congregation of God's people, for the church is gathered by the Word of God to hear the Word of God. Like the children of Israel at Mount Sinai who were gathered by God to hear his covenantal word, Christians have been gathered by God to hear his Word. It is a better, more gracious word than Abel's cry for retribution. For our Lord's death, murdered as he was by his own people, just like Abel, was a sacrificial death declaring forgiveness and mercy.

The warning is corporate and not just for individuals. As God says: "Take care, brothers, lest there be in any of you an evil, unbelieving heart, leading you to fall away from the living God. But exhort one another every day, as long as it is called 'today,' that none of you may be hardened by the deceitfulness of sin" (Heb. 3:12–13). Our concern is for each other's hearts. So we have this corporate responsibility to take care and to exhort one another every day as long as it is called "today."

The time to preach God's Word is in the last days, as we love one another and use the gifts that God has given to us when "whoever speaks, as one who speaks the oracles of God." This is "preaching the Word today." It is an activity of fellow pilgrims. We love one another by mutual exhortation to hear the Word of God today and today and today.

11

Challenges for the Twenty-first-century Pulpit

D. A. Carson

The title of this essay (originally prepared as an address)[1] was suggested to me by David Cook, the visionary behind the founding of the new School of Preaching at Sydney Missionary and Bible College. Although I accepted with pleasure the invitation to speak, the more I thought about the invitation, the more I wondered if the title was a bit of a cheek. Indeed, I ruefully had to face my own hubris in accepting the assignment. In 2005, what could I possibly know about the challenges of the remaining ninety-five years of the century? If in 1905 I had been asked to address the challenges facing the twentieth-century pulpit, would I have managed to reflect on two world wars, the great depression, the end of the British Empire, the rise and fall of fascism and of (much of) communism, Vietnam, the deployment of nuclear weapons, men on the moon, the digital world, jet travel, global economics, the reshaping of communities by the impact of the automobile, the Holocaust and other instances of genocide (including that perpetrated by buffoons like Idi

---

1. This address was first prepared as the inaugural lecture, March 2005, of the School of Preaching founded by Sydney Missionary and Bible College. It is a pleasure and a privilege to present it in this slightly revised form in honor of my friend Kent Hughes, whose ministry has been remarkably dedicated to the strengthening of the pulpit. I have purposely not removed most of the evidence that this piece began its life as a lecture.

Amin and idealogues like Pol Pot), massive expansion of the church in Africa and China, horrendous accounts of martyrdom and unbelievably encouraging medical advances, the resurgence of militant Islam, the remarkable stiffening of the processes of secularization in much of the West, the unforeseen yet massive expansion of Pentecostalism and the charismatic movement, and the dawning of that array of perspectives and epistemologies we label postmodernism?

And what should be said about the theological moves from widespread residual confessionalism through the classic liberal theology of the early decades of the twentieth century to Barthianism, ecumenism, and post-colonial theology, and the rise of major theological colleges and seminaries? The shift in Christian numbers from the North to the South and from the West to the East has still not been adequately explored. The transformation of social structures brought about by advances in contraception and by multiplying abortions have combined to give us throughout Europe, and now increasingly elsewhere (e.g., Japan), a birth rate below the 2.1 figure needed to sustain a stable population. We have traveled from the horse and buggy to supersonic speed, from telegraph and early telephones to instantaneous transmission of gigabytes of information, from rural life and pace to megalopolises, from realism to surrealism to virtual worlds.

All of these changes had at least *some* impact on the distinctive challenges of preaching in the twentieth century—yet which pundit living in 1905 would have predicted more than a tiny handful of them? So if the end is not yet, what changes are likely to occur by the year A.D. 2100? For someone who in 2005 is nearing the end of his sixth decade to pronounce on the challenges of the remaining ninety-five years of the twenty-first century is simultaneously an implicit claim to a prophetic gift and a charge to a lot of preachers to do what he is not going to live long enough to do himself.

For a start, then, I ought to restrict the immediate applicability of my remarks to the beginning of the twenty-first century. Yet I insist on a further limitation. It would be dangerous to focus on the challenges specific to the twenty-first century without recalling, however briefly, the challenges that confront the pulpit in *every* generation. That would be to ignore the perennially important for the sake of focusing on the temporarily important. The result would be a distorted view both of our challenges and of preaching itself.

So at the risk of stepping outside my mandate, I propose, first, to remind you of some of the perennial challenges in preaching, and only then to outline some of the peculiar challenges preaching faces at the beginning of the twenty-first century.

The Perennial Challenges

Some of the challenges facing preaching are timeless. In fact, we can see hints of them in the Bible. I will discuss four of the perennial challenges.

The Preparation and Qualification of the Preacher

In the nature of the case, the preacher will commonly, but not always, be an elder/pastor. That is why it is worth briefly reflecting on biblical passages that lay out his qualifications. We might begin with 1 Timothy 3:1–7. Perhaps the most remarkable thing about this list is how unremarkable it is. Everything that is required of the elder/pastor, with a couple of caveats, is elsewhere required of all believers. For example, if the overseer is not to be given to drunkenness, this certainly does not mean that all other Christians are permitted to get sloshed whenever they like. The demand that these pastors be hospitable is paralleled by the more general exhortation, "Don't forget to show hospitality to strangers" (Heb. 13:2 NLT). So it is with almost all the other entries. The thrust of all the entries in this list of qualifications, then, is transparent: Christian leaders are not necessarily qualitatively different from their brothers and sisters in Christ, but they *must* present in disciplined form the virtues that the Word of God requires of all believers.

One of the superficial exceptions is the insistence that an overseer/elder not be a novice, a recent convert (1 Tim. 3:6). Of course, that is a relative category. On the return swing of the first missionary journey, Paul and Barnabas appoint elders in each church (Acts 14:23), yet this takes place only months after the conversion of the members of this church. In times of rapid expansion, someone who has been a believer for ten months is "not a recent convert" compared with all the rest who have been converted only during the preceding three or four months—though transparently, that same person would not be qualified to serve as pastor in a church where many people have been Christians for decades.

The other apparent exception is found in 3:2: the overseer/elder/pastor must be "able to teach." That presupposes two things: the pastor must have reliable content (compare, for instance, 2 Tim. 4:1–5) and must be able to communicate it. Those who are mightily endowed with the gift of communication but who have little worth communicating are disqualified from pastoral ministry; those who know a great deal but who are utterly unable to communicate it, whether one-on-one or in larger company, are also disqualified. In one sense, of course, all

Christians should be teachers. If the Great Commission commands all of us to make disciples of all nations, *teaching* them to observe whatever Jesus has commanded (Matt. 28:18–20), and if the readers of Hebrews can be rebuked because by the time of writing they ought to be teachers (Heb. 5:12), then there is some sense in which the responsibility to teach the Word of God is widely distributed throughout the church. Yet there is a narrower usage in the New Testament. James 3:1 reminds us that we are not to multiply teachers, knowing that they will be more severely judged. The church-recognized teaching authority is demonstrably vested in the pastor/overseer/elder; the corresponding lists of qualifications for, say, deacons, never mention this responsibility.

Another passage in the Pastoral Epistles sheds light on what has been said so far. In 1 Timothy 4:14–16, Paul links two other injunctions: "let all see your progress" and "watch your life and doctrine closely." This suggests that both the pastor's understanding of biblical truth and his own conformity to it should be progressing—indeed, progressing in such a way that other believers can *see* the progress. So here we have it again: exemplary living plus the responsibility to know and teach the Word of God—and, in this passage, growing on both fronts.

This suggests that we must work toward the abolition of a disjunction that is very common in the Western world, a disjunction that has no biblical warrant and that is potentially very dangerous. It is the disjunction between the pastor and the preacher. Some church leaders, we are told, are good pulpiteers, good proclaimers, good preachers, but really very poor at pastoral care. Others are wonderfully sensitive pastors but, rather sadly, cannot handle the Scriptures very well, and certainly cannot teach or preach. Yet Paul stipulates that *pastors/elders/overseers* must be able to teach (1 Tim. 3:2; Titus 1:9); theirs is the ministry of the Word and prayer. No matter how good they are at listening, hand-holding, and personal encouragement, if they cannot teach the Word of God they are disqualified from the office/role of pastor/elder/overseer. Of course, some pastors may exercise all or most of their teaching ministry one-on-one or in small groups; not all will be equally adept with the larger crowd. But Scripture leaves no place for the "pastor" who cannot teach. After all, a "pastor" is simply a "shepherd"—that is what the word means. And shepherds must feed the flock of God (cf. 1 Pet. 5:1–4). Conversely, however, preachers who are nothing more than pulpiteers, who display few Christian graces that enable them to love people, work with people, listen humbly, exhort patiently, encourage graciously, and rebuke engagingly, are simply disqualified. They may be "able to teach" in some performance sense, but what is missing is the array of Christian graces that Christian pastors/elders/overseers must display. And all of us engaged in this high calling should be *making progress* in both doctrine and life.

The first perennial challenge, then, is equipping preachers with gospel graces, gospel knowledge, and experience of communicating that gospel, so that they meet the minimal biblically stipulated qualifications for pastoral office.

An Adequate Grasp of What Preaching Is

Countless volumes have been written on this subject, of course. Here I shall restrict myself to five observations.

First, preaching is more than the oral communication of information, no matter how biblical and divine that information may be. Rather, we should think in terms of what might be called "re-revelation." Across the centuries, God disclosed himself—he revealed himself—in great events (e.g., the burning bush, the exodus, the resurrection of Jesus); he disclosed himself supremely in the person of his Son. But very commonly he revealed himself by his words. Perennially we read, "The word of the Lord came to such-and-such a prophet." So when that Word is re-announced, there is a sense in which God, who revealed himself by that Word in the past, is re-revealing himself by that same Word once again. Preachers must bear this in mind. Their aim is more than to explain the Bible, however important that aim is. They want the proclamation of God's Word to be a revelatory event, a moment when God discloses himself afresh, a time when the people of God know that they have met with the living God. They know full well that for the Scriptures to have this revelatory impact the Spirit of God must apply that Word deeply to the human heart, so that preaching must never be seen as a mere subset of public oratory. Both the content (the Bible is God's Word) and the transformative empowering (the Spirit himself) transcend any merely mechanical view of preaching.

Second, to remain true to this basic understanding of what preaching is, the preacher must be committed to the primacy of *expository* preaching. We must take pains to debunk what many people think "exposition" and "expository" mean. They associate exposition with a style that takes not more than half a verse per sermon and casts around widely for every conceivable association, biblical and pastoral. Certainly that is one form of exposition, but that form is not the essence of the matter. Exposition is simply the unpacking of what is there. In a narrative text (e.g., 2 Samuel) or major epic (e.g., Job), fine exposition may focus on several chapters at once. If a sermon takes two or three short passages from disparate parts of the Bible *and explains each of them carefully and faithfully within its own context,* it remains an expository sermon, for it is unpacking what the biblical text or texts actually say. If we expect God to re-reveal himself by his own words, then our expositions must reflect as faithfully as possible what God actually said when the words were given to us in Scripture.

Third, there is an heraldic element in preaching. The Bible sometimes envisages other forms of oral communication, of course: we may be invited to reason together with the Lord (Isa. 1:18), for instance, or enter into a dialogical confrontation with him (e.g., Mal. 1:2–8; Rom. 6:1–2). Yet in the oft-repeated "Thus says the Lord" of the Old Testament, or in the proclamation so common to the New Testament, there is an unavoidable heraldic element—an announcement, a sovereign disclosure, a nonnegotiable declaration. As ambassadors, we are tasked with making known the stance and intentions of our Sovereign; we do not have the authority to tamper with his position.

Fourth, preaching is never an end in itself. It is not an art form to be admired, still less mere high-flown rhetoric that so captures the audience's imagination that the content is of little importance. This is not to deny that artistry and rhetoric may be traced in sermons; rather, it is to keep ultimate ends in constant view. The faithful preacher will care little what folk think of his oratorical skills; he will care a great deal about whether he has faithfully represented the Master and his message. This includes a passionate commitment to make the Word wound and heal, sing and sting.

And that means, fifth, that we must study our own people, the culture of the people to whom we minister. Inevitably there are commonalities from culture to culture, but there are countless distinctives as well. To communicate effectively we must address the people of the time and place where God has placed us. This is a perennially urgent need in the thoughtful and faithful preacher, of course, but the peculiar shape this takes in the twenty-first century is part of what takes us into the second part of this essay.

A Firm and Growing Grasp of Scripture

This is implicit in Paul's injunction so to advance in "life" and "doctrine" that others see our progress. Yet two further reflections may be of use:

First, what we mean by teaching "the whole will of God" needs some p.   g. When Paul attests that this is what he proclaimed to the believers in Ephesus, the Ephesian elders to whom he makes this bold asseveration know full well that he had managed this remarkable feat in only two-and-a-half years. In other words, whatever else Paul did, he certainly did not manage to go through every verse of the Old Testament, line by line, with full-bore explanation. He simply did not have time. What he must mean is that he taught the burden of the whole of God's revelation, the balance of things, leaving nothing out that was of primary importance, never ducking the hard bits, helping believers so to grasp the whole counsel of God that they themselves would become better equipped to read their Bibles intelligently, comprehensively. This doubtless included not only what to believe but how to act. It embraced God's purposes in the history of redemption (truths to be believed and a God to be worshiped), an unpacking of human origin, fall, redemption, and destiny (a worldview that shapes all human understanding and a Savior without whom there is no hope), the conduct expected of God's people (commandments to be obeyed and wisdom to be pursued, both in our individual existence and in the community of the people of God), and the pledges of transforming power both in this life and in the life to come (promises to be trusted and hope to be anticipated).

Second, to pursue a firm and growing grasp of Scripture ideally demands an improving grasp of Scripture, of historical theology, of biblical theology, and of systematic theology. These disciplines may be distinctive, but they are certainly not mutually exclusive: growth in any one of them deepens growth in all of the others, and sustained ignorance of any one of them hampers growth in all the rest of them.

A Deep Commitment to Making the Important Things the Important Things, to Making the Central Things the Central Things

There is a kind of "biblical" preaching that is not so much unbiblical as trivial. Not long ago I heard a sermon on Luke 1:26–38, in which the angel Gabriel announces the birth of Jesus to the Virgin Mary. The entire sermon focused on how God sometimes does unexpected things in our lives. After all, Mary didn't expect to become pregnant in this way. The rest of the "exposition" focused on Mary's psychological and spiritual profile in all of this. A fair bit of what was said had some sort of relation to the text; reasonable inferences were made. *But none of the "exposition," none of it at all, focused on Jesus!* Whatever interest Luke has in saying something about Mary is minor compared with his interest in telling us who Jesus is. Five minutes of the sermon reserved for some reflection on Mary's outlook might have been appropriate; the loss of Jesus was not.

Recently I skimmed a book that included a chapter on "Mrs. Noah." Same problem: the author was so desperate to get the text to answer contemporary questions that virtually the entire account of the flood merely served to help us understand Mrs. Noah's outlook. As it happens, this essay was more restrained than most popular writing of this sort. Even so, the author was terribly far removed from making the main thing the main thing.

Another sermon I recently heard, this one on John 2:1–11 (the changing of the water into wine, in Cana of Galilee), included some interesting comments on the social customs of Jesus' day and reflected for quite a while on the way in which Jesus meets us in the commonplaces of life. Somehow or other, the preacher failed to tie this passage to the other "signs" in John's Gospel, or say much about the miracle itself, or reflect on the "glory" theme (with which this passage ends, 2:11) in the Gospel of John, or comment on the many, many ways in which Jesus in John's Gospel transcends the law, showing himself to be the *true* temple, the *true* vine, the *true* bread of life, and so on—even though the passage carefully mentions that the six stone water pots full to the brim were used for Jewish ceremonial washings, and that it was Jesus' word that brought about the miraculous transformation, not observance of the law. Moreover, the miracle itself prepares the way for the declaration, in the next chapter, that Jesus himself is the bridegroom: the miracle anticipates the messianic banquet. All of this and more was left out. The preacher's comments could not legitimately be charged with false doctrine. They could have been legitimately slipped into a faithful sermon. But as it was, they made the "exposition" merely trivial.

It would be easy to add additional perennial challenges to the preacher's responsibility. But it is high time to focus a little more closely on the topic assigned me.

Some Twenty-first-century Challenges

The following list of six entries is exhaustive neither in quantity nor in quality—i.e., it would be easy to add additional entries to the list, and it would be easy to expand each entry considerably. Moreover, even these six reflect my own primary geographical and cultural location. I have visited many parts of the world in which the challenges to the twenty-first century pulpit look rather different. So part of the purpose of the rest of this essay is modest: to stimulate thinking that will help others flesh out this list and modify it for different cultural locations.

Multiculturalism

Transparently, the move toward multiculturalism is not evenly distributed. There are numerous rural pockets in the United States that have been largely untouched by what is almost a global phenomenon; there are entire countries that have experienced little of the phenomenon of mixed ethnicities (e.g., Japan in the industrialized world and some parts of the still-developing Two-Thirds World). Nevertheless the multiplication of ethnic diversity in our major metropolitan centers around the world is one of the most dramatic changes of the past fifty years. For this reason, ministry in New York City has more in common with ministry in Toronto, London, and Berlin than it does with ministry in Franklin, Tennessee.

In some cities the pace of this change has been stunning. A bare three decades ago, Toronto was still largely white and at least substantially WASP. Now the United Nations says it is the most ethnically and culturally diverse city on the continent—and that includes Los Angeles. Moreover, many major cities that have been immune from such transformation are losing their immunization. Two years ago I spent a pleasant couple of hours walking the streets of Bratislava. Accustomed as I am to the sights and sounds of Western Europe, I was struck, once again, by how mono-racial and mono-cultural a Central European city like Bratislava was. I think I counted three black faces. Similar things could be said a few years ago of Prague and other major cities of the countries of the former Eastern block. But now that so many of these countries have joined the European Union, the entailments for immigration are incalculable. I suspect that within a decade or two Bratislava will be almost as multicultural as London, Paris, Brussels, and Rome. Cities like Johannesburg and Cape Town may not have exactly the same distribution of nonnationals, but they, too, are becoming more and more diverse.

The reasons for such changes are many. Increased mobility, the relative ease of travel and its relative inexpensiveness, the massive movements of refugees on the one hand and of those seeking a better economic way of life on the other (while America has about twelve million undocumented Hispanics, South Africa has just under three million undocumented citizens of Zimbabwe—and similar statistics could be charted in many countries), all play their part. In Europe, one of the most significant pressures undergirding these developments is demographic: not a single European country has a birthrate of 2.1 or higher.[2]

---

2. One may not always like the sometimes sassy and savagely funny analysis of Mark Steyn, *America Alone: The End of the World as We Know It* (Washington DC: Regnery, 2006), but it is difficult to ignore the plethora of documented statistics.

The influx of international guest workers drafted to keep the economies moving invariably has far higher birthrates (e.g., Europe as a whole, about 1.35; Muslims in Europe, about 3.5). Mathematics does the rest. Already there are more worshipers of Allah on any weekend in the United Kingdom than there are Christian worshipers (even with the broadest possible definition of "Christian"); in France, the ratio is now higher than 2.5/1.

Why are such considerations important for the preacher? Certainly I do not want to belong to the doom-mongering crowd. Besides, many of us actually love the diversity now characteristic of many of our big cities. The last thing the church needs in a city like Toronto or New York is a church that hunkers down into ethnically and culturally pure enclaves. That is wrong biblically and stupid strategically. Yet there are at least five facets of these developments that have a bearing on twenty-first-century preachers and preaching.

First, preachers who serve in most of our large urban centers, and even in many small centers, will face increasing cultural diversity in the populace where their church is located. Woe to the church that lags way behind these demographic changes, for it is destined to become a narrow (and narrow-minded) enclave, instead of joyfully anticipating the day, in the new heaven and the new earth, when men and women from every language and people and nation will gather around the throne. Churches comprised of believers from diverse cultures will include people with different senses of humor, different tastes in food, different views on how to bring up their children, different perspectives on individualism and family identity, different traditions with which they choose to identify themselves. Yet what unites them in Christ Jesus is far richer than what divides them. The preacher sensitive to these changes will be eager to establish a growing, empathetic, and biblically faithful distinction between "the faith that was once for all entrusted to the saints" (Jude 3 NIV) and an immense array of cultural differences over which it is unwise to divide. Perhaps nowhere do such matters become more sensitive than when our children express a desire to marry across racial and cultural divides—a phenomenon occurring with increasing regularity, especially in our coastal cities. How families respond to these pressures quickly discloses where their hearts and values are, not least how much they have been shaped by the gospel.

Second, preachers will have to distinguish between, on the one hand, the empirical pluralism and multiculturalism increasingly characteristic of our big cities, and, on the other, the dogmatic "PC" form of multiculturalism that refuses to make any moral or cultural distinctions. Are we so very sure that the culture of Nazism is morally indistinguishable from the culture of the Dutch folk who hid so many Jews? We shall want to eschew alike the traditionalism that always sides with our own inherited culture, the sentimental love of the esoteric that always sides with whatever is foreign, and the postmodern blinkers that refuse to allow much moral and cultural distinction and discernment at all. The preacher who is speaking from the whole of the Bible to the whole of human life will not be able to duck such issues.

Third, preachers in these environments need to take extra time to prepare *themselves* for ministry characterized by these challenges. It used to be that the better theological colleges and seminaries required *of missionary candidates* certain courses in cross-cultural communication. Nowadays pastors serving metropolitan areas need similar help. It is important to read up on the major groups in your area; it is even more important to develop friendships among the various people of your area, for such interaction will supplement your reading with experiences that no amount of reading can ever cover. One of the valuable things that pastors can do is spend time with more senior pastors who have already crossed a lot of the bridges, and who are willing to mentor a new generation coming along behind.

Fourth, these developments are generating in preachers the need to revive the debate over the validity or invalidity of "the homogeneous unit" principle. Several decades ago, this principle was especially associated with the name of Donald McGavran, who taught missions at Fuller Seminary. McGavran argued that the gospel advances far more quickly and fruitfully if missionaries and evangelists target discrete ethnic and cultural groups. The countervailing argument was that the New Testament demands one unified people of God drawn from all races and cultures—in short, that McGavran's formula was a betrayal of the gospel itself.

Thus cast, the two outlooks allow no common ground. In fact, some common ground is possible. Evangelistic outreach may demand special sensitivity to definable groups: Paul himself could make himself a Jew to Jews, a Gentile to Gentiles (1 Cor. 9:19–23), with the aim of by all means saving some. What Paul will not sanction is that once they are converted, people may constitute churches separated by race or culture: the church in Antioch must be made up of both Jews and Gentiles. A church that begins, say, an outreach Bible study into the Greek community nearby, or into the Mandarin-speaking community, may be working faithfully. But faithfulness equally mandates that the church attempt to bring disparate people together under the lordship of Christ. One can sympathize with immigrant churches that cater to folk of similar language and culture. On the long haul, however, the priority of preserving the language and culture can easily trump the gospel itself—and in any case the second or third generation is going to start voting with their feet unless attempts are made to integrate with at least some larger parts of the broader culture. All of these things a preacher must think through as he plans a course of teaching and preaching in a complex, multicultural city.

Fifth, in some geographical locations special thought must be given to the very large groups of one kind of new immigrant: often (in North America) various Hispanic groups; often (in many cities in Europe, and in some places in North America) the Muslim population. In other words, addressing something abstract like "multiculturalism" may actually become an excuse for *not* thinking through the impact of *specific* cultures in our own neighborhoods.

Rising Biblical Illiteracy

The reasons for this illiteracy are many, of course, and have often been probed. This is not the place to review those reasons again. Yet few observers would deny the phenomenon, however unevenly it may be distributed. Two years ago I was giving some fairly academic lectures in Paris. Students had distributed handbills announcing the content, and a young woman living on a boat on the Seine came across a handbill and decided to attend. The first lecture included a lot of historical allusions to major figures in Western Christendom; the second lecture was much more focused on the Bible. The woman came and chatted after the second lecture. She told me she followed the first address much better than the second; because she was a young lass, she had attended a Catholic school where she had been exposed to the thought of Augustine and others, even though she had never found out much about the Bible. But I am quite sure that for every Parisienne who could follow even the first lecture, there are many more for whom both the Bible and subsequent church history are pretty much closed books.

I have sometimes said that when I began doing university missions more than three decades ago, the atheists I met were mostly *Christian* atheists—i.e., the God in whom they did not believe was the Christian God, which is a nice way of saying that the conceptual categories were still largely on my turf. Nowadays one cannot count on even this minor alignment. Most university students are so utterly ignorant of the Bible today that the responsible preacher cannot make biblical allusions without unpacking them and cannot use biblically "loaded" words without explaining them. Even the smallest subset of our cherished Christian vocabulary—grace, faith, God, sin, atonement, resurrection, and the like—is either a list of meaningless expressions or will prove to be deeply misunderstood by the folk we are addressing. A preacher who is able to proclaim the gospel only to believers who are already deeply Christianized in vocabulary and concept will not be able to proclaim the gospel to people who are not only ignorant of basic biblical content and terminology, but who have already adopted stances toward spirituality and religion that are deeply at odds with what the Bible says. We are not simply writing fresh data on the blank hard drives of their minds; we are required to help them erase certain files and parts of files that clash irremediably with the truth of Scripture that we are trying to write onto their minds. These are challenges that exerted few pressures on most Christian preachers in the Western world a bare half-century ago.

Shifting Epistemology

The word *postmodern* and its cognates have come to mean slightly different things to different groups of people, and in particular to mean different things in different countries. In France, for example, people do not speak of postmodern*ism* precisely because the "ism" suffix suggests a stability that the movement itself disavows. Even the preferred word *postmodernity* is nowadays rarely used, in part because the movement called postmodernity was closely tied to certain literary and philosophical commitments that are no longer *de rigueur* in French intellectual circles. By contrast, in America the French postmoderns of a generation ago are still being read in translation. Here everyone talks happily about *postmodernism* and the presses keep churning out a disheartening number of books on the subject.

Although some have tried to tie postmodernism to anti-consumerism and other current agendas, most concur that in much of the Anglo-Saxon world the heart of the issue is epistemology. "Hard" postmoderns exaggerate the difference between moderns and postmoderns, depicting the former as being fixated on certainty, infatuated with propositions, invariably arrogant and intolerant, and largely blind to the ambiguities and artistries of life. By contrast, postmoderns recognize the relativity of all truth claims, embrace the wide possibilities of a word like "truth," approach other groups with tolerance and cultural sensitivity, and embrace the subtleties and complexities of life. The caricature intrinsic to these stereotypes may be laughable to serious historians, but millions buy into it. More importantly, "soft" postmoderns avoid the worst antitheses but insist nevertheless, not inaccurately, that there are only two kinds of perspectivalists: those who admit it and those who don't. Only Omniscience is not burdened with being a perspectivalist. Moreover, many hold that perspectivalism so limits our capacity to know very much with certainty that firmly held beliefs are read as narrow-minded dogmatism, theological exclusivism is taken to be intolerance, and most moral distinctions must remain nothing more than private preferences.

At very least we must see that the focus of interest has changed. It used to be that someone giving evangelistic addresses on a university campus could provide a full-blown defense of the resurrection of Jesus and thereby precipitate discussions about the truthfulness of the Bible's claims. Nowadays it is more likely such a presentation will elicit the entirely tangential question, "Yes, but what about all the Hindus?" There was a time when one could easily talk about sex and its good purposes in God's creation. Nowadays the same presentation will probably call forth the question, "Are you homophobic?" In short, what starts off as the perception of a tectonic shift in epistemology works down into ten thousand small but vital shifts in perspective and priority.

What I must do, then, is outline a handful of ways in which this epistemological shift ought to affect the preacher and his task. I shall mention only four, though many more could be added.

First, it has become more difficult to get across what the Bible says about sin. When more people lived in a world where "right" and "wrong" were widely perceived to be transcultural categories, it was easier to get across something of the enormity of violating the law of God.

Second, the current focus on narrative preaching has rightly broadened the older emphasis on discourse passages from the Bible. If it helps us better handle all the genres of Scripture faithfully and responsibly, it will be to the good. If it merely tips us from one cultural preference (viz., discourse) to another (viz., narrative), we have not gained anything. Indeed, because narrative is intrinsically more hermeneutically "open" than discourse, the move may merely contribute toward moving us away from truth. How much better to remain faithful to biblical truth yet simultaneously focused on Scripture's existential bite.

Third, because for many people in today's world, "faith" and its cognates refer to one's personal, subjective, religious choice—a choice abstracted from any pretensions of public truth—it does no good to encourage people "to believe" unless one explains what "to believe" means, how important the object of belief is (see 1 Corinthians 15), and how faith and truth relate to each other. Many such links were simply presupposed by our hearers several decades ago. Few of the links are today culturally presupposed.

185

Fourth, the structure of apologetics needs to change somewhat. A great deal of the earlier intra-evangelical debates about presuppositionalism and evidentialism were themselves parasitic, in whole or in part, on the subject-object distinction as it developed in the modern period. That debate today takes on a raft of new emphases with the move to various kinds of postmodernism.

Each of these four points could easily be developed into a long chapter. Thoughtful Christians will not want to align entirely with either modernism or postmodernism, of course, but the kindness of God in his "common grace" ensures that there are useful things in both epistemological structures that a Christian may usefully exploit, and things in both structures to confront.

The last three points—multiculturalism, rising biblical illiteracy, and shifting epistemology—combine to remind us that challenges like these are not new. When Paul preaches the gospel in a synagogue in Pisidian Antioch (Acts 13), he does not sound exactly the way he does when he preaches the gospel to biblically illiterate intellectuals in Athens (Acts 17). On any reckoning, Paul has been in the ministry for more than two long decades when he preaches in Antioch. He is not shifting his message because he is intimidated. Rather, he recognizes that he is now in another cultural "world" than the one he inhabited when preaching in a synagogue. He perceives that the biblical illiteracy in Athens, combined with such alien frames of reference as Stoicism and Epicureanism, means he must start farther back and talk about monotheism, creation, who human beings are, the aseity of God, the nature of idolatry, and a view of history that includes teleology and final judgment, before he can help his hearers make sense of Jesus and the resurrection.

Integration

This category needs a little unpacking. What I have in mind is the need for Christian preachers so to think through God's Word that they can wrestle discerningly, penetratingly, critically, and integratively with the manifold movements and cultural (including moral and ethical) questions of the day. This does *not* mean that the agenda of an age becomes the preacher's agenda. It means, rather, that we must not pretend we can preach the Bible in a cultural vacuum.

Most of us have met preachers who have spent years of their lives reading the Puritans (or the Reformers, or the Fathers) and little else, and whose entire imaginations are locked in a time warp several centuries old. They should not deter us from reading history, of course:

history opens our eyes to other cultures, introduces us to brothers and sisters in other times and places, and weaves depth and perspective into our lives. Nevertheless, we must address the challenges of *our* time and place. Preachers whose every point of integration and application springs from the Donatist controversy or the debate over Socinianism or the Revocation of the Edict of Nantes or the legitimacy or otherwise of the Hooker principle, but who never address abortion and other sweeping bioethical issues congregating around the beginning of life and the end of life, are living in the wrong century.

At a time when internet porn now outsells cigarettes, booze, and hard drugs combined, when digital worlds open up new horizons and yet shut down human intimacy, when globalization reminds us that we are one world and yet sometimes exploits the weak, when AIDS threatens tens of millions of human beings, and when Islam, fueled by oil, strengthened by demographic trends, and disgusted by the immorality of the West, is once again resurgent, the preacher who never demonstrates how the gospel of Jesus Christ addresses these things has, at best, retreated to an individualistic form of piety not sanctioned by the biblical prophetic tradition.

Christian preachers are not authorized to duck important issues. At the same time, these issues must not determine his message. Yet failure to show the bearing of the gospel on such issues is merely to trumpet that there is no bearing. Our task, then, is to be expositors of the Word of God yet to exercise that ministry in the time and place where God has providentially placed us.

Pace of Change

At the beginning of this essay I briefly drew attention to some of the changes that took place in the twentieth century. The pace of change in that century was staggering. But virtually all quantifiers promise that the pace of change in the twenty-first century will accelerate and prove to be far more rapid.

At one level, of course, this should matter little to the preacher. We deal in eternal realities. Indeed, endless analysis about change and its pace may distract us from the eternal gospel, the faith "once for all delivered to the saints." Nevertheless, our task is to communicate the truth of God's words, which are forever settled in heaven, to men and women who very much live on earth—a rapidly changing earth. What this suggests is that along with the primacy the preacher must give to the study of Scripture and ancillary disciplines, he must also set aside time to try to understand his own times. This may be done through reading, discussion groups of various sorts (e.g., analyzing books and films), seminars with the most experienced and insightful preachers, and much more. But to ignore the pace of change is to lust after a false security, the security of stability, that will not characterize any part of the twenty-first century.

Modeling and Mentoring

For much of the last three decades my primary task has been to teach students at Trinity Evangelical Divinity School. I have sometimes said that if, God forbid, I were suddenly appointed evangelical Pope, the first thing I would do on my first day in office would be to bring ten or fifteen of the ablest pastor-preachers to churches within a short driving distance of Trinity. The reason is obvious: a great many things are better caught than taught. I wish more of our students were exposed to great preaching. Some of the most important lessons I have learned about preaching have been gleaned by sitting under the ministry of able preachers.

This suggests we ought to be thinking hard about mentoring and apprenticeships. Various organizations, such as The Proclamation Trust in the United Kingdom, have developed preaching workshops that devote time to (a) listening to able preachers, and to (b) mutual criticism of sermon outlines that each participant prepares in advance. Other networks prepare preachers for urban ministry or cross-cultural ministry. The apostle Paul understands how much of his own *life* must shape Timothy (e.g., 2 Tim. 3:10–11). Considering the challenges ahead of us, preachers are more likely to multiply their fruitfulness if they pay attention to the importance of mentoring than if they persist in "Lone Ranger" ministries all their days.

Concluding Reflections

It would be easy to conjure up more trends unwinding before us in the twenty-first century that will have some bearing on preachers and their task. Preachers cannot responsibly ignore these things, for they stand between the speaking God and the listening people—people who are not empty ciphers but culturally located men and women who must be addressed where they are, even if our hope and prayer is that they will not remain where they are, but begin by God's grace the march down the King's highway, the narrow road that leads to life.

Our motivation to understand and address people in the twenty-first century is not to domesticate the gospel by constant appeal to cultural analysis, but to prove effective ambassadors of the Sovereign whose Word we announce. For one day the kingdom of this world will become the kingdom of our Lord and of his Christ, and he will reign for ever and ever (Rev. 11:15). It is precisely because we are anchored in eternity that we are so utterly resolved, like Paul, to address lost men and women who must one day meet their God.

12

Preaching That Reforms

Philip Ryken

Preaching has fallen out of vogue in most of the contemporary American church. "Stop preaching at me!" people say in these post-Christian times. "Spare me the sermon." If we consult a dictionary, we find that the first definition of the word *preach* is "to deliver a sermon," but the second is "to exhort in a . . . tiresome manner." For many churchgoers today, the second definition is the operative one: a sermon is assumed to be boring and probably annoying as well.

Preaching is also falling out of favor not only among nominal churchgoers but among Christians as well, which is a sign that our post-Christian culture is producing a post-Christian church. The listener rather than God is sovereign. There is an overall "dumbing down" of doctrine. Sermons are getting shorter; if they go longer than twenty minutes, people start to get restless. Churchgoers demand to be entertained, so in many churches the sermon has been replaced by music, testimonies, drama, or even videos.

Such preaching as there is tends to be more experiential than biblical, more humanistic than evangelistic. One popular trend is for preachers to tell "a simple story designed to teach a moral lesson, as opposed to a traditional dissection of a biblical text. Often it is a very personal tale of the preacher's trials and triumphs, with lots of emotional content and little thorny theology."[1]

Apparently ministers who resort to this form of communication have lost their confidence in the inherent power of God's Word. As a result, their congregations rarely hear the voice of God's Spirit speaking in Scripture. The post-Christian church no longer believes in the power of biblical preaching. Writing "An Appeal to All Pastors," online theologian Sam Storms states:

> I can't tell you how many times I've asked people all across America, "Tell me about the strengths and weaknesses of your church," only to hear something like this: "Well, we've got a great youth program. And there's plenty of parking space. . . . But honestly, it doesn't seem like our pastor spends much time in the Word. He'll read a passage here and there, but he never goes very deep into its meaning. I get the feeling he doesn't think it's very relevant to our lives today. He shows some interesting video clips from recent movies and he's up to date on political events. But Scripture doesn't play a huge role in our services. I've even stopped bringing my Bible to church. I never seem to need it."[2]

A decline in biblical preaching is disastrous because the sermon is a divinely ordained means for bringing sinners to Christ. Consider this biblical line of reasoning: "'Everyone who calls on the name of the Lord will be saved.' But how are they to call on him in whom they have not believed? And how are they to believe in him of whom they have never heard? And how are they to hear without someone preaching?" (Rom. 10:13–14). The emphasis here is on preaching—not just the personal witness of someone who is living for Christ (although that is often part of what the Spirit uses to bring someone to faith), but the public proclamation of the gospel of Jesus Christ. By the sheer force of divine logic, we are forced to admit that without hearing the Word preached in this way, sinners cannot be saved. In these post-Christian times, ministers are sometimes told to stop preaching to the unchurched. Yet gospel preaching is a necessary part of God's plan for their salvation.

Preaching is equally necessary for the Christian life. The gospel is not a form of self-help; it is a transforming message. Thus it is through the explanation and proclamation of God's Word—with exhortation—that believers grow in grace. Therefore, what the church needs in post-Christian times is preaching—biblical, expositional, practical preaching that proclaims Christ from all the Scriptures.

---

1. Nancy Gibbs, "How Much Does the Preaching Matter?" *Time*, September 17, 2001, 55.
2. Sam Storms, "An Appeal to All Pastors," Enjoying God Ministries (April 23, 2005).

No Tolerance for Truth

Two problematic features of spiritual life in the twenty-first century are relativism and narcissism. Relativism is the denial of absolute meaning. The relativist says, "The truth is whatever you want it to be." Narcissism is the worship of the self. The narcissist asks, "What's in it for me?"

These attitudes are in the culture and in the church, where leaders who call themselves evangelicals openly advocate a more flexible approach to theological orthodoxy, and practice a more consumer-oriented style of congregation life. This attitude is exposed in the condemning review that *Publisher's Weekly* gave of a bestselling book by one of America's hottest preachers. This book, said the reviewer, is "a treatise on how to get God to serve the demands of self-centered individuals."[3]

If we are living in an age of relativism and narcissism, what are the implications for preaching? Obviously, Bible teaching will be out of favor. As sinners, we generally do not like to have our selfishness exposed; but this is one of the primary purposes of preaching the Bible. In a post-Christian culture, the last thing people want to hear is the truth about their self-centeredness. What preaching there is, therefore, tends to be therapeutic rather than prophetic. It aims to make people feel better about who they are rather than to challenge them to become, by God's grace, what they are not.

When *The New York Times Magazine* visited one mega-church in the desert southwest, it found the messages "light on liturgy" and heavy on "successful principles for living—how to discipline your children, how to reach your professional goals, how to invest your money, how to reduce your debt." The pastor "never talks about transforming your life through struggle, surrender or sacrifice; he talks about being happier by accepting Jesus." "If Oprah and Dr. Phil are doing it," the preacher said when interviewed, "why shouldn't we? We should be better at it because we have the power of God to offer."[4] But how can we have the power of God unless we are using the Word of God, which is the only divinely empowered instrument for spiritual change?

This is the kind of preaching people are getting in the church today. But most people can be counted on not to want anyone to preach to them at all. The apostle Paul anticipated this centuries ago: "For the time is coming when people will not endure sound teaching, but having itching ears they will accumulate for themselves teachers to suit their own passions" (2 Tim. 4:3).

---

3. From a review of Joel Osteen's *Your Best Life Now* that appeared in *Publisher's Weekly.*

4. Lee McFarland, quoted by Jonathan Mahler in "The Soul of the New Exurb," *The New York Times Magazine*, March 27, 2005, 33, 37.

When Paul said, "the time is coming," what time did he have in mind? Probably the whole time between the first and second comings of Christ, between his resurrection and his return, which would include our own post-Christian times. The twenty-first century is one of the times when "people will not endure sound teaching." They will not have the patience to listen to theological instruction. And when they do hear what the Bible says, they will deny that it is truth from God. Instead, they will believe whatever they want to believe, listening only to teachers who tell them whatever they want to hear, so that they can do whatever they want to do. As the Scripture says, "They will turn their ears away from the truth and turn aside to myths" (2 Tim. 4:4 NIV).

The New Evangelicalism

When the apostle Paul spoke about myths, he was referring to what people were thinking in the church. His concern was with those who had the appearance of godliness but denied its power (2 Tim. 3:5). In other words, he was worried about people who called themselves Christians but did not know Christ, who were unorthodox in their theology and unbiblical in their practice, who were still "doing church," even though their ministry was no longer animated by the gospel power of the Holy Spirit.

All of which leads us to ask this question: What dangerous doctrines confront the contemporary church? Each generation faces its own theological challenges, so it is necessary to identify the ideas that threaten to harm the church in the twenty-first century. What are the post-Christian denials of the power of God?

The winds of doctrinal change are sweeping through the evangelical church. Some colleges and seminaries are heading in the direction of what has been termed "post-conservative" evangelicalism. The new evangelicals move beyond the boundaries of the historic confessions, in some cases by introducing postmodern perspectives to Christianity. They are trying to get beyond what they see as the old conservative/liberal dichotomy. As a result, the following doctrines are coming under attack.

The doctrine of Scripture. This was an area of dispute starting in the nineteenth century and continuing throughout the twentieth century, culminating in America with "the Battle for the Bible." In many evangelical churches, the battle was won on behalf of infallibility and inerrancy—the Bible cannot and does not err. Yet the war may still be lost. Today there is widespread ignorance about what the Bible actually teaches. Even those who believe that Scripture is true deny that it is sufficient for evangelism, guidance, spiritual growth, or social change.[5] They say that in addition to Scripture, other methods and techniques are needed.

Then there are the evangelical Bible scholars whose hermeneutical assumptions and exegetical methods are virtually indistinguishable from those employed by liberal scholars. The evangelical doctrine of biblical inerrancy is becoming notional rather than foundational. There is a rising suspicion of the term *inerrancy*. Scholars introduce so many questions and qualifications that they no longer clearly affirm the full truthfulness and authority of Scripture.

The doctrine of God. There is a movement among some evangelicals to advocate the "openness of God," or "open theism." This is an attempt to solve the mystery of divine sovereignty and human responsibility by denying that God has full knowledge of the future. The new evangelical deity is a risk-taker whose will is sometimes thwarted and whose plans often change in response to the actions of human beings. This doctrine of God is purported to be more faithful to the Scriptures. However, it is a radical departure from biblically orthodox teaching about divine foreknowledge. The true God is all-knowing. He says, "I am God, and there is no other; I am God, and there is none like me, declaring the end from the beginning and from ancient times things not yet done" (Isa. 46:9b–10a).

The doctrine of Christ. Here the trend is towards religious pluralism, as relativism comes to church. Many people believe that all religions are equally true, that they all provide equally valid perspectives on ultimate reality. In the church this takes the form of denying that Jesus is the only way to God. Today some scholars who claim to be evangelicals nevertheless claim that explicit personal faith in Jesus Christ is unnecessary for salvation. Under the influence of other world religions, they conclude that God must also offer forgiveness through non-Christian religions. Jesus Christ is one possible expression of salvation, but not its exclusive means.

This is yet another example of the way a post-Christian culture produces a post-Christian church. The truth is that God really does require faith in Jesus Christ for salvation. It is only by believing in him that anyone will not perish but receive everlasting life (John 3:16). "There is salvation in no one else, for there is no other name under heaven given among men by which we must be saved" (Acts 4:12).

---

5. See James Montgomery Boice, *What Makes a Church Evangelical?* Today's Issues (Wheaton, IL: Crossway, 1999), 19–27.

The doctrine of salvation. Evangelicals are forgetting and in some cases denying vital Reformation teaching on the doctrine of justification. Partly out of an eagerness to find common cause with Catholicism and also as the result of new perspectives on Paul and the law, some post-conservative evangelicals dismiss the necessity or even the possibility of receiving Christ's righteousness by faith alone. The biblical view is that God imputes or credits his righteousness to the believer, so that when we stand before him we are covered with the perfect righteousness of Jesus Christ (e.g., Rom. 3:21–24). We are not justified by anything we do for ourselves, but only what Christ has done for us (see Eph. 2:8–9). By contrast, the Roman Catholic view includes good works as part of the basis for our justification, while the new perspectives on Paul and the law downplay the centrality of justification for the New Testament gospel.

Under these influences, some evangelicals are losing their grip on the Reformation principle of *sola fide,* the gospel of justification by faith alone. It is sometimes hard to get pastors and teachers to make a clear statement about what justification teaches, or about where it is found in the Bible, or about why the Reformers were right to say that the church stands or falls with its doctrine of justification.

These new theological trends are not peripheral matters but strike at the vitals of Christianity. They concern such fundamental doctrines as the sufficiency of Scripture, the sovereignty of God, the uniqueness of Christ, and the imputation of his righteousness. Each of these attacks on evangelical orthodoxy is a denial of God's power, just as Paul warned: a denial of God's power to give us a true word, or to rule over the world and the future, or to save us through the righteousness of Christ, and only through the righteousness of Christ. Unless these post-conservative denials are denied themselves, they will destroy evangelical theology and eventually the evangelical church. Whereas the twentieth century witnessed the decline of liberalism, the twenty-first century may well see the end of evangelicalism as a coherent Christian movement.

The Word That Is Preached

How should the church respond to these challenges? In a time of wide-spread biblical ignorance and increasing doctrinal confusion, how can Christians maintain their theological integrity? Paul's answer is very simple: "preach the word" (2 Tim. 4:2).

What ministers are to preach is the Word—that is, the Word of God. A faithful minister does not preach the latest news. He does not preach his private opinion, his personal experience, or his political agenda. He does not even preach his own theological tradition. What he preaches is God's eternal, infallible Word, as written in the Scriptures of the Old and New Testaments. Bryan Chapell defines expository preaching like this: "to say what God says" in such a way as "to make the meaning of the passage the message of the sermon."[6]

What kind of Word has God given us to preach? Paul reminded Timothy of several of its significant features. First, *the Word comes from God.* The Bible has a divine origin. People sometimes say that the Bible is inspired, and what they mean when they say "inspired" is "true." Yet the Bible actually teaches that God's Word is *ex*-spired: "All Scripture is breathed out by God." The Bible is the creative product of the Holy Spirit, and thus it bears God's own perfection and authority.

This is the problem with views of Scripture that emphasize the human element above the divine. Yes, the Bible is a human book, written by real human beings, who had their own experiences and abilities. But the humans who wrote the Bible were under the sovereign compulsion of God the Holy Spirit. Here Paul says "all Scripture" in order to show that each and every verse in the whole Bible is *ex-spired* in this way. This doctrine is sometimes called "plenary verbal inspiration." What it means is that all the words of Scripture are the very words of God, which is why we believe they are infallible and inerrant in the original manuscripts. The Bible is fully trustworthy and absolutely true in every respect. Therefore, what the minister reads and preaches is God's own Word—provided that he is committed to preaching what the Bible says and nothing else.

Second, *the Word brings salvation through faith in Christ.* This had been Timothy's own experience, as Paul reminded him: "But as for you, continue in what you have learned and have firmly believed, knowing from whom you learned it and how from childhood you have been acquainted with the sacred writings, which are able to make you wise for salvation through faith in Christ Jesus" (2 Tim. 3:14–15). Timothy had been raised on the Bible. His mother and grandmother taught him the Scriptures of the Old Testament, and in time, this brought him to a saving knowledge of Jesus Christ.

The reason the Bible has this saving influence is that it is all about Jesus Christ. We do not have the Bible simply for its own sake, but because it brings us into a relationship with Jesus Christ, which it has the power to do because it is all about him! After he was raised from the dead, Jesus walked to Emmaus with two of his disciples, who were having trouble understanding the meaning of the crucifixion and the

---

6. Bryan Chapell, "The Future of Expository Preaching," *Presbyterian* 30/2 (Fall 2004).

resurrection. Jesus wanted to help them, so "beginning with Moses and all the Prophets, he interpreted to them in all the Scriptures the things concerning himself" (Luke 24:27). Not only is all Scripture God-breathed, but all Scripture is also Christ-centered. The salvation that was expected in the Old Testament is exhibited in the Gospels and then explained in the rest of the New Testament. From Genesis to Revelation, God's Word is all about Jesus, and thus it has the power to bring salvation through faith in him.

The Bible does more than bring people to faith in Christ, however; it also helps them to grow in grace. So a third great truth is that *the Word prepares the Christian to do God's work.* This is the main thing that Paul wanted Timothy to know: "All Scripture is breathed out by God and profitable for teaching, for reproof, for correction, and for training in righteousness, that the man of God may be competent, equipped for every good work" (2 Tim. 3:16–17). Having been breathed out by God, Scripture is of inestimable practical benefit for knowing and serving him.

Paul uses four words to describe its usefulness—two that pertain to doctrine and two that pertain to life. God's Word is useful for *teaching;* in other words, for communicating theological truth. It is also useful for *reproof,* which means to refute doctrinal error. Taken together, these terms show that the Bible distinguishes between truth and error in theology. How important that is today, when the relativism of our postmodern context makes many people reluctant to say that anyone's views are wrong—even views that contradict Scripture. But that is what the Bible is for: telling truth from falsehood.

Scripture is equally useful for *correction,* which has to do with personal conduct. The Bible warns us away from sin, reproving our tendency to serve ourselves. More positively, it is profitable for *training in righteousness.* God's Word disciples us by teaching us the difference between the right way and the wrong way to live. It is not just our thinking that the Bible needs to correct, but also our living, especially because we are so self-centered.

To summarize, the Bible is useful for both doctrine and life, for creed as well as conduct. It is so useful that it provides total preparation for doing God's will. A Christian who knows the Bible is fully trained to serve God at home, at work, in the church, and everywhere else in a post-Christian culture. In the words of a hymn by James Montgomery Boice, "God's Word is all the Christian needs to grow in grace and do good deeds."[7]

---

7. James Montgomery Boice and Paul Steven Jones, "God's Amazing Word," in *Hymns for a Modern Reformation* (Philadelphia: Tenth Presbyterian Church, 2000), 27.

Preaching the Word

What the minister is to do with this Word—this Word from God that brings salvation and prepares the Christian to do God's work—is to *preach it*. In his instructions to Timothy, the apostle Paul indicates what that preaching ought to include.

In the first place, preaching must be *evangelical*, which simply means that it takes as its central theme the gospel of Jesus Christ. The Greek word for preach (*kerygma*) is the word for proclamation. So when Paul told Timothy to preach, he was telling him to proclaim the good news of the gospel. A minister is a herald who makes the royal announcement of salvation through the death and resurrection of Jesus Christ.

Good preaching is always evangelistic, which perhaps is why Paul went on to remind Timothy to "do the work of an evangelist" (2 Tim. 4:5). Even though he was the pastor of an established church, Timothy still needed to reach the lost. Proclaiming the gospel was a necessary part of his ongoing work as a minister. A preacher is an evangelist who in one way or another is always pointing people to the cross and the empty tomb, and who is always saying to people, both in public and in private, "Believe in the Lord Jesus, and you will be saved" (Acts 16:31).

This kind of proclamation requires boldness, a virtue that is sadly lacking in the contemporary church. One of the reasons evangelicalism is in decline is because Christians have lost their nerve. In these post-Christian times, we tend to be a subculture rather than a counterculture. We are all too content to live in our own private enclaves, reinforcing our own opinions by attending our own schools, forming our own clubs, and reading our own magazines. But it is not the herald's job to stay at home. His task is to go out and confront people with his message, which in this case is the most important message ever proclaimed: the free gift of eternal life through faith in Jesus Christ.

In addition to being evangelical, preaching must also be *doctrinal*. Preserving sound doctrine is a major emphasis in the Pastoral Epistles. According to Paul, anyone who wants to be a good minister must keep a close watch on himself and on his teaching (1 Tim. 4:16), "rightly handling the word of truth" (2 Tim. 2:15). He must maintain "the words of the faith" (1 Tim. 4:6), also described as "the sound words of our Lord Jesus Christ" (1 Tim. 6:3), and "the pattern of . . . sound words" (2 Tim. 1:13).

Paul understood that the future of the church depends on the defense of its doctrine. When he charged Timothy to preach the Word, therefore, what he had in mind was the preaching of biblical doctrine. This is clear from the end of 2 Timothy 4:2, where Timothy is told to preach "with complete patience and teaching," which again means "doctrine." The reason he needed to preach this way is given in the following verse: "For the time is coming when people will not endure sound teaching" (2 Tim. 4:3). If the problem is unsound doctrine, then obviously the solution is good, doctrinal teaching.

In order to meet the challenges of the twenty-first century, preaching must be theologically informed. We face the same problem that Timothy faced: people are turning away from sound theology. They prefer what novelist David Brooks has termed "flexidoxy," or flexible orthodoxy.[8] In response, we must apply the same remedy that Paul recommended to Timothy: Preach sound doctrine. This is especially important at a time when most people (including many churchgoers) have never been introduced to the basic principles of Christian theology. In these post-Christian times, a major pastoral task is to explain Christianity to people who really have no idea what it means. And once people come to Christ, they need to be taught the basic doctrines that will help them think and act the way a Christian should.

It would be a mistake to think that doctrinal preaching is something different from evangelical preaching. The New Testament makes little or no distinction between teaching and evangelism. The apostles understood that the gospel is for Christians as well as non-Christians. Thus their teaching was always evangelistic and their evangelism included a heavy dose of teaching. In keeping with their example, Christian preaching for post-Christian times must be squarely doctrinal as well as solidly evangelical. There can be no preaching for conversion without an announcement of Christ's divine person and saving work, both of which need to be explained in clear doctrinal terms. Similarly, no aspect of Christian theology should ever be taught apart from its relationship to Jesus Christ and his gospel, because when theological instruction is Christ-centered, it has the power to draw people to salvation in him. Our doctrine should always be evangelical, and our evangelism should always be doctrinally sound.

Preaching must also be *practical*, and this was Paul's primary concern for Timothy. The eternal truths of Scripture must be applied to contemporary culture and the needs of daily life. To that end, Paul reminded Timothy to be practical in his preaching. A good sermon serves to "reprove, rebuke, and exhort" (2 Tim. 4:2). To *reprove* is to correct; it is to warn those who persist in sin. To *rebuke* is to censure those who are in error, especially theological error. Here again there is a dual emphasis

---

8. David Brooks, *Bobos in Paradise: The New Upper Class and How They Got There* (New York: Simon & Schuster, 2000), quoted in *Modern Reformation*, January/February, 2002, 36.

on life and doctrine, and thus a remedy for the narcissism and relativism of our times. The preacher has a responsibility to teach the Scriptures in a way that reforms belief and transforms conduct. Then to *exhort* is to encourage, pressing the truth of Scripture home to the heart. Biblical teaching is not effectively applied unless it comes with life-changing persuasion. Correcting, rebuking, and exhorting—these are not the only ways to apply a sermon, but together they remind us that good preaching is as practical as it is evangelical and doctrinal.

The Great Need for Bible Exposition

There is more than one way to preach a sermon. Not every minister should preach exactly the same way on every occasion. Even the sermons we read in the Bible show that different preaching contexts call for somewhat different sermons. But if faithful preaching includes these three elements—gospel presentation, theological explanation, and practical application—then not just any sermon will do. A minister who wants to preach in the biblical way will not spend all his time preaching revival sermons, such as an evangelist might preach at an evangelistic rally. Such sermons would be evangelical but probably not very doctrinal. He will not deliver theological lectures, such as a scholar might deliver at a seminary. Although such lectures presumably would be doctrinal, they might not be all that practical. Nor will a minister preach about his own spiritual experience every week, which could be practical, in a way, but might not be biblical.

If the church needs evangelical, doctrinal, practical preaching, then the kind of sermon that best satisfies the need is an expository sermon. The most effective way to keep Paul's charge to preach the Word is through biblical exposition: the careful and thorough communication of what the Bible actually says. This is the kind of preaching—I think really the only kind of preaching—that can re-form a deformed church back into the biblical pattern.

Expository preaching means making God's Word plain. It is the kind of preaching Paul was talking about in 2 Corinthians 4:2, where he said, "We refuse to practice cunning or to tamper with God's word, but by the open statement of the truth we would commend ourselves to everyone's conscience in the sight of God." In an expository sermon the preacher simply tries to explain what the Bible teaches. The main points of his sermon are the points made by a particular text in the Bible. The minister not only begins with Scripture but also allows the Scripture to establish the context and content for his sermon. The way he decides what to say is by studying what the Bible has to say, so that the Scripture itself sets the agenda for his interpretation and application.

Expository preaching does not mean merely beginning with a biblical text and then communicating the preacher's own spiritual ideas or the values of contemporary culture. Rather it is preaching that is driven by Scripture and derived from its divine authority, so that God's Word is declared to God's people. Expository preaching carefully and thoroughly communicates what the Bible actually teaches. It involves explanation and proclamation with exhortation. In each worship service the minister preaches a particular Bible passage in a way that explores its context, explains its meaning, expounds its doctrine in connection to the person and work of Jesus Christ, and applies its gospel to the spiritual needs of those who listen, exalting the glory of God. Expository preaching, says Sinclair Ferguson, is preaching in which "the explanation of Scripture forms the dominant feature and the organizing principle of the message. . . . It sees as its fundamental task the explanation of the text in its context, the unfolding of its principles, and only then their application to the world of the hearers."[9]

I believe that this kind of preaching is most helpfully done when a minister follows the logic of the Scriptures, systematically preaching chapter by chapter and verse by verse through entire books of the Bible. This helps ensure that a congregation hears what God wants them to hear, and not simply what their minister thinks they ought to hear. But expository preaching is not so much a method as it is a mind-set. A minister who sees himself as an expositor knows that he is not the master of the Word but its servant. He has no other ambition than to preach what the Scriptures actually teach. His aim is to be faithful to God's Word so that his people can hear God's voice. He himself is only God's mouthpiece, speaking God's message into the ears of God's people, and thus into their minds and hearts. To that end, he carefully works his way through the Scriptures, reading, explaining, and applying them to his congregation. On occasion he may find it necessary to address some pastoral concerns in a topical fashion, but even then his sermons come from his exposition of particular passages of Scripture. Rather than focusing on his own spiritual experience, or on current events, or on what he perceives as his congregation's needs and interests, the minister gives his fullest attention to teaching what the Bible actually says.

During the Protestant Reformation John Calvin made a claim, which we can only pray to make about evangelical churches in the twenty-first

---

9. Sinclair B. Ferguson, "Exegesis," in Samuel T. Logan, *The Preacher and Preaching* (Phillipsburg, NJ: P&R, 1986), 192–93.

century. He said: "It is certain that if we come to church we shall not hear only a mortal man speaking but we shall feel (even by his secret power) that God is speaking to our souls, that *he* is the teacher. He so touches us that the human voice enters into us and so profits us that we are refreshed and nourished by it. God calls us to him as if he had his mouth open and we saw him there in person."[10] God can only speak this way through a sermon if it is expository—that is, if it makes God's Word plain. As Martin Luther said, "We must get the Word from our lips to people's ears; the Holy Spirit can carry the Word from their ears to their hearts."[11] Expository preaching is preaching that uses human lips to get the Word of God from the biblical page to people's ears, and from there, into their hearts.

Expository preaching is able to do all three of the things that Paul said good preaching is supposed to do. It is evangelical because in expository preaching the minister preaches God's Word. We noted earlier that the whole Bible is about Christ. Therefore, when the Bible is preached, Christ is preached, and sinners are saved. As long as he is careful to preach Christ from all the Scriptures, an expository preacher is an *evangelical* preacher.

He is also a *doctrinal* preacher. All true and sound theology comes from the Word of God. A good expository preacher is careful to explain the doctrines that are taught in each passage of Scripture. As he preaches the Word, therefore, he is preaching biblical theology. Furthermore, he is preaching Christian doctrine in its biblical arrangement and according to its biblical proportions. As a preacher, how do I know what my people need to hear, and when, and how often? Generally speaking, I don't know. So the best thing to do is to preach the Scriptures in a systematic and comprehensive way, and then they will hear what God wants them to hear.

Expository preaching is also *practical*, which is precisely why Paul told Timothy to preach the Word. The Bible is the most practical book ever written. As Paul understood, practical preaching is biblical preaching—and the more biblical it is, the more practical. We believe that God's Word is what it says that it is: "profitable for teaching, for reproof, for correction, and for training in righteousness" (2 Tim. 3:16). If that is what the Bible is good for, then it should be used for that purpose. It is astonishing how many personal problems can be resolved when someone hears even a few months of solid expository preaching. Of course, sometimes there is a need for personal counsel, for the private

---

10. John Calvin, *Ephesians* (Edinburgh: Banner of Truth, 1973), 42.
11. Quoted from an address by Albert Mohler, First Presbyterian Church, Chattanooga, June 2006.

ministry of God's Word. But over time, good expository preaching—in which a minister is careful to draw out the practical implications of the biblical text—addresses the vast majority of spiritual needs.

The Final Analysis

Expository preaching may seem rather old-fashioned. This is an age of dialogue, and it is often said that preaching needs to become less dogmatic, more conversational. People want the minister to share, not preach. We are also told that Bible exposition is out of place in the information age. We should be going video, not audio. People need more stories and fewer propositions. They want preachers to be more personal, less doctrinal.

There are many reasons to be cautious about this kind of thinking. For one thing, information technology has its limitations as well as its strengths. Recently a United States history teacher at a first-rate Christian school conducted an informal survey of a class of eleventh graders who had been studying the Great Awakening. To illustrate the power of preaching, one Monday he asked them what they remembered about the sermons they had heard the day before. Roughly half of his students attended churches that were generally expository in their approach— the spoken word—while the other half attended churches with videos and Power Point presentations. Of the former group, nearly all of the students remembered the topic of the sermon, and in many cases they could reproduce a full outline. Of the second group—the group from the high-tech, visually-oriented congregations—half of the students admitted to sleeping during the sermon and the other half couldn't remember the main point of the message, let alone the outline. This admittedly unscientific survey points to an important truth: few things are more powerful and persuasive than a living voice preaching a living Word, and thus the personal proclamation of God and his gospel will never become obsolete.

Here it helps to know a little church history, because wherever systematic expository preaching has been practiced, it has brought great blessing to the church. This is well documented by Hughes Oliphant Old in his seven-volume history of preaching.[12] The technical term for this method is *lectio continua*—the reading and teaching of consecutive passages of Scripture in their biblical context. One notable example is John Chrysostom, the great preacher of the fourth century, who trans-

---

12. Hughes Oliphant Old, *The Reading and Preaching of the Scriptures in the Worship of the Christian Church*, 7 vols. (Grand Rapids, MI: Eerdmans, 1998–).

formed the city of Constantinople by expounding large sections the Bible, especially from the New Testament. Or consider Ulrich Zwingli and John Calvin, who reformed the church primarily through their daily expositions of God's Word. There are more recent examples as well. From his pulpit in Aberdeen, William Still influenced an entire generation of Scottish ministers by preaching and teaching through the entire Bible in fifty years. Similarly, men like Martyn Lloyd-Jones, John Stott, and Dick Lucas exercised a widespread influence from their pulpits in London. And here in America the late James Montgomery Boice and R. Kent Hughes have inspired many men to become better preachers by publishing substantial expositional commentaries on Genesis, Psalms, John, Romans, and many other books of the Bible. The point is that systematic Bible exposition is always beneficial in life-changing and culture-transforming ways. And it will remain beneficial as long as there are sinners who need to be saved and sanctified.

The best reason to practice expository preaching is not simply that it works, however, but because it brings glory to God, which ought to be the ultimate purpose for everything we do. Expository preaching does this by making it clear that all spiritual blessing comes from God's Word and not from any human being. Expository preaching is the kind of preaching that is most in keeping with our belief that the Bible is the very Word of God. When a church grows through the plain teaching of God's Word, it becomes obvious that whatever has been accomplished is not due to the gifts of men but to the grace of God, who alone deserves all the glory.

The apostle Paul was well aware that preaching would not always be popular. This reality seems to lie behind his exhortation to "be ready in season and out of season" (2 Tim. 4:2). Usually this is taken as a comment on Timothy's own personal circumstances. Whether it is convenient for him or not, he must always be ready to preach at a moment's notice. However, the word for "season" (*kairos*) more properly refers to the times in which he lived. Sometimes preaching seems to be in season; at other times it is out of season, according to popular opinion. But whether it is in season or out of season, Bible exposition is the minister's God-given responsibility, and he must keep doing what God has told him to do. Preaching is God's primary and *permanent* method for converting sinners and teaching them to grow in grace.

It is an awesome responsibility to preach to the glory of God. Consider again the charge Paul gave to Timothy: "in the presence of God and of Christ Jesus, who is to judge the living and the dead, and by his appearing and his kingdom: preach the word" (2 Tim. 4:1–2a). This is a solemn charge, urgently given with a view to Christ's second coming.

A calling to pastoral ministry is serious business—a matter of spiritual life and death. Charles Spurgeon said:

> Today there is not very much gospel about; the church has given it up; a great many preachers preach everything but the living truth. This is sad; but it is a strong reason why you and I should teach more gospel than ever. I have often thought to myself—Other men may teach Socialism, deliver lectures, or collect a band of fiddlers, that they may gather a congregation; but I will preach the gospel. I will preach more gospel than ever if I can; I will stick more to the one cardinal point. The other brethren can attend to the odds and ends, but I will keep to Christ crucified. To the men of vast ability, who are looking to the events of the day, I would say, "Allow one poor fool to keep to preaching the gospel." Beloved teachers, be fools for Christ, and keep to the gospel. Don't you be afraid: it has life in it, and it will grow: only you bring it out, and let it grow.[13]

---

13. Charles H. Spurgeon, "The Mustard Seed," in *The Metropolitan Tabernacle Pulpit* 35 (1890; repr. Pasadena, TX: Pilgrim, 1970), 576.

PART FOUR

TRAINING AND EXAMPLE

13

The Seminary and the Sermon

Peter Jensen

Some years ago Kent Hughes and I discussed the question of homiletics training in seminary and the usefulness of a preacher's becoming a professor. Not all good preachers can teach others how to preach. In fact, the two skills do not necessarily belong together at all. Kent himself combines the two abilities, and a seminary might therefore feel that its homiletics instruction would be set to rights by the addition of Dr. Hughes to its faculty.

But would that be a correct judgment? If I were advising a preacher who had been offered a position as homiletics professor, I would suggest a close analysis of the seminary. The question I would ask is this: why is this seminary looking for a practicing preacher as its homiletics professor? Is it because it sees itself as having a weakness in this part of its offering, a weakness that it plans to fix by the simple expedient of adding a good preacher to its faculty? If this is the case, it is likely that the appointment will not succeed and that the new professor will end up frustrated by the experience.

It Takes an Entire Seminary to Produce a Preacher

Classes on homiletics, even classes by master preachers, do not by themselves yield good preachers. It is the business of the whole faculty and the whole curriculum to produce preachers. If the total aim of the seminary is not the sermon, there is no way in the world that the addition of a preaching luminary is going to make much difference. I would advise the would-be professor not to contemplate joining a faculty unless it is clearly the aim and reality of the whole program to graduate good preachers. The instructor in the biblical languages, the church historian, and the pastoral theologian must share this goal, and the curriculum, indeed the life of the community, must be based on it.

This is not such a strange idea. In an earlier day it was the clear aim of Protestant seminaries to graduate preachers. This accounts for some of the features that we still observe in the program. The offering of the biblical languages, for example, is an indication that the graduate is expected to use them in fulfilling his chief pastoral duty, namely, the instruction of the people of God through preaching the Word of God. When seminaries began to make the languages optional, it was a sign that the preaching ministry was no longer regarded as the central role of the pastor. It was also an invitation to those who taught the languages not to teach them in a way that would help with the exposition of the Word. Professors were invited to become scholars or technicians instead of academic pastors, chiefly interested in helping students to acquire and use the skills that they themselves possessed.

This was brought home to me while visiting seminaries in order to learn better how to be the principal of Moore College. The lack of a clear focus on preaching troubled me. I could, of course, understand this in seminaries devoted to shaping the next generation of priests in the Catholic tradition. The formation of such priests in a tradition of heavy emphasis on the sacraments animating pastoral ministry might include preaching, but the priestly role did not center on the Word. However, I discovered in colleges and seminaries of an alleged Protestant persuasion a certain coyness about taking preaching as the main business for which they were set up. This all became strikingly apparent in one famous institution where I asked about preaching. I was promptly told that the student body of the college in question was an expression of the body of Christ. Just as in the body there are many gifts, so one would expect to find in the college a similar range of gifts, with preaching only one of them.

This was an evangelical Protestant college dedicated to graduating ordinands. There was a time when such an institution, clear as to its goal of preparing men for the ministry of the Word, would glory to be known as "a school of the prophets." It is true, of course, that during the twentieth century many of the great Protestant seminaries widened their scope. They accepted many students who did not have a preaching ministry in mind but who wanted to study the Word of God in order to equip them for other ministries. But this hardly seems like a fair reason to set at risk the one fundamental ministry that must be the mark of every church, the ministry of the Word.

Indeed, the effort to produce such ministers would have been entirely consistent with graduating those who labor in other ministries. But a generalist path became dominant. Electives multiplied, and academicians became self-chosen specialists rather than academically gifted pastors. In such a context, it is of hardly any use to employ an eminent preacher to carry the burden of making sure that those who want to be ministers of the Word are properly prepared for such a ministry. By the time they take his courses, the die is cast. Students have not been shaped by teachers or a curriculum or fellow students who have the preaching ministry in mind.

Why It Takes a Whole Seminary to Produce a Preacher: The Nature of a Sermon

Is the issue as crucial as I am suggesting? Consider the reality of the sermon. The wise and godly pastor will minister the Word in a number of ways. There will be the visitation of the sick and dying; there will be the visitation of the home; there will be the one-to-one occasion; there will be the Sunday school class and the lecture; there will be opportunities for question and answer. But basic to all these is that moment when, on a Sunday, as the people of God gather to meet the Lord Jesus Christ in his Word and by his Spirit, their pastor stands before them all to declare and apply the Word. It is the Head of the church supplying the church with his wisdom, exhortation, direction, and rebuke through his under-shepherd. It is the minister's weekly confession of faith—his faith, their faith, the faith. It is a solemn and fundamental occasion for the church.

The Sermon as Truth

The sermon ought to be marked by at least three elements. It must be true, applied, and listenable. First, a sermon must be true. We cannot waste our time on such a solemn occasion with the opinions and the speculations of men. The people gather with all their life experiences, all their needs, all that burdens them and distracts them, all their sins that need to be dealt with, their false and worldly thoughts, their lack of love for one another. They need to hear a word from the Lord. Their needs can be met only through the preaching of the Scriptures, and the best way to accomplish that on a regular and consistent basis is by what we call exposition. There is a place for doctrinal preaching, a place for what we may call topical preaching. But the steady and constant diet of the people of God needs to be the preaching that conforms most closely to their own daily reading of the Scriptures.

There is no substitute for exposition. The basic rule of biblical interpretation is this: the Scriptures interpret the Scriptures. A theological education is a very wonderful experience and almost indispensable for the preacher. But the truth of the matter is that it is only adding marginally to an attentive reading of Scripture based on a confidence that what we are reading is the infallible word of God and that it will interpret itself. It is the good rule of the Reformation that the Scripture is clear enough to be studied by the unlettered and to speak powerfully even to the person whose only book is the Bible. It is the communication of the God who loves to communicate and is well able to speak to us by this method.

The method of exposition by which we move through the Scriptures in an orderly manner is the only one that will deliver us from the conceit of trying to feed the people each week with the husks of our own spiritual experiences or, worse, the heated up version of what we have read during the week in a newspaper. It allows God to set the agenda for the church; it allows Christ to have his right as the head of the church to rule over it with his word and not merely the word of man. If it were not for expository preaching, I would not know what to say to the congregation, and I would fear to stand before them.

Whatever else a theological education does, it must help the pastor to be able to preach in an expository manner. It has failed if it cannot help him do that. The theological education of the pastor has to deliver to him, as far as possible, an understanding of the whole of Scripture. Each part of the Bible has its context both in the book in which it may be found, but also in the Bible as a whole. The skill of the expositor is not in principle different from the skill which any faithful Christian may bring to the task of reading. The more we read the Bible, the better able we are to interpret the individual parts of the Bible.

But the time of intensive study that the pastor is able to give the Scriptures in his seminary days and then, as he is freed to do so, during the week, enables him to have a deeper grasp of the all-important context. In particular, he should be fully aware of the narrative of the Bible, its unfolding theological story, so that he can locate a particular passage on the theological time line; and he should be aware of the overall teaching of the Bible on the subjects that belong to it, so that his reading and exposition of any passage will be enriched by the total revelation of the knowledge of God. In other words, he must have a biblical theology, a theology of the whole. These understandings may legitimately be expected by any congregation of its pastor. The lack of them would constitute a severe disability in the task of pastoring. But is a seminary education geared to produce them?

The Sermon as Application

First, then, the sermon must be true. Second, it must be applied. If we recollect that it is through the Word that Jesus Christ as the head of the church rules his people, we are entitled to expect that the preacher will make clear the connection between the Word that he is expounding and the life of the church. To say that this is often handled poorly is an understatement. Sometimes no attempt is made at all, and the preacher simply delivers exegesis in the place of exposition. At other times the application is the same on every occasion ("we must evangelize more—please bring people to church with you!") no matter what part of the Word is preached. At other times the Word becomes merely the source of illustrative material for the preacher's doctrinal or pietistic or political fantasies. Often the call to repentance is muted or trivialized, like the "mint, dill and cumin" of the Pharisees. It seems very difficult to listen to the Word itself and accept its direction for our thoughts and lives.

I have used the word *application* for this process, but it is inadequate for what needs to occur. For a start, it suggests two processes, exegesis and application, two tasks that have to be attended to separately in the process of sermon construction. But we do not read the Bible like that. We are looking for it to edify and instruct us more directly than the word *application* suggests. It gives some grounds for the results I have portrayed above. I wonder whether the word *implication* may be better—not so much the application but the implication of a text. We need to draw out what is there rather than to add on something that we hope is consistent with what is there.

The task still remains difficult. It requires a knowledge of human nature, of the life of the church, of the world around us, and of the meaning of the text that addresses us as the Word of Christ. But here we come to the indispensable part played by Christian doctrine in preparing the preacher. The homiletics professor cannot do his job unless the teachers of theology are doing their job. Indeed, if a seminary that is genuinely trying to graduate preachers has to choose between having an instructor in preaching and a theologian, there should be no hesitation in choosing the theologian. The job of the theologian in training preachers is far more important. The role of the homiletics professor is secondary. It cannot be remedial for a prior failure in theology.

Systematic theology is the central, organizing subject of the theological curriculum. It is most close to the knowledge of God that is the one great theme of the whole curriculum. It summarizes the teaching of the Bible on all the major subjects of the Bible and shows how they interrelate. It deepens and corrects exposition in the light of the whole biblical Word. It enables the student to begin the task of comparing and critiquing the theological systems that lay claim to being Christian. It sets the foundations for the study of theological ethics and pastoral theology. It is the bridge over which Christian truth marches to confront and interact with the ideas and practices of the world.

It is tragic that much of the way in which systematic theology is approached leaves the student wondering what it has to do with his chosen task of preaching the Word. Where theological study consists of extended expositions of the great names in theology, where students are expected to know a great deal about Barth or Calvin but not the scriptural sources from which these giants of theological study drew their inspiration, the student is never equipped to do his main job. The study of contemporary theology, the study of classical theology, have their place. But they cannot take the place of the study of God's Word. The business of the theological professor is not to introduce his students to Berkhof or Pannenberg but to introduce them to God with whatever help Pannenberg and Berkhof and Calvin and Athanasius may give to this enterprise. The student must be left with the impression that the supreme textbook of the theology course is the Bible itself.

A failure at this point is fatal to the enterprise of producing preachers. The Sunday morning congregation could quite easily exist without ever knowing that a man called Calvin ever walked the earth. They are not looking to be fed Barth. They seek the Lord in his Word. Systematic theology is a crucial discipline for bringing out the implications of the Word and showing its relevance to the world we inhabit. If the theologian does not consistently handle the Scriptures in a way that shows these links, we cannot expect his students to do it. The aim of the theology class cannot be less than to help students know God and be equipped to make him known.

The Sermon as Listenable

The third necessary element of the sermon must be that it is listenable. To state the obvious, the sermon must obey the laws of genuine communication; the boring sermon is a deadly thing. Now it may be thought that here at least the homiletics professor is on home ground. In some cases he has been appointed precisely because he has mastered the art of communication and is adept at getting people to listen to him. It is hoped, although the hope may well be confounded, that he has sufficient self-knowledge to be able to analyze his own success and pass the secret of it on to others. In fact, of course, it may well be that the best professor, like the best athletics coach, may not be outstanding at doing the task himself; he may be outstanding in his insight as to what needs to be done. However, let us assume that the fine preacher and the fine teacher are found in the best person. Let us assume that he can do the (admittedly important) work of training preachers to communicate effectively. It may still do nothing to save the seminary from producing poor preachers.

We are not, after all, looking for mere rhetoricians. Indeed, some of the best preaching, even the most listenable preaching, does not meet the usual criteria for style and communication. Or, to put the matter another way, its communication is of a truth so powerful that it grips by its substance, not its style. Its essence is dramatic, not because it tries to be dramatic, but because, in this world, truth is inherently dramatic. Let me explain.

The essence of drama is conflict. That is what makes audiences turn out night after dreary night to watch television. The hook that brings us back is conflict, conflict of persons, of ideas, of events, of moral choice. Television is soul-destroying because it uses the cheapest of tricks to create drama, such as in the endless deployment of the crisis in human lives caused by murder. Conflict creates suspense and uncertainty; it exposes the nature of human beings and life; it exposes the audience to moral and spiritual dilemmas. Interestingly, it is very rare for drama to succeed over any extended period if it does not contain a morally appropriate end. We actually prefer virtue to triumph; we do not like programs in which evil wins consistently. Of course in the world of television this is low-grade stuff, morally deadening and often demeaning. But in the hands of a master, drama can shake and transform. There is a high moral purpose at work, which we recognize as something that intersects with our world and even challenges our sense of identity. It can create profound change by telling the truth with power.

I do not suppose that Amos went to homiletics lectures or would have benefited much from such attendance. It is true that we can see rhetorical device and technique in how he delivered the Word of the Lord. But his technique was not the essence of his potency and his ability to arrest his audience. Classes in Hebrew rhetoric would not have made him a better prophet. The truth that he had from God contradicted everything his contemporaries believed and hoped in. It placed him in deep conflict. He was an unforgettable—and eminently listenable—prophet because he was first of all confronted by the word of God in his own person and then spoke it with a blazing passion and boldness which were startling and provoking.

Why It Takes a Whole Seminary to Produce a Preacher: The Nature of the Preacher's Message

The preacher is a living contradiction: as a sinful and finite creature, he preaches on behalf of the eternal and holy God. That contradiction is both his despair and his hope. It is his despair, because he sees contradiction in all he does and recognizes that the root cause of it is sin. He cannot keep to the high standards that he preaches. He finds that his own love for the world is greater than his love for God. He also recognizes that the truth that he preaches is contradicted by the world he lives in at innumerable points. He is angered by the very sin of which he is part. Furthermore, the Scriptures are beyond his intellectual, moral, and spiritual grasp. He sees in them depths and difficulties that cry out for investigation and understanding.

Struggling with the Text

And yet these contradictions are also his hope as a preacher. The difficulties of the text force him to struggle and wrestle with it until light comes. I am not suggesting for a moment that it is the duty of the preacher to share his doubts with the congregation; a man in the grip of systemic doubts should step down from the role of ambassador of Christ until those doubts come to some sort of resolution. I am saying that there is an interrogative mood in which Scripture is to be approached—submissive and yet questioning. There is a variety of smooth preaching that replicates what it sees as the main theme of a text but does not bring to the surface anything in the text that surprises, contradicts, creates tension. Smooth preaching rushes too easily to solutions, or more frequently, fails to see or fails to mention the stress points. In doing so, it becomes dull; more important, it dulls the Word of God and fails to challenge.

But it is not simply a matter of a difficulty of exegesis. The preacher must also struggle against a text that contradicts his life as a sinner. Personal repentance is a priority for the preacher. His listeners will sense that struggle in what he says, and they themselves will begin to recognize their human position as sinful and yet beloved creatures. His struggle against sin, his own striving to be holy, will be apparent in his intensity, in the moral force and power with which he speaks. This is not something of which the preacher will be aware; you cannot manufacture it; an artificial godliness will soon expose itself as a sham. But the most powerful prophetic preaching comes from those who have themselves met sin and evil on the field of battle and triumphed in the Lord's strength.

Struggling with the World and Contemporary Culture

The preacher struggles against sin. But he must also struggle against the world, against the culture in which he and his listeners live. Entering that contest will enable him to speak transformingly into the ears of those who themselves are being tempted to conform to the world. Exegesis is the indispensable groundwork of the sermon, but only the groundwork. If expository preaching is merely the deliverance of exegesis, it fails in its duty. From exegesis through biblical theology to systematic theology and so to the culture beyond is the route that must consistently be followed. If it is followed, and if the culture is understood, the sermon will inevitably have all the drama of truth about it.

How can the Christian faith so preached be anything else but dramatic? We live in a culture of the closed world order. Instinctively, our educated contemporaries believe that the world is governed by unbreakable laws of science; that, if there is a God, he lolls on his throne, letting the world run its own aimless course while he fails to intervene. The Christian preacher is charged with the impossible task of declaring that a resurrection has occurred in history, and that of a man born of a virgin. These are utter impossibilities. So great is the confrontation that our society turns its face away by treating these claims as though they are myths. You may have your consoling story, the world declares, as long as you do not trouble me to think not only that they did take place, but that such things could take place in a world such as this one. Announce them as myths and I will smile at you; announce them as facts and I will scorn you, so says our world.

And yet, Sunday by Sunday the preachers of the faith announce the resurrection as though it were as important and confronting as a suburban train journey. There is no shock, no drama, no conflict, because we choose not to confront the world that declares that such things do not happen. We may believe that we are announcing an historical event, but we announce it in such a way as to make the congregation yawn and our culture smile. We do not analyze unbelief and call it out. We do not even seem to have the intellectual resources to do so. I would gather a crowd more easily to a speech on climate change than to a speech in which I announced that a man has risen from the dead.

217

The genuineness of the preacher will also be tested by his willingness to speak the unpopular and divisive truth to the congregation on whom he depends for a living. In our day, the unpopular truth is about such matters as sexual ethics, divorce, and the ministry of women. True expository preaching will lead a preacher to these subjects as he expounds the Scripture systematically. The cowardly and man-pleasing evangelical preacher will ensure that he is missing in action when it comes to teaching these difficult parts of the Word. His preferred option will be to expound them in such a way that he does not have to make a choice. He will prefer peace to war; he will sound right to those who pay his stipend, but he will not speak with a prophetic voice, and the blessing of God will not attend his ministry no matter how eloquent he may be.

What Kind of Seminary Can Produce a Preacher?

Whether a preacher will be such a prophet should not be determined in the homiletics class. It has to do with what sort of man he is rather than what sort of communicator he is. It is true that a course in sacred rhetoric may be of benefit. It is true that a good professor of homiletics will raise the very points that I am making. But it is also true that if the seminary is such that it relies on the professor of homiletics alone to make these points, it has failed. For the shaping of the person of the preacher, his own personal encounter with the living God, his capacity to struggle and wrestle with the Bible and to struggle and wrestle with the world, his capacity, in short, to see in himself the contradictions and conflicts which go to make up prophetic drama, do not occur first and foremost in the preaching class. If they do not occur in the study, in the library, in fellowship with other students, in the classroom, and preeminently in the chapel, they will not occur in a course of lectures on preaching. If a preacher is not a man of God, it will be difficult to preach the Word of God.

Will a seminary produce preachers? Only if it actually tries to do so and if the whole program and the whole faculty are geared to that end. Only if it is God-centered and student-centered. There are few greater challenges than those involved in preaching the Word of God. In a relatively short, uninterrupted discourse, the preacher must expound the Bible in a way that is true, applied, and listenable. Furthermore, it is to be done to the same audience week in and week out. To do so effectively requires intellectual and spiritual qualities of the highest order. Indeed, it is a more demanding task than that of being a professor. The professor in a seminary is usually able to specialize in one branch of Christian knowledge. He or she may become an expert in the Old Testament, or in philosophy or church history. Professors can communicate with less than optimal skills, since their students are assessed and have to take the course. They can afford to dig deep and to take the odd excursus. They are not faced with the relentless demands of the pulpit.

If the seminary program is intended to train preachers, it must be assumed that the different disciplines that make up the program have some relevance to the preacher's task. Certainly I would argue that studies in subjects such as church history and philosophy contribute critically. But the preacher has to do what no professor does: he must bring together, focus, and use all the resources that the seminary gives him at one moment in time. Even if he makes no formal reference to church history in his sermon, his knowledge of history is what helps create the depth and texture of the sermon, part of what gives it authority. In other words, the preacher has to *integrate* all his learning as well as all his experience in a few moments.

And this is the final challenge for the seminary. Seminary education has become fragmented. The different disciplines ignore each other; the experts are interested in their own field of expertise; the student is permitted to choose his own courses to a significant degree. The very person in the seminary least able to integrate the learning—namely, the student—is being required to perform this feat on his own and thus equip himself for his major role as a preacher of God's Word. It is not surprising that even amongst evangelicals there has been a move away from exposition of Scripture to topical preaching with its accompanying dangers of shallowness and repetition. Where this occurs, it reflects the inability of the seminary to make its own studies coherent and actually useful for the task of training pastors who are preachers.

I believe that the seminary must center its program on the knowledge of God before it begins to think about any particular academic discipline. This knowledge of God, which is the basic aim of every course, comes via the Scriptures and has a necessary impact on the lives of students and faculty alike. This is the key to the integration of the seminary, not just the program of the seminary.

In short, the professor of homiletics has a great job. But it is worth doing only if he can be assured that the whole seminary is committed to producing expository preachers and that this is evident in the faculty as well as the program. The seminary that does this will not be less adept in its other roles of teaching the faith and apologetics and ethics and pastoral counseling and the rest, since preaching demands a skill in these roles. But if in the course of its history the seminary has wavered from this task, and has become a nursery for professors or church musicians or educationists or lay training, even the great Chrysostom himself would have difficulty in fostering preachers if he had the misfortune to be employed as the professor of homiletics in such a place.

14

Multiplying Men:
Training and Deploying
Gospel Ministers

Jon M. Dennis

The theme for this volume in honor of Kent Hughes is taken from 2 Timothy 4:2: "Preach the word." Every preacher knows the glory of those words. They resonate in the marrow of our bones. To preach the word—it is the divine privilege of a pastor. It is the thing to which the apostle Paul—and Kent Hughes as well—gave his life. In a day and age when preaching God's Word is often treated as irrelevant, marginal, or unimportant, the voice of the apostle Paul rings out with urgency to restore the dignity to the preaching of God's Word that it deserves.

"Preach the word," writes the apostle Paul. As he writes, Paul looks back over the history of his life with a sense of eternal finality and upward to the presence of God and of Jesus Christ. Paul charges Timothy to preach the Word, not in view of the world, not in view even of the lost, but in view of God the Father and Jesus Christ who will judge the living and the dead. Paul writes, in a sense, on the brink of eternity sensing what Kent, now entering a new phase of gospel ministry, must sense as well: that he has poured out his life as a drink offering for the gospel.

This essay is written to examine 2 Timothy 2:2 as a model and call to train and deploy gospel ministers. It is not intended to be scholarly, but pastoral—written from a pastor's heart to the church and to the next generation of pastors and church planters. I intend to look closely at this single verse and its context and draw out eight principles for training and deploying gospel workers.

The context of 2 Timothy is well known. Paul writes to Timothy in the last stage of his life while imprisoned, most likely in Rome. Though Paul expects to live for a bit longer (he asks Timothy to come to him in 4:9), he certainly writes as a man who knows he is in the final phase of life. He writes, in fact, as if his life is already ebbing away: "For I am *already* being poured out as a drink offering, and the time of my departure has come. I *have* fought the good fight, I *have* finished the race, I *have* kept the faith" (2 Tim. 4:6–7).

Paul envisions his life as if it is nearly over. He writes as if he is in the presence of God already—yet with his feet placed firmly on the earth. One senses that Paul balances on the edge of eternity. What is on his heart and mind? What are Paul's last thoughts in this final stage of life and ministry? As Paul sees the finish line of his ministry, his life-ending thoughts are upon the critical importance of the preservation of the gospel. The gospel is what he has lived and suffered for.

He writes, "I charge you in the presence of God and of Christ Jesus, who is to judge the living and the dead, and by his appearing and his kingdom." In other words, the apostle Paul writes to Timothy with a blood-earnest intensity and with the vividness of eternal realities before him.

So let us take this one verse from the letter and meditate on its urgent call for training of others for gospel ministry. From this single phrase, familiar as it is, we can draw a number of principles for training and deploying men into ministry:[1] "and what you have heard from me in the presence of many witnesses entrust to faithful men who will be able to teach others also" (2 Tim. 2:2).

Entrusting the Gospel with Care

The first thing we see when we look closely at 2 Timothy 2:2 is the *care* that Paul envisions that the training and deploying of ministers must take. The word Paul chooses when he commands Timothy to multiply men for gospel ministry is the word "entrust."

---

1. In this context, Paul is thinking mainly of the training of men here, as his interest is likely in leaving behind elders. See William D. Mounce, *Pastoral Epistles*, Word Biblical Commentary (Nashville: Thomas Nelson, 2000), 504. However, Paul is not unconcerned with training of women and writes elsewhere concerning this subject (Titus 2:3–5).

The word literally means to "entrust for safekeeping, give over . . . commend" or "to deposit, commit to one's charge."[2] It is the same word, for instance, that Jesus uses when he cries out to the Father on the cross, saying, "Into your hands I *commit* my spirit" (Luke 23:46). At the desolation of the cross, the Son knows the one safe place for his spirit is the Father's hands. Jesus uses the word elsewhere in a parable to emphasize faithful stewardship. He says, "To whom they *entrusted* much, they will demand the more" (Luke 12:48). For Paul the gospel is not merely a message, but a deposit or trust given to him.

So it is that the apostle Paul, looking over the span of his life, clings to the necessity of the gospel's being instilled or deposited in others with great care and intentionality. The gospel must not die with him! One can almost sense the hushed breath of holy presence when Paul speaks of transmitting the gospel to the next generation. For Paul the gospel message is a holy treasure committed by none other than God to his charge.

Part of the reason Paul thinks of the gospel as something so valuable to entrust to others is that *God* himself had first entrusted the gospel to Paul. Earlier in 2 Timothy Paul wrote, "But I am not ashamed (of suffering for the gospel) for I know whom I have believed, and I am convinced that he is able to guard until that Day what has been *entrusted* to me" (1:12). The gospel is the divine treasure that God directly entrusted to Paul. God placed the message in Paul's possession to guard *in God's strength*, not his own. How long? How long is Paul to guard the gospel in God's strength? Verse 12 says, "Until that Day." "That day" is the eschatological return of Jesus Christ to reward his saints for their labor. Later he writes, "Henceforth there is laid up for me the crown of righteousness, which the Lord, the righteous judge, will award to me *on that Day*, and not only to me but also to all who have loved his appearing" (4:8).

So the gospel is a treasure to guard—in God's strength. This is not just true for Paul, but for Timothy too. If God gave the message to Paul, Paul also deposits the same gift, the same gospel, with Timothy to guard in the strength of the Spirit. Paul writes, "By *the Holy Spirit* who dwells within us, *guard* the good deposit *entrusted* to you" (2 Tim. 1:14). So we see the beginning of a chain of entrusting—from God to Paul to Timothy. Each is participating in guarding the gospel.

What we must not lose sight of in the training of others is a simple truth: *The gospel is a treasure.* It is a possession of the highest value. It is

---

2. Frederick William Danker, ed., *Greek-English Lexicon of the New Testament and Other Early Christian Literature*, 3rd ed. (Chicago: University of Chicago Press, 2000) s.v. "entrust."

a message to be cherished. It is a responsibility, a privileged possession, a trust. If we guard our earthly possessions, invest them in banks and put them under lock and key—it is no wonder that we can guard the gospel only in God's strength.

Paul, as he sees his own life receding from him, thinks about what is most important. What will he leave behind? What will be his legacy? What will he entrust to others? Only that which was entrusted to him. This he will entrust to others.

So it is for us in our day. As we watch Kent make his way to the finish line of his local ministry—the urgency of entrusting the gospel to others is heightened.

What a high calling for the pastor and for all of God's people! God has given the church and the pastor a coin of infinite value. Martyn Lloyd-Jones in his classic book *Preaching and Preachers* has written, "The moment we realize man's true need and see the only answer, it becomes clear that *only those who are in possession of this understanding can impart this message* to those who lack it."[3] We have the gospel! Lloyd-Jones goes on to emphasize the importance of preachers. "The preacher alone is the one who can do this. He is the only one who is in a position to deal with the greatest need of the world."[4] Both the church and preachers in particular have a great responsibility to pass on the gospel.

Could anything be more valuable than the message of life and death, the message of salvation? When we see the care with which Paul speaks of the gospel it motivates us to also pass on the gospel with the same care. If the financial investors of our day, Goldman Sachs and others, take such care with the deposits they receive, how much greater care must the pastor and the church take with the coins of the priceless gospel? We will never multiply men as we might until we feel, as Paul certainly did as he finished his ministry, the exceeding eternal value of what has been entrusted to us.

Passing on the Apostolic Message

Related to the *value* of the gospel in training gospel workers, we must also think about its *content*. Notice that when Paul tells Timothy *what* is to be passed on, he speaks of the gospel itself—the apostolic message. Paul writes, "What *you* have heard *from me* . . . entrust to faithful men."

---

3. Martyn Lloyd-Jones, *Preaching and Preachers* (Grand Rapids, MI: Zondervan, 1972), 29 (emphasis in original).

4. Ibid.

What Paul wants transferred is not merely his lifestyle or personality, it was Paul's teaching, it was content, it was the message that Timothy had heard Paul preach so many times. Timothy was not at liberty to simply invent a gospel or to change Paul's. He was constrained to "rightly handling the word of truth" (2:15). Paul emphasizes the centrality of the gospel a few verses earlier in 2 Timothy 2:8 where he writes, "Remember *Jesus Christ*, risen from the dead, the offspring of David, as preached in *my* gospel." As Paul felt his life ebbing away and sensed the awe of Christ as eternal judge, his emphasis was on the transference of the *gospel* itself.

So, let us train men to preach the gospel. It is the gospel centered on Jesus—his life and his work—that saves the lost; it is the gospel centered on Jesus Christ that strengthens the church. Paul was inflamed with the gospel. He could preach nothing else. He awoke thinking about it, preached it during the day, and sometimes went far into the night heralding it.

The men that our churches and seminaries train for gospel ministry must know all of the Scriptures, the facts and details, from Genesis to Revelation—but they must know how it all centers on the person and work of Jesus Christ. We can preach in a way that does not remember Jesus Christ risen from the dead as preached in Paul's gospel, and we must train our men to avoid it. Jesus himself taught the disciples after the resurrection how everything in the Law and Prophets and Psalms were fulfilled in himself (Luke 24:44).

Charles Spurgeon recounts a moment when someone complained that he had gone to hear a preacher the previous Sunday who had not preached Christ. In response another remarked that "perhaps it was not the due season." Spurgeon then writes, "But, my brethren, the due season for preaching Christ is *every time you preach*. God's children are always hungry and no bread will satisfy them but that which comes down from heaven."[5]

Charles Simeon's aim was to preach in such a way as to "humble the sinner, exalt the savior and to promote holiness."[6] Lloyd-Jones called this giving the listener a sense of God. He wrote, "Preaching is theology coming through a man who is on fire."[7] "What is the chief end of preaching? I like to think it is this. It is to give men and women a sense of God and his presence. . . . I can forgive the preacher almost anything if he gives me a sense of God, if he gives me something for my soul . . . if he

5. C. H. Spurgeon, *An All-Round Ministry: Addresses to Ministers and Students* (Edinburgh: Banner of Truth, 2000), 265.

6. Charles Simeon, *Expository Outlines of the Whole Bible* (Grand Rapids, MI: Baker, 1988), xxi.

7. Martyn Lloyd-Jones, *Preaching and Preachers*, 97.

gives me some dim glimpse of the majesty and the glory of God, the love of Christ my Savior, and the magnificence of the gospel."[8] This must be our aim in our training—to give a sense of the majesty of God and the magnificence of the gospel. Paul's message was something alive, dynamic—not static, not inconsequential. Paul's message stirred cities, shook homes. This is what he wanted Timothy to transfer: the power and content of his message.

As Nehemiah wept upon hearing that the wall of Jerusalem was broken down, so should we also weep to see neighborhoods or churches without gospel witness in them, or churches that have turned to politics or psychology rather than the gospel-centered preaching of Jesus Christ. Gospel centered expository preaching is uncovering the raw glory of God from a particular passage and showing how it relates to Christ.

If we want to fulfill a ministry of gospel multiplication, then gospel-centered *content* in our training is critical. As Paul nears the finish line of ministry and remembers the turning away from the gospel in Asia and foresees the hardness of days to come for Timothy, it is his own words that he emphasizes must be passed on. The apostolic message of the gospel is at the heart of multiplication.

There are so many things that might be multiplied in the modern church today—good things even. We can multiply music, we can multiply churches, we can multiply services; we can multiply people, marriages, and ministries. But if we do not multiply the gospel-centered message of the apostles, then we are merely building monuments to ourselves. Teaching is what Paul wants passed on. He writes later, "You, however, have followed my teaching, my conduct, my aim in life, my faith" (2 Tim. 3:10). It is teaching he is concerned about. It is the message that Paul wants Timothy to guard with his life: "guard the good deposit entrusted to you."

It would be impossible to overstate how important the gospel is in Paul's understanding of multiplying men. It is the gospel for which Paul suffers (1:8, 12), the gospel for which Paul has been appointed an apostle and teacher (1:11). Elsewhere Paul emphasizes that the gospel is not only what we are saved by (1 Cor. 15:2; Rom. 1:16), but it is what is to be taught as of first importance. Why? Why Paul's finish-line emphasis on the gospel in multiplying ministers? Certainly one reason is that it is the gospel that the teachers of the day were turning away from. He writes of his opponents, "Their talk will spread like gangrene. Among them are Hymenaeus and Philetus, *who have swerved from the truth,* saying that the resurrection has already happened" (2 Tim. 2:17–18). Earlier in the

---

8. Martyn Lloyd-Jones, *Preaching and Preachers*, 97–98.

same letter, Paul wrote, "You are aware that all who are in Asia turned away from me, among whom are Phygelus and Hermogenes" (1:15).

As Paul nears his own execution he sees that much of his fruit has turned away. It is with a sense of abandonment that he writes later in the letter, "Do your best to come to me soon. For Demas, in love with this present world, has deserted me and gone to Thessalonica. Crescens has gone to Galatia, Titus to Dalmatia. Luke alone is with me" (2 Tim. 4:9–11).

In the gospel, Paul tells us, God manifests "the appearing of our Savior Christ Jesus, who abolished death and brought life and immortality to life through the gospel." (2 Tim. 1:10) The gospel is our life, our salvation! The gospel is not a matter of secondary importance but of first importance (1 Cor. 15:3.) All of our efforts in deploying and training men for ministry must have at their very heart the gospel itself.

Entrusting the Gospel in a Context of Community

The next important principle from Paul's charge on multiplying the next generation of gospel leaders is the principle of *training within the context of community*. Paul writes, "What you have heard from me *in the presence of many witnesses* entrust to faithful men." In other words, when Paul entrusted the gospel to Timothy personally, it was not in isolation, merely in one-on-one contexts—though Paul did take Timothy with him when he traveled. Rather, Timothy learned the gospel message and how to do gospel ministry from Paul as Paul taught publicly in places like the synagogue in Corinth or the homes of believers like Titius Justus (Acts 18:5–8).

Jesus used the same principle. He sometimes trained the twelve disciples alone behind closed doors, but just as often Jesus taught them through his *public* ministry throughout all the cities and villages. For instance, the Sermon on the Mount was preached to his disciples with the crowds pressing in behind (Matt. 5:1). His classroom for training the disciples was on-the-job, the mobile environment of the dusty road, the noisy market, and the open plain. Even the training of his closest circle of disciples, Peter, James, and John, was done within the community of the other nine disciples.

In other words, Jesus trained in community. He *would* speak to individuals such as the woman at the well or Nicodemus. But he intentionally built a community of men around him. So it must be for us. Pastors need to train other younger men within the context of the local church. Our churches must build training communities within the local ministries that specifically recognize, challenge, and train younger men for gospel ministry.

One of the most beautiful and enduring marks of Kent Hughes's legacy is not merely the growth of the church he pastored or the many books that he wrote. It is the men that he trained—in the context of community. Many younger men have learned to preach by hearing him preach. Fathers and mothers had the gospel passed on to them in the presence of many witnesses. On November 19, 2006, I had the privilege of watching Kent "finish" twenty-seven years of pastoral ministry at a retirement celebration in an evening service at College Church. What struck me most was what happens when the gospel is faithfully preached in a single location for many years: the ministry of the gospel is multiplied, young pastors are trained and mentored for ministry, and hundreds of committed Christians are equipped for the gospel. God allowed Kent to create a ministry that reinforced dedication to the study of God's Word.

Put differently—as a principle—preaching is often more caught than taught. What will multiply godly expository preachers more than anything else? It will be men devoting themselves to pastoring and preaching in their local contexts and at the same time intentionally training younger preachers "in the presence of many witnesses." I thank God for the classroom instruction of my own seminary training. But I also thank God for the training I received within the context of the local church. As a freshman in high school, I watched my youth pastor preach and teach. But it was later, when he challenged me to join him in ministry by teaching junior high students, that I began to see how to do ministry.

Later, in seminary, I had a similar experience. As I finished up my coursework, I was on a dynamic pastoral staff. So I had the chance to wrestle through the theological issues from the classroom within the context of the community of a pastoral staff. More churches will be planted this way and more future pastors will be trained if we stay faithful to preaching and pastoring in our local contexts—all the while training up others.

For a number of years in the church in America there has been a strong emphasis on "discipling." Usually we think of discipling as meeting with someone one-on-one for Bible study. This is important. But it wasn't Jesus' or Paul's primary method. Yes, Paul brought Timothy and Barnabas with him. But their training was on the dusty roads of Palestine, learning as they went in community together. The main way that both Jesus and Paul multiplied preachers was in the context of community.

They taught others to do ministry, to preach by equipping within the context of community.

A Vision of Multiplication

Related to training within the context of *community* is *training for multiplication*. In his little volume *The Art of Prophesying* William Perkins (1558–1602) has a chapter called "The Scarcity of True Ministers." There he argues that "good ministers are one in a thousand."[9] He sees what Paul saw—the need for the gospel to be entrusted to others—the principle of multiplication. He writes, "If ministers are few in number, then all you can do is *increase* their number."[10] He adds, "So, let every minister both in his teaching and his conversation work in such a way that he honours his calling, so that he may attract others to share his love for it." This is multiplication. We attract others to the ministry of the gospel in such a way that they *share* our love for it.

For Paul the increase of ministers comes by thinking "generationally." Often we only think about teaching or preaching the gospel to those who are directly in front of us. We counsel with an aim to help solve the immediate problem. We instruct in a classroom to instill biblical knowledge. But our teaching ends with the people before us.

Not so with Paul. Paul looks out on four generations in his charge to Timothy to train others:

* generation 1: Paul
* generation 2: Timothy
* generation 3: Faithful men
* generation 4: Others

He writes, "and what you [generation 2] have heard from me [generation 1] in the presence of many witnesses entrust to faithful men [generation 3] who will be able to teach others also" (generation 4).

The principle of multiplication for several generations might be illustrated this way. I remember as a youth pastor complimenting a parent on how well I thought he was doing in raising his children. The parent turned and looked me straight in the eyes and said with all seriousness, "How do you know?" A little taken aback I said that I knew the parent's children. The parent remarked, "You won't know how good a parent I

9. William Perkins, *The Art of Prophesying* (Edinburgh: Banner of Truth, 1996), 96.
10. William Perkins, *The Art of Prophesying*, 98.

am for several more generations—until you see if my children's children are still praising God." The parent had the same generational view that Paul had. Our training of others—even our children—should look out far beyond this generation.

This is in fact what we find elsewhere in the Scriptures. In Psalm 78 we read that God "established a testimony in Jacob and appointed a law in Israel, which he commanded our *fathers* [generation one] to teach to their *children* [generation two], that the next generation might know them, *the children yet unborn* [generation three], and arise and tell them to their *children* [generation four]" (vv. 5–6).

We need a vision for multiplying the gospel beyond us! As we seek to train new pastors and plant new churches, we need the same view. When we come to the end of our ministries as Paul did, we want to be able to say that the gospel has not only been passed to us from our mentors, but from us to new churches and new gospel ministers beyond them. May our churches entrust the gospel in a way that multiplies throughout the world!

Entrusting the Gospel to Faithful Men

Critically related to the *multiplication* of the gospel for several generations is the matter of the *character* of those to whom we entrust the gospel. Robert Coleman makes this point in his classic work *The Master Plan of Evangelism*. He calls it the principle of selection. He writes, "It all started by Jesus calling a few men to follow Him. This revealed immediately the direction his evangelistic strategy would take. His concern was not with programs that would reach the multitudes, but *with men whom the multitudes would follow . . . men were to be his Method of winning the world to God*."[11] Men of character—and men who would be able to invest their lives in others—were the ones that Jesus chose. Coleman writes later, "Jesus devoted most of his remaining life on earth to these few disciples. He literally staked His whole ministry upon them."[12]

Paul charges Timothy to select some—not all—to entrust with the ministry of gospel multiplication. So, whom to select for gospel ministry? The criterion for who is to be selected could not be more simple. It is "*faithful* men who will be able to teach others also." A faithful man is one who is "trustworthy, dependable."[13]

---

11. Robert Coleman, *The Master Plan of Evangelism* (Old Tappan, NJ: Revell, 1987), 21.

12. Robert Coleman, *The Master Plan of Evangelism*, 27.

13. Frederick William Danker, ed., *Greek-English Lexicon of the New Testament and Other Early Christian Literature.*

Paul himself gives faithfulness as the reason that God chose him for ministry. He writes, "I thank him who has given me strength because he judged me *faithful*, appointing me to his service, though formerly I was a blasphemer" (1 Tim. 1:12–13). Likewise, those whom Paul personally selected for ministry alongside him were often listed as faithful. Of Timothy he writes "That is why I sent you Timothy, my beloved and *faithful* child in the Lord" (1 Cor. 4:17). He speaks similarly of his associate Tychicus in Ephesians 6:21, calling him "Tychicus the beloved brother and *faithful* minister in the Lord." In Colossians 4:9, he calls Onesimus "our *faithful* and beloved brother, who is one of you," and he calls Epaphras "our beloved fellow servant . . . a *faithful* minister of Christ on your behalf." (Col. 1:7) Such are the men to whom Paul personally entrusted the gospel.

Faithful men are those to whom we entrust the gospel. Of course whether someone is faithful is not always immediately clear. How do you know if someone is faithful? Phillip Jensen in Australia speaks of having a category of young men that he calls "Blokes Worth Watching." These are men to test against the descriptions of faithfulness in Titus 1:5–9 and 1 Timothy 3:1–7.

The gospel needs to be multiplied. Faithful men are the ones to whom we look to entrust it to.

The Role of Suffering for the Gospel

Related to the principles of community, multiplication, and faithfulness is what comes next in Paul's charge. The men we train must be ready to *suffer* as soldiers, athletes, and hardworking farmers. The next verse from Paul following the charge to Timothy to entrust the gospel to others is, "Share in suffering as a good soldier of Christ Jesus." (2 Tim. 2:3) It is an apt image. Soldiers know that the discipline of warfare requires personal sacrifice. They understand how to enter the tough arena of boots and blood and mud. They commit themselves to physical discipline.

Soldiers are not the only image Paul presents for preparing to share in suffering. He also writes of the athlete and farmer. He writes in 2 Timothy 2:4-6, "No *soldier* gets entangled in civilian pursuits, since his aim is to please the one who enlisted him. An *athlete* is not crowned unless he competes according to the rules. It is the hardworking *farmer* who ought to have the first share of the crops." All three are images of discipline with the final two promising reward. The soldier disciplines himself single-mindedly to obey the orders of his commanding officer. The athlete disciplines himself with self-control hoping to be crowned.

And the farmer disciplines himself to work knowing that he will share in the harvest. So our curriculum must train men to be physically and spiritually disciplined.

The men whom Timothy trains need to be ready to suffer. Nearly the entirety of the letter trumpets this call to Timothy. In 1:8 Paul writes, "Therefore do not be ashamed of the testimony about our Lord, nor of me his prisoner, but *share in suffering* for the gospel by the power of God." Later in his the famous and magisterial charge "to preach the word" Paul writes, "As for you, always be sober-minded, *endure suffering*, do the work of an evangelist, fulfill your ministry" (2 Tim. 4:5).

What an amazing call! How easy it is for us to overlook the suffering in training. How often do we hear today the call to suffering? How often do we as Christians heed the words of Paul to embrace suffering? In the Western church in particular this is a very difficult reality to embrace. Yet, it is part and parcel of the call of Paul in 2 Timothy.

So, we ask the question: as we seek to multiply men—as we seek to take faithful men and train and deploy them for ministry—will suffering play a part? It isn't an easy virtue to weave into the seminary curriculum. But it certainly was a part of the apostle Paul's curriculum for Timothy. Share in suffering. Endure suffering.

Certainly Jesus expected suffering. Who can forget those piercing words of Christ's, "If anyone would come after me, let him deny himself and take up his cross daily and follow me" (Luke 9:23). If this is the call for every Christian, should it not be even more so the path for those we train to lead and teach others?

Let us train men to suffer. Let's train preachers who feel called not to live on flowery beds of ease but to wade in the mud of the soldier. Let's raise up not merely those "who wear soft clothing in kings' houses" but those like John the Baptist who are called to a lifestyle that goes against the prevailing culture.

Jesus' call to *all* Christians is to take up their cross and follow. How much more acquainted with suffering must the preacher be, who leads a procession of crossbearers. We must raise up a generation of men who are willing to suffer as good soldiers, athletes, and hard-working farmers.

Relationship as a Requirement

Part of the reason Paul could so easily call Timothy to suffer is that Timothy was familiar with Paul's own life and suffering. Paul mentored Timothy. Timothy saw Paul suffer. Paul can write, "*You, however, have fol-*

lowed my teaching, my conduct, my aim in life, my faith, my patience, my love, my steadfastness, *my persecutions and sufferings* that happened to me at Antioch, at Iconium, and at Lystra—*which persecutions I endured; yet from them all the Lord rescued me*" (2 Tim. 3:10–11). Timothy was there as a firsthand witness with Paul through his hardship including Paul's stoning in Lystra (Acts 14:19) when they left Paul for dead. So the appeal to multiply the gospel in others was founded on an intimate and comprehensive mentoring relationship.

Notice the fatherly affection of Paul in writing to Timothy. He calls him in the greeting (1:2), "My beloved child." He says, "I remember you constantly in my prayers night and day" (1:3) and writes, "As I remember your tears, I long to see you, that I may be filled with joy" (1:4). Is this merely apostolic? Or is it inherently part of Paul's success in training?

Affection must have a place in the training and deploying of gospel ministers. We are not producing robots. We are producing shepherds. We are trying to raise up those who will love the sheep. Does the generation we are training know our affection for them? Our children can tell if we love them! Cannot also our spiritual children—our sons and daughters in the faith?

This pastoral affection in training is so apparent in men like Charles Spurgeon. When one reads his *Lectures to My Students*, one senses that he indeed truly loves the men to whom he speaks. He understands their trials in their small rural parishes, the difficulty of contending for the gospel. So it is with other ministers. Homer Hodge tells of his attraction to E. M. Bounds, the great man of prayer. He says, "He drew me to him with hooks of steel."[14] Bounds prayed fervently for Hodge, asking God to anoint him for ministry. And Hodge was drawn to early times of prayer (4 AM) inspired by Bounds's example.

Certainly Timothy was drawn to Paul in a similar manner. As a church planter, Paul specifically desired Timothy to join him in the ministry of beginning new churches. Luke tells us in Acts 16:3 that "Paul wanted Timothy to accompany him." The reason is clear. Besides his godly character, Timothy was uniquely suited as a church planter to reach both Jews and Greeks, since his mother was a Jewish believer and his father was a Greek (Acts 16:1).

Nor was Paul's mentoring relationship to Timothy distant. Their relationship was one of gentle intimacy. The vision for multiplication itself is preceded by the endearing address, "You then, *my child*." For Paul,

---

14. Lyle Wesley Dorsett, *E. M. Bounds: Man of Prayer* (Grand Rapids, MI: Zondervan, 1991), 58.

ministry multiplication was not a program but a relationship founded on and framed as gospel family. Paul writes remembering Timothy's tears, longing to see him.

As we seek the multiplication of the gospel, our churches and we as leaders need the same language and lifestyle of mentoring. We need Christians who self-consciously invest in others. It is the only way multiplication will happen. And yet, as important as Paul's relationship with Timothy was to create a context for the multiplication of gospel ministers, there was one relationship more critical, namely, that of Timothy's with Christ. This brings us to our final principle.

A More-than-human Venture

If we are to multiply the gospel as a treasure for generations to come, we must remember the source of our strength for training. Training others for gospel ministry requires divine strength. Paul writes just prior to his charge, "You then, my child, *be strengthened by the grace that is in Christ Jesus*" (2 Tim. 2:1).

This is the ever-present irony of human weakness and divine strength in Paul's writing. Essentially he tells Timothy to be strong: "be strengthened." And Timothy obviously will need it as he trains and deploys men in the face of terrible suffering and fierce opposition. Yet, what is the source of that strength? Irony of ironies—it is not Timothy's own strength but the grace that is in Christ Jesus. We are made strong in grace.

Paul is the model of strength in weakness. The classic statement of the concept comes in 2 Corinthians where Paul tells how God reassured him: "'My grace is sufficient for you, for my power is made perfect in weakness.' Therefore I will boast all the more gladly of my weaknesses, so that the power of Christ may rest upon me" (2 Cor. 12:9). In fact, earlier in 2 Corinthians Paul writes of his trials in Asia that "we were so utterly burdened beyond our strength that we despaired of life itself. Indeed, we felt that we had received *the sentence of death.* But that was to make us r*ely not on ourselves but on God who raises the dead*" (2 Cor. 1:8–9). Paul's philosophy of power in ministry and, by extension, training others for ministry, was founded on the irony of weakness—when we are weak, we are strong.

Paul illustrates this philosophy elsewhere. In Colossians he writes of his labor for the maturity of the church, saying, "For this I toil, struggling with all his energy that he powerfully works within me" (Col. 1:29). The irony is that it is *Paul* working ("for this I toil"), but as he works he struggles with *God's* strength ("with all *his* energy")—yet God's energy is within *him* ("that so powerfully works within me"). This principle is the one upon which Paul bases Timothy's charge to train. As Timothy trains, he is to do so "strengthened by the grace that is in Christ Jesus."

Those who raise up gospel ministers today need the same understanding. Church planters seeking to multiply gospel ministry must know the experiential reality of being strong in weakness. Seminary professors must instill the content of the gospel, but also the lifestyle of dependence that fits with the gospel. Lay trainers seeking to train others in evangelism need to personally experience strength in grace and then instruct others in this principle. Indeed, those who have been most mightily used of God and have multiplied others have understood this philosophy.

This grace that is in Jesus—what is it particularly? It is a divine strengthening by the power of the Holy Spirit, who makes us adequate to do our work, to guard the gospel when we are not adequate and when we may grow discouraged. Related to 2 Timothy 2:2 is 1:14, "By the Holy Spirit who dwells within us, guard the good deposit entrusted to you."

This is the final principle for training other gospel workers. The entirety of the ministry must be done in the power of the Holy Spirit. Spurgeon writes, "To us, as ministers, the Holy Spirit is absolutely essential."[15]

Conclusion

It is a privilege to honor Kent with these essays as he enters into a new stage of the race of his ministry. As he does so, may God continue to multiply men through him and through the church. The prophets speak of a day when "the earth will be filled with the knowledge of the glory of the Lord as the waters cover the sea" (Hab. 2:14; Isa. 11:9). And George Whitfield, seeing such a day, spoke not of water, but of fire, saying: "Surely our Lord intends to set the world in a flame."[16] When this day comes it will be because God uses the church to enormously multiply ministers—ministers who view the gospel as a treasure—and are willing to pass it on, even while suffering, in the power of the Holy Spirit. May God fulfill Paul's vision for multiplication even in our day. The world awaits the word of the Lord.

---

15. Charles Spurgeon, *Lectures to My Students* (Grand Rapids, MI: Zondervan, 1954), 186.
16. Iain H. Murray, *The Puritan Hope: Revival and the Interpretation of Prophecy* (Edinburgh: Banner of Truth, 1998), 117.

15

Few Are Not Enough:
Training a Generation of Preachers

David Helm

A Convergence of Gospel Commitments in Early Tudor Puritanism[1]

Norwich, England, 1576— Preaching Workshops

The preacher slowed his horse to a walk as he came upon the final upward slope of Elm Hill. For three long autumn days, he had been pushing his horse from London. He had preached a sermon to his

---

1. The genesis of this narrative/essay was a sabbatical extended to me by College Church in Wheaton, a vibrant body of Christ known for expository preaching. Their kindness to me has been lifelong, and my family cherishes this abiding partnership in the gospel. And the preaching ministry of Kent Hughes has greatly informed my own commitments. Further, I want to thank Dick Lucas and the congregation of St. Helen's Bishopsgate (with a special nod to the "East Enders"). Dick's kind invitation to my family to come and "sabbatical" among them for the first half of 1996 allowed access to the right libraries. From St. Helen's we also experienced the richness of Christian community and learned the importance of practicing hospitality to those living in urban contexts. In addition, gratitude goes to my friend and colleague Robert Kinney, director of ministries of the Charles Simeon Trust. This essay is much better than it might have been without his constant help, vision, and meticulous oversight. Finally, I want to express my appreciation to Jon Dennis, brother-in-law, friend, and pastoral colleague of sixteen years. It is with Jon's co-laboring that everything outlined here in Part 4 is being attempted in living color.

own congregation there early last Thursday. But by now, the Lord's Day was drawing to a close, and this last little mound was all that kept his eyes from seeing the place of his birth. Even so, he wasn't in a hurry. He never tired of that moment when his eyes would meet it all over again. Bringing his horse to a walk only heightened his childlike expectation. At last, reaching the crest, he halted his mare altogether. Looking up, he gazed upon the rich soil of the region he called home.

Before him lay the sprawling, familiar land of Norwich. The great limestone cathedral still rose in the distance. It had been constructed nearly 500 years before, in A.D. 1096, under the direction of Losinga, then bishop of Thetford. That the town warranted such a great structure was in part due to the fact that it had its own mint. Every coin bore the local inscription, *Norvic.* Indeed, even in the preacher's day the ancient coins were considered keepsakes and treasures and the bishop was still proud to sign himself *Norvic.*

The seasoned preacher stood alone on the good earth. He enjoyed the harvest view from here. Looking out over the River Wensum he liked to imagine the connections these waters had to larger tributaries, waters unseen. His mind filled with the pleasant thought that the entire world was somehow within reach from here.

At last he climbed upon his mare again. A meeting of sorts would begin in the morning. It was a gathering he attended as often as he could. In fact, this particular assembly had come to mean more to him than all the coins minted in town and all the miles these rivers could run. To his own peculiar way of thinking, the coin of the gospel was being minted at this meeting. So he prodded his mount toward town, convinced that God's good news—news already beginning to be treasured in this countryside—would one day wind its way to the ends of the earth.[2]

The next morning, he took up his Bible and arrived at Christ Church by 8:30 AM. His punctuality was the result of his knowing that the meeting was "kept every Monday from nine of the clock in the morning till eleven."[3] Once inside he saw the familiar faces of friends. Most of them also were preachers. Norwich had long been known for its many

---

2. Roland Allen captures this sentiment with a description of the apostle Paul's strategic evangelism of cities: "In his hands they became the sources of rivers, mints from which the new coin of the Gospel was spread in every direction. They were centres from which he could start new work with new power." Roland Allen, *Missionary Methods: St. Paul's or Ours?* (Grand Rapids, MI: Eerdmans, 1962), 17.

3. Roger Morrice, "The Order of the Prophefie at Norwich in Anno 1575," MSS, B, 1:268–70; C tran. fols. 204–6, Dr. William's Library, London. Please note: throughout the essay we have modernized all English quotations.

churches, and a good number of their pastors attended this weekly gathering.[4] Like him, others resided elsewhere and had charge of congregations both big and small. In fact, a few prominent ministers here today—the more travel-weary among them—had come all the way from Cambridge, which lay more than sixty miles to the south and west.

Pastors were not the only ones present, however. A few layperpersons were also in attendance. Four years before, in the year 1572, the preachers had opened this meeting to the public.[5] After many warm embraces, handshakes of reunion, and conversations spent in catching up on life and ministry, the entire lot assembled in the pews. And at 9:00 AM, the moderator rose to his feet, made his way to the lectern, welcomed everyone kindly, and opened the meeting in solemn prayer.

Holding in his hands *The Order of the Prophecy at Norwich in Anno 1575*,[6] a document that this group had put to paper the year before, he began speaking to the forty or so present about the urgency of the hour. In doing so, his voice began to rise: "The great need of our day, brethren, is for preachers—and not merely preachers, but preachers of a particular sort—preachers who will simply expound God's Word. I do not need to remind you that this great land of ours, now under Elizabeth the Queen, stands at a pivotal juncture."

Then, as if reticent to disclose a secret, he went on: "Given what I have heard this morning from one who arrived from London last evening, news which has been confirmed by two men who are here today from Cambridge, the Queen is not at all pleased with the proliferation of meetings resembling this one. I am told that she may seek to suppress these gatherings. Thus, we must pray all the more diligently for the Archbishop of Canterbury. The future of these events may in the end rest upon his ability to mediate for us." This last line, of course, caught the attention and imagination of all who were present.

Thus, it was only after a lengthy pause that he was able to go on, "Brethren, we need preachers who will be faithful to the Word of God." Then, spotting a dear friend and minister sitting near the back, he motioned toward him and said, "As our own John More has told us on more than one occasion, 'Get your preachers into your parishes,'

---

4. The Norwich prophesying was attended by "a great number of good and godly people." Patrick Collinson, *The Elizabethan Puritan Movement* (Oxford: Clarendon Press, 1967), 172.

5. The chancellor to the bishop of Norwich Thomas Becon altered the meetings to monthly gatherings in 1578. Collinson, Elizabethan, 183.

6. Roger Morrice, "The Order of the Prophefie at Norwich in Anno 1575."

and 'bestow them labor, cost and travail to get them, ride for them, run for them, stretch your purses to maintain them; we shall begin to be rich in the Lord Jesus.'"[7] At these words, the ministers were truly gripped, and a few turned to affirm the distinguished minister who sat among them. The moderator then moved toward the conclusion of his opening remarks, "Well, brethren, we meet here today, and every week, to do our part in raising up a generation of gospel preachers."

With that he introduced the morning preacher. A young man rose and made his way to the lectern. He knew, of course, as *The Order* had made clear, that he could not "exceed three quarters of an hour"[8] in his sermon. In fact, just this past week, as part of his preparation, he had visited the moderator's home to read *The Order* afresh, for it outlined in detail just how the exercise would unfold. Thus he was keenly aware that he must "be careful to keep to the text"[9] and "abstain from heaping up too many testimonies and annoying . . . diversions," which do not "aptly grow out of the text."[10] Firmly convinced that his task was to take "special care to rip up the text, to show the things of the Holy Ghost, and briefly, pithily, and plainly apply"[11] his message in a manner that would honor God, the young man began to preach.

Preaching workshops of this sort were beginning to emerge throughout the land.[12] These practical conferences were initiated and run by pastors, many of whom had grown tired of waiting for the queen to take action herself.[13] Five years ago, Reverend Edward Deringe had preached a fearless sermon in the presence of the queen on the need for improved preaching. Deringe's death earlier that summer[14] had only emboldened these pastors to continue gathering weekly. In fact, there was hardly a man listening who had not previously read the published transcript of Deringe's sermon to the queen, where he said quite plainly, "Of all the miseries wherewith the Church is grieved, none is greater than this: That her ministers be ignorant, and can say nothing. . . . And

---

7. John More as quoted in Collinson, *Elizabethan*, 186. John More, who is often referred to as "the Apostle of Norwich" due to his seniority at St. Andrew's, had considerable influence throughout much of the Norfolk province. For more than twenty years he attended to the affairs of Norfolk as a sort of "bishop" and, at one point, coauthored a catechism with Edward Deringe.

8. Roger Morrice, "The Order of the Prophefie at Norwich in Anno 1575."

9. Ibid.

10. Ibid.

11. Ibid.

12. Collinson, *Elizabethan*, 174.

13. Ibid., 42.

14. Edward Deringe died in June 1576.

yet you in the meanwhile . . . you at whose hands God will require it, you sit still and are careless."[15]

Momentum for these workshops had gathered under other preachers. John Field, an instigator for church reform, one of whom we shall hear more later, had enlisted others to send "An Admonition to the Parliament" demanding that they "displace those ignorant and unable ministers already placed, and . . . appoint to every congregation a learned and diligent preacher."[16] Therefore, when neither the queen nor Parliament took direct steps to assist the development of preachers, these men at Norwich and others like them took matters into their own hands. Of the proliferation and influence these weekly gatherings would have, history would later record that "these were conferences of the preaching clergy devoted to systematic biblical exposition" and "by the popular interest which they attracted and . . . homiletical training which they offered to the more ignorant clergy, the prophesyings did more than any other agency to propagate and establish the new religion in Elizabethan England."[17]

By this point in the morning, the young preacher was bringing his sermon to a close: "the learned brethren coming together, and the first speaker for that time put apart."[18] In the young preacher's absence, the older men candidly evaluated the "soundness of his doctrine, how he kept and followed his text, wherein he swerved from it, how aptly he alleged his testimonies out of the Scripture . . . how modest his speech and gestures, how sound, reverent and sober his whole action was or wherein he failed."[19] At last they called upon him to return. Taking his place among them, it fell to the moderator "in the name of the rest of the brethren"[20] to humbly encourage and instruct him in how he might exalt Christ more fully and rightly handle God's Word.

---

15. Edward Deringe, "Two Godly Sermons. The first preached before the Queenes, Maieftie, the 25 daye of Februarie, 1569," *Maifter Derings workes*, from the Early English Books microforms at the University of Chicago Library, 6733.3.

16. John Field and Thomas Wilcox, "An admonition to the Parliament holden in the 13 yeare of the reigne of Queene Elizabeth of blessed memorie, Begun anno 1570 and ended 1571," British Library, MS G. 19929; and MS 854. a. 5. The *Admonition*, authored by John Field and Thomas Wilcox, was a public and quite provocative exhortation submitted to Parliament late in the summer session of 1572. It was written out of a frustration, suggesting that the leaders of the Church of England were not Protestant enough as they enforced reforms aimed at suppressing "preaching-centered" movements like the prophesyings.

17. Collinson, *Elizabethan*, 51.

18. Roger Morrice, "The Order of the Prophefie at Norwich in Anno 1575."

19. Ibid.

20. Ibid.

The format was striking for its simplicity. The two hours had passed quickly and these preachers had given their morning to the task of working together on their preaching. On this particular day, the young preacher went home grateful—not only for the chance to proclaim the gospel message, but for the advice he had been given by those he greatly respected. He departed satisfied. Clearly his little flock would be better fed next Sunday.

The others who had come that day were also much encouraged. The time of exposition had nourished them, and their mutual interaction over the text of Scripture had advanced their own understanding of and love for God's Word. At last, the meeting adjourned. The preachers rose, although many were in no hurry to leave. After all, they treasured the weekly fellowship that this conference afforded. Conversations that had begun earlier with dear friends and colleagues in ministry resumed. Some went off to lunch together in smaller groups and, of course, others needed to depart before they would have liked. There were appointments to keep and pastoral visits to make.

Cambridge: A Residential Training Scheme

Before all departed, the preacher who had come on horseback made his way across the room. He needed to speak with the men who had come from Cambridge. He knew them well and was hoping to catch up on the gospel work undertaken at the great university. "Good day, my dear friends!" he said. "A fine message this morning, wasn't it?"

"Yes, it was!" one replied. "That young man will do the church much good if he keeps his nose in the feedbag of God's Word."

"Indeed," said the preacher from London, "May we find a way to train more like him. But, tell me, what news of Cambridge have you? How are our efforts proceeding to train a generation of learned and godly preachers?"

"Ah, Cambridge!" said the other. "I love it as much now as ever. And we are still praying that God will see fit to raise up a host of gospel men from her."[21]

The Church of England "had the benefit of two famous universities, Oxford being the other, and both contained many good schools and

---

21. The men of Cambridge were discussing Luther and his ideas as early as 1521 at the nearby *White Horse Tavern*. It would become known as the birthplace of Protestantism in England. See Arthur G. Dickens, *The English Reformation*, 2nd ed. (University Park, PA: Pennsylvania State University Press, 1964), 91–92.

Cathedral Churches."[22] However, and this was what troubled these three men most, while there were more than "10,000 parishes, the great schools had been able to raise up but 2,000 preachers to serve them."[23] The resulting failure was clear. Vast numbers of men and women in England, the majority by far, were living week to week without able-minded, learned, and godly preachers committed to expounding the Scripture.[24]

The Cambridge man went on, "We are nearly done with our initial study and are convinced that "unworthy preachers abound." We must find a way to thrust them out, so that able men may replace them. In fact, Oxford will be able presently to yield 194 such men. Cambridge, by our computation, would yield 140 and above, fit men all."[25] "This is good news!" the seasoned preacher replied. "But now, what of Chaderton? Surely, he must be the one to lead these men through formal training."[26]

On this day, Laurence Chaderton was far removed from Norwich. Christ College was nestled between Jesus Lane and Gonville and Caius College. Thus, Chaderton's rooms lay not far from where William the Conqueror had built his Cambridge Castle and were only a short walk to the bridge overlooking the tranquil River Cam. But while the Cambridge University setting of Chaderton's life was idyllic, his recent gospel work did not have the luxury of a moment's peace. One of the Cambridge men said, "Chaderton has just finished up his fellowship at Christ's and recently had engaged in a 'public dispute with Dr. Baro, a professor who holds Arminian tenets.'"[27] In the debate, so they now told the preacher from London, Chaderton "displayed his great learning, piety, and moderation."[28]

---

22. Roger Morrice, "Meane for the Establishing of a Learned and Sufficient Ministry," MSS, B, 1:195–97; C tran. fols. 206–7. 1586, Dr. William's Library, London.

23. Ibid.

24. The early Puritan preachers were meticulous about tracking both the numbers and the quality of preachers around England. One register, or written record of a survey with hundreds of entries, tracked the number of preachers compared to the number of openings by geographic province. Another tracked each practicing preacher and graded them—from "as badde a curat as may be" to "one that feareth the lord unfainedlye," noting particular characters with colorful observations such as "a drunkerd and a quarreler with other bad qualities." For a fascinating study of the subject, see Albert Peel, *The Seconde Parte of a Register* (Cambridge: Cambridge University Press, 1915), 88–89, 108–11.

25. Roger Morrice, "Meane for the Establishing of a Learned and Sufficient Ministry," 206–7.

26. Laurence Chaderton would later serve as a founding master of Emmanuel College, founded by Sir Walter Mildmay in 1584. The college was intended, from its beginning, to be a place for training pastors and Protestant preachers in opposition to the successful Roman Catholic theological schools. Many notable Puritan preachers would later attend.

27. Benjamin Brook, *The Lives of the Puritans* (Pittsburgh, PA: Soli Deo Gloria, 1994), 2:445.

28. Ibid.

"Yes, we are likewise convinced that he must lead if we are to train an emerging generation of preachers. Indeed, we have been in conversation with one of Chaderton's pupils whom you well know, William Perkins. He is likewise in agreement."[29]

At this point in the conversation, the other Cambridge preacher pulled a handwritten resolution from his bag. "Take a look at this," he said. "It is something we want you to bring back to the preachers in London. We are anxious for their comments." As the seasoned preacher took the paper in hand, he read at the top of the page, "*An order to be used for the training up and exercising of students in divinity, whereby they may be made fit and made to discharge the duties belonging to that profession.*"[30] Glancing down the page he saw enough to tell him that these men meant business. They were already laying the groundwork for some great gospel work that leaned on residential biblical training. And he was pleased to see that everything was "to begin with the Bible." He took note of the need for "the knowledge of the tongues, especially of the Hebrew and Greek." And he was happy to note that the kind of residential training these men had in mind would include the classical disciplines of "rhetoric and logic and disputation."[31]

"I will gladly bring it to London," said the preacher as he tucked the document away for safekeeping. "Well, I asked you of news from Cambridge and I now see that much good is happening. Perhaps, God being with us, we might expect that within a few short years there will be a college in Cambridge completely devoted to 'the propagation of the pure Gospel of Christ, our only mediator, to the praise and honor of God almighty.'"[32]

At last the three men prayed together. They prayed for the growth and proliferation of these workshops. They prayed for a learned and godly ministry. They prayed for residential training, and then they prayed for one another, that each would know God's peace and blessing. When they finished, the two from Cambridge readied themselves for the two-

---

29. William Perkins would become one of the great preachers of the Puritan age. He was educated at Christ's College in Cambridge and went on to author "The Art of Prophesying," a tract aimed at helping all Christians and particularly preachers to both read and use the Bible intelligently. He did so by advocating the so-called "plain style" of preaching that would later become known as "expositional preaching."

30. Roger Morrice, "An Order to be used for the training up and exercising of Students in Divinity. Whereby they may be made fit and made to discharge the duties belonging to that Profession," MSS, A O.L.P. 191; C tran. fol. 151, Dr. Williams' Library, London (emphasis in original).

31. Ibid.

32. Emmanuel College Charter. For more on the history of Emmanuel College, see n. 26.

day ride home. As they mounted their horses, they promised to bring the preacher's greetings to Chaderton and to Perkins especially. Fall term was coming to a close.

It was only after their horses disappeared from sight that the preacher turned down a side street that would take him to the home of his birth. His mother was still living, and he intended to stay with her for a week before returning to his pastoral duties in London.

London: Connecting Point for Pastoral Community

London was a thriving, dirty city. Increasingly, it was becoming the center of commerce and trade. Its own history dated back hundreds of years, with the monarchy and Tower marking its strength. The great River Thames cut its way through the city, presenting itself as flowing waters of some great expanse. Its width, of course, was in large part due to the many smaller rivers and streams that emptied into it at various places from the north. All waters, it seemed, flowed through London before going on to the ends of the earth. The moving Thames allowed boats quick access from one end of town to the other. At the north end, the houses of Parliament stood on one bank. The Archbishop's residence stood opposite.

As the seasoned preacher made his way back into town, he found himself praying again for Grindal, Archbishop of Canterbury. True to his Christian name, Edmund, Grindal served as *benevolent protector* to the growing number of gospel men who desired to see the land filled with expository preaching. However, the Archbishop's efforts to assist these preachers would soon come at personal cost. As history shows, the queen was not at all enthralled with Grindal.[33] In fact, she was increasingly set on suppressing the more radical advocates of the movement who harped at continual reform.

London's own John Field was one such radical. With underground-like tendencies, Field, perhaps more than any other, had pricked the goads of reform. Although he had been born and grown up in London, Field attended university at Oxford and was ordained by Edmund Grindal on March 25, 1566, at the age of twenty-one. As a Bible lecturer in London

---

33. Grindal the Archbishop of Canterbury played a significant role in shaping the trajectory of Elizabethan Puritanism, both as the bishop of London and the Archbishop of Canterbury. One of his most significant contributions was his refusal to be the queen's tool in suppressing the prophesyings by means of a letter in December 1576. This strongly worded letter resulted in his suspension from office until February 1577. He would be restored to office after apologizing with another letter to the queen carried by Sir Walter Mildmay. See n. 27. Collinson, *Elizabethan*, 195–96.

he quickly developed into a leader amongst the most radical Puritans, which landed him several suspensions from preaching between 1571 and 1579. And when the *Admonition* came out in tract form, Field was sentenced to twelve months of imprisonment. In fact, he received a visit during his imprisonment from none other than Edward Deringe in 1572,[34] demonstrating London to be the connecting point for a growing community of like-minded preachers.

Still in the saddle, and in prayer, the preacher made his way along the Thames to the Archbishop's residence. Nearly two weeks had passed since he had last seen Grindal, and winter was now coming on. The archbishop had requested a firsthand report on the preaching workshops. Arriving at last, the preacher dismounted and knocked upon the smallish wooden door framed in the wall running adjacent to the Thames. Through this side entrance he was admitted. And after introductions were made, he was told to wait for the archbishop in the library.

Grindal appeared, looking tired. Greeting the preacher solemnly he said, "Good evening, my dear friend. I am so very sorry. Things are not well." He held a document in his hands. "I have been upstairs writing a letter and intend to have it delivered to the Queen. It appears that she will soon move to suppress the informal gatherings we have established for preachers to gather around God's Word."

"We have all been anticipating this," the preacher replied. "And this is your decided response?" he asked, casting a glance at the document in the Archbishop's hands.

Grindal, steadied by the seasoned preacher's strength, held his recently written document to the light and began to read, "But surely I cannot marvel enough, how this strange opinion should once enter into your mind, that it should be good for the church to have few preachers. Alas, Madam! Is the scripture more plain in any one thing, than that the gospel of Christ should be plentifully preached; and that plenty of laborers should be sent into the Lord's harvest; which, being great and large, standeth in need not of a few, but many workmen!"[35]

---

34. Paul S. Seaver, *The Puritan Lectureships*, (Palo Alto, CA: Stanford University Press, 1970), 78, 207. While Field later overcame any separatist tendencies he may have had (rejecting the notion of dissolving the national Church of England), some emphasis on alternate church meetings was established. Field began holding meetings for preaching and prayer in houses and gardens throughout the city starting in 1568. One of the six or so that he started was conducted in a garden outside Bishopsgate. These meetings were, in some sense, an early Puritan form of what later generations would think of as a church-planting movement.

35. Edmund Grindal in a letter to Elizabeth I on December 20, 1576, as quoted in William Nicholson, ed., *The Remains of Edmund Grindal* (Cambridge: Cambridge University Press, 1843), 378. Exact wording varies with other manuscripts of the same letter.

He paused, but the preacher only filled the silence by standing calm and erect. And after some further discussion and a time of prayer together, the preacher bade Grindal goodnight. Departing the residence, he passed through the same door he had entered some time before. By now the night sky was pitch and the winds blew cold off the Thames. But this troubled him not. He remained convinced that the activity and hand of God was at work in the land. For years he had desired to see the day when God's Word would wind like the rivers to the ends of the earth. And on this winter's night, he believed it still.

An Agenda Relevant for the Church Today

Within a very short period of time, the English landscape would be watered from an overflow of learned and godly gospel preachers. Through the eyes of faith, the seasoned preacher had seen that night what historians would later recognize as the "preacher-led movement" of Puritanism. In all its fullness, as able historians have shown, Puritanism was largely an expository movement, flooding city and countryside alike with the force of abundant headwaters.[36]

Today, we have ample reason to emulate our sixteenth-century preacher's optimism, faith, and hard-working vigor. Indeed, the world in which we live is very much like the world into which he was born. Two contemporary comparisons help demonstrate this point. First, the need for expository preachers was as great in his day as it is in our own. Second, the rising confusion and dissatisfaction among pastors today could foreshadow a return to our primary calling as preachers, just as it did for the discontented preachers in the Elizabethan era.

Trends in the American Pastorate

The need for expository preachers was as great in their day as it is in our own. One of the documents that I cited earlier is a sixteenth-century resolution titled *A Mean for the Establishing of a Learned and Sufficient Ministry*. The document speaks of ten thousand parishes around England, some eight thousand of which had no parson or preacher. Today, recent labor statistics indicate that there are about seven hundred people for each pastor in the United States, or roughly 1.7 pastors per one thousand people.[37]

---

36. See William Haller, *The Rise of Puritanism* (New York: Columbia University Press, 1965), 49–82.

37. There were 422,000 pastors/priests/clergy in the U.S. in 2004 according to the Bureau of Labor Statistics 2004. The corresponding population of the U.S., according to the U.S.

But this void of preachers is really only one facet of a trend. When we take into account what congregants today actually believe, it only heightens the need for a new generation of preachers to faithfully expound God's Word. According to George Barna, a church trend researcher, the shocking reality is that "only 9 percent of all born-again adults have a biblical worldview—meaning that less than one out of every ten Christians age eighteen or older believes that absolute moral truth exists, believes that such truth is contained in the Bible, and possesses a handful of core beliefs that reflect such truth."[38] Other research says that today's listeners prefer to interpret the Scriptures for themselves rather than "permit the preacher to impose his interpretation on them."[39] In other words, the very task to which the preacher commits himself—preaching the Word of God—has gravity for a very small number of the people who even bother to show up and listen.

The second and perhaps more elemental trend is the effect this disparity seems to have on the preacher. The quality of a pastor's life, including everything from salary to the demands of a sixty-three-hour workweek, is often cited as one symptom. One recent survey of pastors concluded that "90 percent feel they're inadequately trained to cope with ministry demands."[40] This survey also found that "80 percent believe that pastoral ministry affects their families negatively,"[41] while other research places it as high as 89 percent.[42] The result is that "45.5 percent of pastors say that they've experienced depression or burnout to the extent that they needed to take a leave of absence from ministry."[43] It is no wonder that pastors express a profound lack of confidence in both the substance of their work and the effectiveness of their preaching.

H. Richard Niebuhr, an early-twentieth-century theologian and researcher of theological education at Yale Divinity School, points to an often overlooked cause and effect of this pastoral depression. After observing the American pastorate, he concluded that "perplexity and

---

Census Bureau estimate for 2004 and based on a 2000 decennial census, was 293,656,842.

38. George Barna, *Revolution* (Carol Stream, IL: Tyndale, 2005), 32.

39. William O. Avery and A. Roger Gobbel, "The Words of God and the Words of the Preacher." *Review of Religious Research*, 22, no. 1 (1980), 51. Other research affirms this reality, concluding that "the expertise of the preacher appeared to be limited to fact and information in the Bible and the contents of the Faith."

40. Fuller Institute of Church Growth, "1991 Survey of Pastors," as cited in H. B. London Jr. and Neil R. Weisman, *Pastors at Greater Risk* (Ventura, CA: Regal, 2003), 20.

41. Ibid.

42. Robert L. Tauber, "Pain in the Pulpit, Panic in the Pew," *The Clergy Journal* (May/June 2006): 32.

43. "I See That Hand," in *The Parsonage* (April 6, 2002), as cited in London and Weisman, *Pastors*, 172.

vagueness continue to afflict thought about the ministry." The effects of this ambiguity are troubling. Niebuhr asserts:

> The minister who knows what he is doing, they say, is able to resist the many pressures to which he is subject from lay groups in the churches, from the society, from denominational headquarters, and from within himself, however hard he must fight to keep his ship on its course; but the man who has no such determinative principle falls victim to the forces of all the winds and waves that strike upon him.[44]

Niebuhr links the preacher's dissatisfaction with ministry to his deteriorating comprehension of his role in the church. Others concur. From his own research on the evolution of pastoral roles in the twentieth century, David Wells lends an important observation. In contemporary culture, "technical and managerial competence in the church have plainly come to dominate the definition of pastoral service."[45] In other words, "the older role of the pastor as broker of truth has been eclipsed by the newer managerial functions."[46] And there is, undoubtedly, no aspect of ministry where this confusion is more dominant than in preaching.

These two trends can seem discouraging. The need for preachers *is* great, and discovering this need at a time when preachers are experiencing nothing short of an identity crisis is distressing. There are days in ministry when a military metaphor seems appropriate: "We are losing the war and, it seems, there are no reinforcements." Yet, the study of history can be a great help to us in these times of seemingly hopeless tumult. It is in periods of instability that new gospel movements are born. The sky is at its darkest pitch just before the coming of the dawn.

---

44. H. Richard Niebuhr, *The Purpose of the Church and Its Ministry* (New York: HarperCollins, 1977), 54. Niebuhr continues, "There may be a connection also between indefiniteness in the sense of vocation and the fact that sloth or 'downright laziness' is often mentioned by ministers as a reason for failure in the ministry. Doubtless a significant temptation to sloth or 'accidie'—as this vice was called in older days—is to be found in the frustration a man experiences when he has no clear sense of his duties and no specific standard by means of which to judge himself."

45. David Wells, *No Place for Truth, or, Whatever Happened to Evangelical Theology?* (Grand Rapids, MI: Eerdmans, 1993), 232–33.

46. Ibid., Wells cites a 1934 study by Brown and May that "identified five clerical roles" for pastors: teacher, preacher, worship leader, pastor, and administrator. By 1980, according to a study by David Schuller, the list of roles had increased to nine. Wells continues to trace this development to 1986, wherein the list swelled to fourteen including "spiritual development of the congregation, pastoral counseling for those in need, visiting the sick, and support of the church's stewardship program" as well as "providing administrative leadership, involving the laity in the church's programs and supporting the church's mission to the world."

A Convergence of Ideas

The dawn, at least for the preacher-led movement of the late sixteenth century, was born out of a convergence of preaching workshops, residential training schemes, and the effects of an emerging community of biblical expositors in London. It was this synergy of seemingly independent activities that God used to form the foundation of the Puritan movement and a widespread recovery of the authority of the Scriptures. And these preachers, through their commitments to training and supporting pastors in the art of biblical exposition, shaped a generation. Could these convergent ideas be at work again in this age? Might God be pleased to restore a preacher-led movement to bring about a recovery of God's Word? What should these strategies look like in the twenty-first century?

Strategy: Preaching Workshops

The preacher's experience in Norwich narrated earlier in this essay was not atypical of preachers in that era. The prophesyings, or preaching workshops, were held in Burton-on-Trent, Durham, and Yorkshire as well as abroad in places like Zürich and Geneva. A modern corollary is the work of Dick Lucas and The Proclamation Trust in London over the last three decades.[47] Lucas's singular priority has always been to confront the poverty of expositional preaching around England. His gatherings, which he calls "expository preaching conferences," consist of instructions on exposition, model sermons, and time for the preachers to speak on passages and analyze each other's work. The goal of these workshops is that those pastors attending "will not rest satisfied with their initial thoughts, but will work hard, hour after hour, to sit under God's Word, and to enable other people to become more Godly."[48]

The model Lucas implemented intuitively in London bears resemblance to the model devised in the same city some four hundred years earlier. Similar to what the preachers in Norwich codified in 1575 to govern their "prophesying" conferences, Thomas Cartwright and William Travers issued the *Book of Disciplines*—a book that would ultimately reach far beyond the streets of London. The *Book of Disciplines* also suggested a course of events for the typical "prophesying" conference to be held "as often as it may conveniently to be had" and "in every

---

47. Christopher Green, "Preaching That Shapes a Ministry," from *When God's Voice Is Heard* (Leicester: Inter-Varsity, 1995), 17.

48. Ibid.

church where it may conveniently be done."[49] Their process would simply begin with the preacher choosing "some part of the canonical Scripture to expound," such that it would be "applied fitly according to the natural meaning." Then others present would "judge and admonish the speaker" with a hope of sharpening his skill in preaching. This practice, accordingly, had a role in determining the fitness of a preacher for the pulpit as their times of "expounding the holy Scripture" should result in the young being "taught and trained up to preach." Indeed, these same goals can be traced through the work of The Proclamation Trust in our present day.

A recent North American counterpart to The Proclamation Trust's network of conferences is an enterprise known as the Workshops on Biblical Exposition.[50] In September 2006, sixteen pastors convened in Chicago for three days to consider the future of these workshops. The work of this gathering was then collected into a report aimed at articulating a coherent direction for these workshops as well as exploring what methodologies should be assumed to achieve their goal.

The mission of the workshops is fourfold. First, in order for expository preaching to take hold of a preacher and subsequently edify and evangelize his congregation, he must be confident in setting to the task of preaching. We must convince the pastor that the heart of pastoral ministry is the proclamation of the Word. Second, as he is convinced, he must also grow in his confidence to practice expositional preaching. We must encourage him in his own lifelong ministry and in his soul by ministering to him from the Word. Third, as he is encouraged, he must also be given the tools to apply specific principles such that he both understands and is equipped for true expositional preaching. We must show him how to rightly handle the Word of God. Finally, showing him how to faithfully exegete the text assumes a common understanding of the fullness of the biblical framework, a comprehensive understanding of the big picture of the Scriptures and the Christological prom-

---

49. Thomas Cartwright and William Travers, "A Directory of Church Government," from Early English Books, British Library, Thomason Collection, LPL H 9178 2.3 MSS 6539 fols. 76-78 and fol. 81. This document is also known as "The Book of Discipline."

50. The Workshops on Biblical Exposition are a series of approximately ten workshops per year around North America coordinated by the Charles Simeon Trust, which was founded in 2001 and modeled after The Proclamation Trust. The aim of these workshops is to equip and encourage pastors in biblical exposition through principles, preaching model sermons, and practice in small groups aimed at refining the pastor's preaching work. Another organization, Leadership Resources Inc., has begun to implement this approach in Africa, Eastern Europe, and Asia with great effect through the initiative of staff member Todd Kelly.

ise/fulfillment pattern contained within. We must reveal to him the geography of the text.[51]

A condensation of these goals for the attending pastors became their simple refrain. "Convince him that it must be done. Encourage him that it can be done. Show him how it is done. Reveal the big picture of what God has both said and done." The group also gave time and attention to studying other aspects of the preaching workshops.

They considered what the term *expositional preaching* means. One of the subgroup teams submitted a definition that would later become the basis of the commission's statement on exposition. Their definition particularly demonstrates the heart as well as the content of such preaching:

> Expository preaching is the public and passionate teaching, proclamation and application of a biblical text in its context in the power of the Holy Spirit and, inasmuch as the preacher's message is faithful to the original meaning, it is authoritative and binding—the very Word of God. Such preaching exalts Christ Jesus as He is revealed in all the Scripture, and calls its hearers to exalt Him in their lives.[52]

This collegial gathering of sixteen proceeded to articulate a rationale for expository preaching from the practice of preaching found in Scripture. To put the argument succinctly: when we read the Bible, we are reading the authoritative revelation of God, who is communicating to us in the manner of his choice. Thus, when we examine what preachers are doing in the Scripture, we must believe them to be doing God's work in God's way. The type of sermon found in the Bible is the simple exposition of God's Word, and the type of preacher found in Scripture is generally an expositional preacher.[53]

---

51. This material comes from the collected notes of a meeting of sixteen pastors hosted by the Charles Simeon Trust and convened to discuss the *Workshops* at the Quadrangle Club on the University of Chicago campus, September 10 to 13, 2006. The pastors present were R. Kent Hughes, David Helm, Steve Bickley, David Camera, Jon Dennis, David Hegg, Carey Hughes, Arthur Jackson, Jim Johnston, Todd Kelly, Oscar Leiva, Aaron Messner, Paul Rees, James Seward, David Short, and Paul Winters.

52. This material comes from one of the subgroups convened at the meeting (see n. 51) and consisted of R. Kent Hughes, David Hegg, Oscar Leiva, and Aaron Messner.

53. Three examples of such preachers are Moses, Ezra, and Jesus Christ. (1) The bulk of the book of Deuteronomy is compiled out of three sermons, chaps. 1–4, 5–26, and 27–30. This is not a second law being given by God but an exposition of the law being given by Moses. (2) Nehemiah 8 recounts a staggering moment in Israel's history, a moment in which they came together to sit under the reading and explaining of the law. Verse 8 tells us that "they read from the book, from the Law of God, clearly, and they gave the sense, so that the people understood the reading." Ezra preached an expository sermon that lasted much of the day. (3) The Sermon on the Mount is, perhaps, the most extensive exposition of Old Testament

Realizing that expositional preaching is the model of preaching presented in Scripture, we must train today's preachers to exalt Christ Jesus as he is revealed in all the Scriptures. Preaching workshops will not only strengthen a new generation of preachers, but they could very well be the best means of uniting the present generation of preachers and supporting every generation.

Strategy: Residential Training

In early summer of the year 2000, St. Helen's Bishopsgate (the church that has served as the primary connecting point for a growing community of like-minded preachers in England) played host to their annual Evangelical Ministers Assembly. The theme for the conference that year was "church planting." Nearly one thousand pastors attended. Don Carson, research professor of New Testament at Trinity Evangelical Divinity School, located just outside of Chicago, made the trip, not only to speak at the general sessions, but to lead a workshop for attendees on the importance of the relationship that exists between church planting and *training* men for ministry.

In his breakout session, Carson highlighted the convergence of three ideas necessary to train preachers. They are *classroom instruction*, *ministry experience*, and *pastoral mentoring*. Put differently, the indispensable components for building learned and godly ministers are threefold. First, the next generation of preachers needs a strong foundation of biblical doctrine—including but not limited to theology, original languages, and an understanding of church history. Second, preparation for gospel work will be best enhanced if those in training can be placed in a local church setting where they have opportunity to test and grow their gifts and usefulness. Third, preachers are best grown under the watchful and supportive eye of an older preacher already seasoned by years of gospel ministry.

Carson is correct. The fusion of these three seemingly independent factors can produce what is needed to build a generation of preachers. Interestingly enough, they are the very three things the preachers of the early Elizabethan period were intent on providing for those who would follow them.

---

texts in the New Testament. For example, by looking at the corresponding chronology of this sermon in Luke 4, an insight into his stop in Nazareth reveals that he quite literally preached out of Isaiah 61 (quoted in vv. 18–19). It is no surprise that the first two beatitudes in Matthew 5 are drawn directly from Isaiah 61. A cursory study of Isaiah will also reveal that "comfort" and "mourn" are melodic themes of Isaiah. Further, the Sermon on the Mount follows with Jesus' explication of the law (see Matt. 5:21–48).

In speaking with the visitors from Cambridge, the seasoned preacher referred to above was introduced to "A Mean for the Establishing of a Learned and Sufficient Ministry."[54] At its core, the document described a collegiate strategy to address the problem. It referenced the efforts at the universities at Cambridge and Oxford to train young men for the pastorate. One of these efforts was a regular event hosted by Laurence Chaderton of Cambridge. Chaderton, himself a preacher for more than five decades at St. Clement, held a number of academic posts: fellow at Christ's College and later master of Emmanuel College from its founding. A man with one foot in an academic setting and the other in the practical ministry, Chaderton's "prophesyings" were meetings for students meant to complement the rigors of scholastic education with training in the practical exposition and application of the text in a pastoral setting.

Some years before Chaderton, Richard Greenham had seen the importance of connecting training to mentoring and ministry exposure. His commitment in ministry was such that "he might train up some younger men to this end, and communicate his experience with them."[55] Much later, in Puritanism's flowering moment, preachers were still intent on making the same point. It was Richard Baxter who said, "But (if you can) at first settle a competent time in the house with some ancient experienced pastor, that hath some small country chapel, that needs your help."[56]

Fortunately, this synthetic and localized training model, a marrying of practical and educational techniques, has parallels in our culture. One of the more influential documents in evangelicalism in the last quarter century is certainly the Lausanne Covenant. In the section on education and leadership, the covenant provided the renewed impetus for training preachers and teachers from local settings:

> We recognize that there is a great need to improve theological education, especially for church leaders. In every nation and culture there should be an effective training program for pastors and laity in doctrine, discipleship, evangelism, nurture, and service. Such training programs should not rely on any stereotyped methodology but

---

54. Roger Morrice, "Meane for the Establishing of a Learned and Sufficient Ministry."

55. Richard Greenham, *The Works of the Reverend and Faithful Servant of Jesus Christ*, ed. Henry Holland, 1605, as quoted in Haller, *Rise*, 28. Greenham spent many years implementing a residential training scheme in Dry Drayton which produced the preeminent preacher of that era, the "silver-tongued" Henry Smith.

56. Richard Baxter, *The Reformed Pastor*, Baxter's Practical Works, ed. J. I. Packer (Ligonier, PA: Soli Deo Gloria, 1990), 4:27.

should be developed by creative *local* initiatives according to biblical standards.[57]

The covenant affirms a need for training leaders and also suggests that this training should occur according to *local* initiatives. What better place is there to train a pastor for a congregation than in that congregation? What better strategy can we concoct for the local church than to train up indigenous leadership with both the benefits of a seminary education and local experience?

The challenge, of course, is that many pastors and churches still need to be convinced. According to the *Field Guide to U.S. Congregations*, only 16 percent of congregants rank "training people for ministry and mission" as one of the three main roles their minister, pastor, or priest actually carries out.[58] This is not nearly enough. We must convince pastors across the country and around the world of the importance of this local-and-learned strategy. We must show them how it can work—as it did for Chaderton and the Puritans who followed him.

Some churches have initiated local initiatives, and in doing so have moved away from a purely seminary-driven model of training pastors. In a 2002 *Christianity Today* interview, Rick Warren said, "We've trained more pastors than all the seminaries combined,"[59] referring to his church's responsibility to teach their principles of ministry to others.[60] Countless churches around the United States hold conferences and training classes for pastors to learn new methods of ministry and focus on current issues in ministry. However, if we are going to succeed in preparing a generation that is equipped to withstand the pressures of the coming years, every local model must begin with and flow from that fundamental aspect of pastoral ministry—preaching God's Word. Simply put, we must rebuild our local endeavors with biblical and intellectual vigor. Merely putting an ever-larger number of men into ministry is not the answer. A movement away from formal seminary education and toward a model of training from the local church settings creates the danger

---

57. John Stott, ed., *Making Christ Known* (Grand Rapids, MI: Eerdmans, 1996), 39.

58. Cynthia Woolever and Deborah Bruce, *A Field Guide to U. S. Congregations* (Louisville: Westminster, 2002), 73–74.

59. Rick Warren, as cited in Tim Stafford, "A Regular Purpose-Driven Guy," *Christianity Today*, November 18, 2002, 48.

60. Rick Warren founded Saddleback Church in 1980 in Orange County, California. The Saddleback conferences for preachers tend to be focused on ideas and themes of contemporary ministry more than on the tools of the particular art and skill of expositional preaching. In some sense, the Saddleback conferences are aimed at practitioners of ministry in a larger sense. The Workshops on Biblical Exposition aim specifically at helping pastors and Bible teachers become better preachers of the Bible in particular.

of placing too many men into ministry without any formal classroom instruction. If our church-led training models produce preachers who are doctrinally impoverished, incompetent in the rudiments of Greek and Hebrew, and void of comprehending or even appreciating the broad strokes of church history, we are going to be ill-equipped to fulfill our gospel calling. We must *all* be ready to adapt and change—not settling for anything less than "godly and learned" pastors.

A few residential training schemes exist that embody the necessary convergence of classroom instruction, ministry exposure, and mentoring. The Ministry Training Strategy (MTS), a training scheme that grew out of Phillip Jensen's ministry in Sydney, Australia, bears mention. It begins with what is called a "challenge," consisting of a series of conferences and an extensive network of coaches designed to challenge young men and women to consider full-time ministry. Participants then work as apprentices under MTS trainers in churches for two years, learning through participation in the church's evangelism and Bible teaching ministries. For those heading into full-time ministry, this apprenticeship serves as a prelude to theological studies at Moore Theological College.[61]

In summary, even though the skills that seminaries teach in language, rhetoric, and theology are essential preparation for preaching, we must nonetheless find creative ways to supplement seminary education in the very center of practical ministry—the local church. Residential training schemes that do not forfeit classroom instruction but instead remain committed to biblical learning, languages, and godly living will not only strengthen a new generation of preachers, but will also provide the framework for training all generations.

Strategy: Pastoral Communities beyond the Sixteenth Century

Central to the logic of *workshops* is the idea of a *community* of pastors gathering together for refreshment in the Word and further training in the preaching of the Word. In that sense, its greatest value is developmental for men established in full-time ministry. And central to the logic of *residential training* is the idea of a *community* in which the experienced preachers lead the less experienced and the skilled preachers lead the less skilled. Its greatest value is for young men at the beginning of full-time engagement in ministry. These aspects of *community* are timeless—from the New Testament, to the early Puritans, to our day. Yet, it is our day that presents both diverse challenges and tools beyond those

---

61. Like MTS in some respects, the Cornhill Training Course, founded by The Proclamation Trust in London, is designed to be a one-year course in English Bible (though it can be done part-time over two years).

of our sixteenth-century English brothers, and at least three strategies should be advanced.

First, one of the greatest advantages to living after the Information Age[62] is that connecting—being in constant relationship to others through technology—is so much easier. We have and will have a myriad of tools—from e-mails to instant messages, blogs to wikis, devices and platforms yet to be created—aimed at giving us the ability to communicate when we must be apart. Imagine working with a small group on your preaching at a conference. You share your outline for next week's sermon and you sharpen each other. When you return home, you are still connected online. You have the ability to share your outlines, discuss your preaching, ask your questions, and discover the secrets of great expositional preaching with the help of the latest technologies. We must find ways to foster such collaborations and such digital communities.

Second, the dominant culture in America must begin serving the ethnically and racially diverse population in this country. From African-Americans to Latinos to Asian-Americans, an increasingly polyglot country affects every aspect of culture on every social level. Intentional efforts must be made to train the next generation of preachers and demonstrate how true exposition of the Scriptures in preaching is not bound by race or tradition. Rather, collaboration across racial lines, with an equal seat at the table for everyone, will lead to the enrichment of all. To this point, the African-American tradition serves as an exemplary model of *residential mentoring* over the last 150 years in the United States. According to one source,

> Early generations of black preachers started predominantly in apprenticeship positions under more mature preachers. This tradition prevails today. God was held certainly as the primary teacher. But the call to ministry and the gifts of preaching were developed in apprenticed positions or on-the-job training. The subsequent generations of preachers have advanced this mentoring model of training.[63]

The opportunity to draw upon such a tradition for the good of the whole church should not be wasted. Rather, we must gather together as a community of preachers—all preachers—unified by a commitment to faithfully expound the Word. Only then will we have a full community, one reflective of our world.

---

62. The Information Age is a period after the Industrial Age but before Knowledge Economy, roughly the early 1970s to the early 1990s.

63. Dale P. Andrews, *Practical Theology for Black Churches* (Louisville: Westminster, 2002), 21. Andrews also cites *Relational Refugees* by Edward P. Wimberly as a "helpful development of the mentoring model."

Third, we must not neglect considering our rapidly changing culture and how biblical exposition might interface with it. Like every major political and economic institution, the church needs think tanks. These could be small centers, strategically located in large cities and near research universities. They could establish community by serving both the academician and the pastor. They could be places where professors and preachers both could go for sabbatical to write and think about issues.[64] The materials they produce could have the credibility of scholarship but the purpose of helping the church. As Jim Packer wrote (while attending a consultation on this very issue), each one could be "a long-term residential community of evangelical scholars and pastors who, through personal research and interpersonal interaction, further the progress of God's Word in the church and contemporary culture."[65] Indeed, we must find ways to foster such communities. They may be the most strategically important communities in an effort to bring about a new beginning.

A Call to Preachers

According to Genesis, the book of beginnings, God's Spirit hovered over the face of the waters. Only then did God speak. Shortly thereafter, we are told that a mist went up from the land and watered the whole face of the ground. Indeed, throughout history, whenever God is gracious to his people, it is attended by Word and Spirit going forth together in great power—and often expressed in the language of water. In writing this essay, I have found myself longing for Spirit and Word to come once more and water the world afresh with gospel glory. Like preachers of old, it would be nice to stand on the good earth in a season of harvest.

With this narrative from the Elizabethan era, I have attempted not only to describe Puritanism as a great movement of the gospel, but also to show how smaller streams and rivers made such a movement possible. In the process, I have come to think that preachers are not so much born as they are made. Clearly, God must raise them up, but we must be engaged as well. First, we must commit to work on our preaching in regularly held gatherings with other pastors. Further, we must carefully consider the young men in our own churches—and we must do everything possible to train

---

64. Perhaps the closest example of one already in existence is Tyndale House in Cambridge. However, we imagine more of a pastoral presence than Tyndale House currently maintains.

65. J. I. Packer at a consultation hosted by the Charles Simeon Trust on creating the Simeon House, one such research community, in Chicago. The event was held in Hyde Park in October 2002 and attended by Hudson Armerding, David Camera, Jon Dennis, Lane Dennis, David Gieser, David Helm, Jane Hensel, Kent Hughes, David Martinez, Archie Poulos, J. I. Packer, Phil Ryken, Eric Stortz, and David Wells.

some of them for Word ministry. This system will require committing our time and resources. Further, these initiatives will not be accomplished by pastors' efforts alone. They will be the result of other deeply committed men and women who, for the joy set before them, enter equally into gospel partnership with us through financial stewardship. Then, we must continue to be in community with one another for the good of the ministry and the glory of God. With this kind of effort, and these kinds of initiatives, the early Puritans launched one of the greatest revolutions the church has known. If preachers in this day will give themselves to the same things, and if God is pleased to pour out his Spirit upon us, we might discover a simple truth—good preachers come from good preachers.

And so the seasoned preacher stood, considering the future and his friend the Archbishop. He was aware that with the morning light Grindal would be leaving his residence to cross the Thames and make his appeal to the queen. With that same resolve, we now must make an appeal to the King of kings. Pray that Jesus Christ would receive all the praise due his name. Pray that God would guide the church and her pastors in enacting strategies that continue the work of the sixteenth-century preaching workshops and training programs. Pray that he will bless those endeavors that have already been established. Consider for a moment the possibilities of training a new generation of biblical expositors to serve in every church, every parish, and every country in the world. Pray that God would raise up a host of vibrant biblical churches in strategic centers of influence that could serve as connecting points for a growing community of like-minded preachers. Then commit to doing something to making it happen. For, as Grindal wrote, the world "stands in need not of a few, but many workmen."[66]

---

66. Edmund Grindal to Elizabeth I on December 20, 1576, in William Nicholson, ed., *The Remains of Edmund Grindal: Successively Bishop of London and Archbishop of York and Canterbury* (Cambridge: Cambridge University Press, 1843), 378.

16

Disciplines of a Godly Pastor: A Biographical Sketch

Randy Gruendyke

I have known Kent Hughes for most of my life—as friend, pastor, and boss. After watching him from the "front row" during all of these years, I am regularly impressed by two seemingly contradictory conclusions. On the one hand, Kent is essentially the same man today as the one whom I met over forty years ago. His unbending commitments to Christ, Bible, church, and family are just as strong today as they were in the 1960s. And in a profession where men are more regularly loosening, or even letting go of, their grip on these fundamental commitments, Kent's enduring discipline is refreshing, even bracing.

On the other hand, while Kent is the same today as he was all those years ago, he is also an entirely different person. That is to say, while Kent's commitment to Christ, Bible, church, and family remains high, his enduring discipline in these areas has made him a far more outstanding man than he could have been otherwise. In fact, Kent is a living example of his own exposition on Caleb, the son of Jephunneh, who grew stronger in the Lord and more ambitious for his kingdom throughout his advancing years.[1] Or, to put it another way, Kent is like a knife that, instead of losing its edge with use, is becoming sharper as time goes by.

---

1. R. Kent Hughes, *Living on the Cutting Edge* (Wheaton, IL: Crossway Books, 1987), 125–33.

This biography traces some of the key figures and events that God has used to make Kent into the disciplined man and pastor that he is today.

Beginnings and Endings

Richard Kent Hughes was welcomed into the world on March 1, 1942, at Las Companas Hospital in Compton, California. He was the first child born to Beth Adelle Bray and Graham Winfred Hughes, a red-headed drill instructor at Camp Pendleton Marine Base in San Diego County.[2] The growing Hughes family, later including Kent's brother Steve,[3] faithfully attended Vermont Avenue Presbyterian Church in Los Angeles. Here Kent was baptized, enlisted on the cradle roll, and later became a faithful Sunday school attendee. It is also the scene of one of his earliest memories.

Like Tiny Tim from Dickens' *A Christmas Carol*, Kent recalls being carried on his dad's shoulder to a church-sponsored, father-son banquet. Beth made matching ties for the occasion, which were worn proudly by both father and son. Even now, Kent can still summon up the memory of his father singing "Shine on Harvest Moon" on that cherished night. But not long after that happy occasion, life for the Hughes family took a terrible turn: Kent's father was killed in an industrial accident.

By the time Graham's tragic death was being reported in the *Compton News-Tribune*, Beth was already receiving condolences from friends and family, including Edward James Caldwell, pastor at Vermont Avenue Presbyterian,[4] as well as Kent's paternal grandparents in North Carolina.[5]

New Town, New Start

The Hughes remained in their Lynwood home immediately following Graham's death. But as Kent was beginning grammar school, Beth de-

---

2. Graham was previously married to Mary Jane Bandy, with whom he had Kent's half-brother, Michael. Mary Jane died from complications following Michael's birth.

3. Born 1944.

4. "We were so distressed to learn of your husband's sudden homegoing and I want to tell you of our prayers for you at this time. The many friends here will be joining in committing you to God's comfort and grace. We do not understand the full reason for these things yet, but Christ our Lord is able to sustain us wonderfully in times of sorrow and we trust you are experiencing God's grace at this time." Edward James Caldwell to Beth Hughes, March 9, 1946.

5. "Dear Beth, Kent and Stevie, As we are experiencing this hour of our lives, we are very deeply impressed with the many times Graham helped us both spiritually and materially, so we want you to accept this little token of love from us. With All Our Love, Mom and Dad Hughes." In the hand of Kent's grandmother Rose, to Beth Hughes.

cided to move her family to the up-and-coming, post-war community of Whittier.[6] Here, on magnolia-lined Edmaru Avenue, the Hughes settled into the house where Kent would finish growing up and Beth would remain for the next five decades.[7]

In 1955 construction commenced on a liquor store in one of the many strip malls along Whittier's expanding border. Phil Martin, a local resident, believed that if a new liquor store was being introduced to the community, a new church should be added as well. Martin was so strongly convinced of this that he told the California Yearly Meeting of Friends Churches that he would pay a pastor's salary for one year if it would plant a congregation in the blighted neighborhood. Not long afterward, Granada Heights Friends Church was founded just two blocks north of the liquor store.

The Hughes family was attending East Whittier Presbyterian Church when they accepted an invitation from Marge and Jim Rhode to visit the new Monthly Meeting. Not long afterward, Beth Hughes and her boys became fully involved with the fledgling Friends congregation. During that opening chapter in Granada's history, Kent was introduced to two people who would become influential lifelong friends.

"Friend of Friends"

David Hamilton MacDonald and his family were living in the ranch house across the street from the soon-to-be-completed church building. Though David was slightly older than Kent, the two adolescent boys became fast friends, and almost immediately the MacDonald family began making an influence on young Kent. David's dad, Joseph, was a role model and paternal figure to the fatherless boy. A career Navy man and one-time boxer, this chief boatswain mate exemplified masculinity and tenderness toward Kent that he, in turn, would someday show his own sons and grandsons.

---

6. In the 1950s, this former Quaker colony, situated twenty miles east of the breakers off Huntington Beach and almost the same distance west of the snow-capped Sierra Madre Mountains, was a Technicolor snapshot of Southern California in its heyday—pervasively young, rapidly growing, and increasingly mobile.

7. Kent's memory of the years following his father's death is that of a "world . . . populated with wonderful women. My mother . . . sometimes worked two jobs to make ends almost meet. My maternal grandmother, Laura Anna Melissa McClurkin Bray, also a widow, gave herself to her 'boys.' Her death was the most traumatic event in our lives. My two adopted, unmarried aunts [were] Beulah and Helen. For a while we all lived in adjacent homes, and then across town. But we spent most weekends together and for two long-anticipated weeks every summer all those women and we boys camped together at Big Sur in California." R. Kent Hughes and Bryan Chapell, *1 & 2 Timothy and Titus*, Preaching the Word (Wheaton, IL: Crossway, 2000), 65–66.

David's sibling, Donna, exercised a sister-like sway over Kent, who was growing up with only brothers. While possessing all the feminine graces, Donna also owned the grit to accept Kent's challenge to a memorable race down Granada Avenue—Donna gripping the reins of her pinto pony, Chico, and Kent clutching the wheel of his 1941 Ford coupe, on the side of which was painted the descriptor *Swing Low Sweet Chariot*!

David, Kent's water polo-playing buddy, is the one who accompanied Kent on the epic, day-long journey to which Kent often refers when re-calling the consummate Southern California adventure from his youth.[8] But while David was endearing himself to Kent as the "friend of friends,"[9] the slender youth was also being influenced by another "Granadan."

A Life-changing Relationship

Verl Lindley was the Friends minister chosen to plant the church down the street from the new liquor store. His broad smile, robust personality, and gospel heart were attractive to twelve-year-old Kent, in whom Verl had taken an interest.

During the early days of Granada Heights, the young pastor and twelve-year-old Kent spent time together working on the construction of the new church building. On one occasion, Verl even took Kent and his brother Steve on a fishing trip to Irvine Lake.[10] But it was over the last week of August 1955 that God used the new pastor, who was work-ing that summer as a camp director in the Sierra Nevada Mountains, to make the most profound and lasting impact on Kent's life.

One evening, after a talk during which campers were introduced to the well-traveled Romans Road[11] thirteen-year-old Kent came to faith in God through Jesus Christ. Later that night, flashlight in hand and hun-kered down in the musty confines of his flannel-lined sleeping bag, Kent

---

8. The morning began with the two teenagers bodysurfing The Wedge located on Balboa Island. Then David and Kent drove one hundred miles east to Apple Valley, where they spun "donuts" on the desert floor in David's 1953 Chevy coupe named *El Chibasco*. Upon regaining their equilibrium, the teenagers made their way to the mountain hamlet of Big Bear where, during a brief stop, they took time to hurl snow balls at one another. Back in the car, Kent and David began racing westward on the final leg of their journey. Arriving in Long Beach, the exhausted but elated boys flopped into two padded theater chairs and spent the rest of the evening at an ocean side movie house watching Orson Wells's *War of the Worlds*—the capstone to a perfect day (based on a conversation with David MacDonald, September 20, 2006.)

9. R. Kent Hughes, *Colossians*, Preaching the Word (Wheaton, IL: Crossway, 1989), dedi-cation page.

10. Recalling the occasion Verl said, "Kent taught me how to fish [that day] and I haven't caught a thing since then!" Conversation with Verl Lindley, September 28, 2006.

11. Romans 3:23; 6:23; 5:8; 10:9, 13; 5:1; 8:1, 38-39

returned to those sacred texts. Tears began falling onto the pages over which he poured again and again and, in the words of John Wesley, Kent's heart was warmed to the gospel. His life would never be the same.

Growing in Faith and Favor

Soon after coming to faith, Kent was given greater responsibilities at church. As a fourteen-year-old, he once presided over Granada's Sunday evening "Inspiration Hour."[12] A year later Kent offered the invocation at the Family Christmas Service[13] and within the next few months, the sixteen-year-old, high school junior announced his intention to become a pastor.

Kent was confirmed in that choice with an invitation to preach his first sermon. He selected the entire book of Jonah for his text and gave his exposition the double title, "The Chicken of the Sea, or God has a Whale of a Plan for Your Life!" The talk enthused Granadans and encouraged the youthful preacher.[14]

While Kent was beginning to grow in the disciplines of the ministry, the Lord was, in the words of early-Victorian divine Charles Simeon, taking care to "grow him downwards." For instance, in the same year that Kent decided to pursue the pastorate, he also wrote this note of apology to his mother concerning an otherwise undocumented incident:

> Dear Momma,
>   I'm sorry I got excited. I really wasn't mad, just nervous. I know I should learn to listen, because what you tell me is important. I know that when I act like a child I don't act too Christian. See you in St. Louis.
>
> Your Loving Son,
> Kent

These lines reveal the disciplining work of God's Spirit on Kent's character. They also show that, even as a teenager, his writing style was to the point and biblically founded, two traits that continue to mark his books and letters even to this day.

---

12. Sunday bulletin, Granada Heights Friends Church, August 5, 1956.

13. Christmas bulletin, Granada Heights Friends Church, December 25, 1957.

14. Upon hearing of her grandson's pastoral ambition, Kent's paternal grandmother, Rose, wrote to his mother, "Beth, we are rejoicing with you about the news of Kent's decision for the ministry. It is an answer to prayer! We haven't seen him in such a long while, but the last time we saw him we thought he had the courage it would take for the ministry." Rose Hughes to Beth Hughes, undated.

Kent did not relegate himself to church activities and friends alone. Newspaper clippings from the time reveal that he was accomplished in a variety of broader pursuits as well. For instance, Kent took first place in a district-wide editorial writing contest, as well as a competition sponsored by the Ford Motor Company for his mechanical drawing of a drill press vise.[15] He also played basketball and received accolades as a topnotch tennis player, and he was a well-known "Condor" yell leader at the newly built California High School.

College and Courtship

Upon graduating from Cal High, Kent enrolled at Cerritos Junior College and then Whittier College, where he majored in history and political science. Kent enjoyed collegiate life and found his classes to be especially invigorating. But as an underclassman Kent found someone even more interesting than his books. Her name was Barbara Triggs.

Barbara grew up thirty minutes south and a world away from Kent in urban Long Beach. The two teenagers met at a Bible study held in the East Whittier home of Barbara and Robert Seelye.[16] Within months, Kent and Barbara had fallen "crazy in love," as Barbara so often puts it, and not long after that the two were engaged to be married.

On May 6, 1962, Kent and Barbara exchanged wedding vows before Verl Lindley at Granada Heights Friends Church. After a poolside honeymoon in Palm Springs, the Hughes moved into a little above-garage apartment on Washington Avenue across from Central Park in the historic uptown district of Whittier. As Kent began his junior year of college, life could not have been better for the twenty-year-old groom and his nineteen-year-old bride.

Studies, Family, and Work

The coming years flew by and were marked by rapid growth. In 1964, Kent received his B.A. from Whittier College and immediately went on to graduate school at Talbot Theological Seminary located on

---

15. Forty dollars and a certificate. Personal correspondence from Barbara Hughes, October 26, 2006.

16. The Seelyes were enthusiastic members of Granada Heights Friends Church and pioneers of church-based, collegiate ministry. Robert Seelye is the one to whom Kent dedicated his volume of sermons on Romans.

the campus of Biola University.[17] While Kent liked college, he loved seminary.

Seminary was the convergence of Kent's greatest and growing interests—biblical studies, theology, church history, and preaching. Immersing himself in the strenuous pursuit of these disciplines alongside other men preparing for the pastorate, such as fellow-student John MacArthur Jr., was supremely exhilarating to Kent. Even his professors recognized Kent's ever-escalating interest and enthusiasm for his studies.[18]

On the home front, the Hugheses had begun their family while Kent was still at Whittier College. Between 1963 and 1968 all four of their children were born[19] and summarily dedicated by Verl Lindley beneath the blue-tiled, stained glass window at Granada Heights.[20] In 1966, Kent added the hectic role of youth pastor at Granada Heights to his already busy life.

Kent assumed his ministerial position as a Copernican cultural shift was taking place in America, especially in Southern California. The typically well-groomed-and-clad pastor let his brown hair grow and began sporting bell-bottomed jeans to more readily identify with his charge. But the power of Kent's ministry, then as now, was not in his sartorial relevance but rather in an unswerving reliance upon the sufficiency of the gospel to change lives. Evidence of that power was never more clearly seen than during five memorable days in Parker, Arizona.

By Kent's own admission, the highlight of his four decades in pastoral ministry transpired at the Colorado River during Easter week 1968. As remains the custom, hoards of Southern Californians had flocked to the river to tan under the strong desert sun, water ski the wide turns and broad inlets of this great American waterway, and, to put it simply, drink too much beer. Amidst that party-minded, tent-dwelling company strewn along the river's edge, the high school group from Granada Heights had come to do evangelism.

By God's grace, the enduring reward of that week was a harvest of four souls—a collection of young men, just a bit older than those by

---

17. Then known as Biola College.

18. One area in which Kent especially excelled at Talbot was biblical languages, and professor Dr. Robert Thomas well remembers Kent's love for New Testament Greek. The aspiring, young pastor was the only student whom Dr. Thomas ever knew that attempted to read A. T. Robertson's massive *Grammar of the Greek New Testament in the Light of Historical Research* from cover to cover! Within a few years, Kent would serve alongside Dr. Thomas as an adjunct professor of Greek at Talbot.

19. Holly Jean, 1963; Heather Bray, 1965; Richard Kent II, 1966; William Carey, 1968.

20. Years later when the Hugheses were grown, married, and raising families of their own, both Kent and Barbara admitted that their only regret as a married couple was that they did not have more children.

whom they were evangelized, who arrived in Arizona sporting the swagger of the late 1960s and returned home to Southern California with the gospel burning in their hearts. The majority of that group went on into Christian ministry. Today, one of those men is the president of a preeminent missionary agency.

During his decade on the pastoral staff at Granada Heights, Kent served in a variety of pastoral roles,[21] each one requiring the preparation and delivery of up to two or more Bible talks per week. Robert Seeyle once observed that the discipline of that weekly regimen was crucial in preparing Kent for the next step that God had in store for him.

A New Challenge

In 1974, the evangelistically minded men and women of Granada Heights set out to establish a daughter congregation in nearby north Orange County. Enthusiasm ran high as Granadans poured the latest in church planting research, twenty of her most active families, and $50,000 into the project. Above and beyond all that, Granada Heights sent her favorite son, Kent Hughes, as senior pastor. His professional stock was at a peak and the prospect for success was great. For a while, the results of the endeavor matched their hopes.

While Kent views the 1968 "river trip" as his greatest moment in ministry, the first Sunday at the newly completed Brea-Olinda Friends Church building was certainly the most satisfying. After months of packing and unpacking their portable congregation, the people of Brea-Olinda had now completed a visible beachhead for the gospel on a prominent corner in a burgeoning community. And the future looked increasingly bright.

But as the months went on, the forecast began to change. "After considerable time and incredible labor, we had fewer regular attenders than during our first six months," Kent writes. "Our church was shrinking, and the prospects looked bad—really bad."[22]

Out of this increasingly desperate chapter in Kent's life rose the principles on which *Liberating Ministry from the Success Syndrome* is based, the book that Kent later coauthored with Barbara. In it, the two review God's definition of success according to the Scriptures versus the numbers-driven version to which Kent had succumbed. Once this matter of true success was settled in their hearts, the Lord lightened Kent's

---

21. Junior and senior high pastor, college pastor, and assistant pastor.

22. Kent and Barbara Hughes, *Liberating Ministry from the Success Syndrome* (Wheaton, IL: Tyndale, 1987), 19.

burden (though attendance persisted at low ebb) and, in doing so, began preparing Kent and Barbara for an unexpected and dramatic move.

Heading East

College Church in Wheaton, Illinois, was founded in 1878 and is located across the street from the sprawling front campus of Wheaton College. While College Church was started as a part of Wheaton College,[23] she assumed independence some fifty years later when the congregation moved from Pierce Chapel to its current location on Washington Street.

In the summer of 1979, Neal Conley, chairman of the pastoral search committee, contacted Kent concerning the now long-vacant position of senior pastor at College Church.[24] That conversation led to others, and within weeks, Kent, with family in tow, was in Wheaton to candidate for the job at College Church. While his morning talk was well delivered and uneventful, the story of Kent's evening sermon is a much-loved and well-traveled tale among the people of College Church.

August 5 turned hot and humid as night began settling on the non-air-conditioned College Church building. A Midwestern thunderstorm, thoroughly foreign to the Hughes, was blowing in from the west. Between the ghastly heat and the noticeable presence of three evangelical luminaries sitting with their wives in the first few rows,[25] the thirty-seven-year-old candidate was starting to perspire.

Upon stepping into the pulpit, Kent began having second thoughts about his sermon. His text for the night, taken from Luke 8, was chosen at the request of his children—not for its expositional punch but because it included an illustration about one of their friends! So, with

---

23. The first two pastors, Jonathan Blanchard and his son, Charles Blanchard, befit the church's historic beginnings, since both men also served as the first two presidents of Wheaton College.

24. In 1977 the much-beloved Nate Goff resigned as senior pastor from College Church. Over the next two years the people of College Church remained well fed from the pulpit. Evangelical stalwarts such as J. I. Packer and John Stott as well as professors from Wheaton College regularly preached to the six hundred or so worshipers who were gathering each week.

25. Kent describes the august presence of these three interested members of College Church as Margaret and Ken "Mr. Bible" Taylor, author of the bestselling *Living Bible*; Phyllis and David "Mr. Missionary" Howard, longstanding chairman of the Urbana Missions Conference; Mary Lou and Joe "Mr. Prophet" Bayly, editor of *Eternity Magazine* and author of the penetrating column "Out of My Mind."

a talk of doubtful origins before him, Kent began preaching with the coming thunderstorm now present and raging outside. What followed was a sermon interrupted fifteen times by a malfunctioning fire alarm, as well as the lights and sirens of arriving fire engines.[26]

The calamity of that Sunday evening cast a pall over Kent's confidence. He returned to Orange County uncertain that he would be getting the job. But within a few days, the phone rang and Kent was receiving an invitation to become the next senior pastor of College Church.[27]

Within days, the Hughes began packing up their Brea home and a few short weeks after that were bidding a tearful farewell to their life-long friends and family. Piling into their pale blue, faux-paneled Ford station wagon, Kent, Barbara and their four children, now ages eleven to sixteen, began heading east on Interstate 10 toward a new and unknown life in the Prairie State.

The Years of Establishment (1979–1988)

Kent's first decade at College Church was devoted to the establishment of his ministry.[28] From his first Sunday in the College Church pulpit, Kent began establishing his approach to preaching, which he regularly referred to as "serial Bible exposition." Beginning with John 1:1–18 on October 21, 1979, Kent took the next two years to work his way, section by section, through the fourth Gospel. Upon completing John, he commenced with a study of Acts[29] and after that the book of Romans.[30]

---

26. Kent Hughes, *Liberating Ministry from the Success Syndrome*, 116.

27. As search committee member David Howard later told him, "Any man who can call down fire from heaven can pastor College Church!"

28. As a former Friends minister, Kent began with the establishment of himself. The quarterly College Church newsletter tried to quell any doubts concerning Kent's Friends background with these words: "The Rev. Kent Hughes is currently pastor at Brea-Olinda Friends Church [and] served previously [at] Granada Heights Friends Church—[modeled] after a community church, attended by many of the students and faculty of Biola College." Later in the piece these words were added: "Although the Friends denomination is largely Arminian in doctrine, the Rev. Hughes is a convinced Calvinist." *College Church Fellowship*, July/August/September, 1979. Also, before coming to Wheaton, Kent had neither served communion nor presided over a baptism. Just before his first Lord's Supper at College Church, Kent was invited to break bread with a cluster of Wheaton College sophomores. Assisted by his associate pastor, Larry Fullerton, Kent carefully and thoughtfully led the underclassmen through a quiet communion in a corner of the Traber Hall lobby. Ironically, a few years later, the one-time Quaker minister would find himself presiding over the midnight New Year's Eve communion for almost twenty thousand men and women at the triennial Urbana missions conference at the University of Illinois.

29. Beginning September 20, 1981.

30. Beginning November 21, 1982.

Over the next twenty-seven years, Kent would preach through sixteen complete books of the Bible.[31]

Kent also began employing successful ideas from both of his Southern California churches that, with God's blessing and some cultural tweaking,[32] became equally well established at College Church. In 1980 a college pastor was added to his staff, a first for any church in the Wheaton area. Next came Summerfest, an attractive entry point for unchurched friends and family members of those in the congregation and surrounding community.[33] Finally, Women's Bible Study, established and developed under Barbara's leadership, would become, in Kent's opinion, the single most effective evangelistic tool in his nearly three decades at College Church. Kent's first ten years are also the ones during which he began establishing some of the most cherished holiday traditions at College Church.[34]

As Kent's first decade in Wheaton was coming to a close, he, along with the elders, established a sabbatical program.[35] In 1987 Kent and Barbara took their inaugural sabbatical to Tyndale House in Cambridge, England, for six months of rest and study. Here, with their days at Brea-Olinda firmly set in providential perspective, the Hughes prayerfully laid down the principles derived from that trying time in their book *Liberating Ministry from the Success Syndrome*.[36]

---

31. In 1981 Kent earned a doctor of ministry degree from Trinity Evangelical Divinity School in the area of homiletics. Almost ten years later, he was awarded a doctor of divinity degree from Biola University, in part for being "a careful scholar in the classical tradition," according to Talbot professors Robert Saucy and Henry Holloman. Clyde Cook, president, Biola University commencement, introductory remarks, December 14, 1990.

32. In some ways, the Hughes stepped back in time upon moving from progressive Southern California to the comparatively staid Midwest. Following one of the Hughes' first Sunday evening services at College Church, Kent's then fourteen-year-old daughter, Heather, stated matter-of-factly, "Well, Dad, I guess you won't be preaching in your Hawaiian shirts on Sunday night anymore."

33. Summerfest features a weeklong, age-graded Bible club for children as well as special interest classes (everything from golfing to gardening, calligraphy to coffee) and an evangelistic, big-group meeting for adults. With lively skits, music, and games throughout the week, as well as a family carnival on the closing night, Summerfest continues to be an annual community attraction.

34. These traditions include a contemplative Good Friday service followed by a celebrative Easter Sunday; a meeting on Thanksgiving Eve featuring a bountiful harvest table and three specially selected testimonies; two Christmas Eve services, an early one for families with small children and a late night, candlelit gathering during which Kent ushers in Christmas with the preaching of God's Word. During these days of establishment, Kent also became known for unpacking the meaning of a child's given name at a baby dedication or baptism as well as offering wonderfully illustrative remembrances at funerals for recently departed saints.

35. A six-month study leave for every seven years of service.

36. Since its release on December 14, 1987, *Liberating Ministry from the Success Syndrome* has sold 46,000 copies and is still in print. *The Christian Wedding Planner* (Wheaton, IL: Tyndale,

The Years of Expansion (1989–1998)

A major decision was facing Kent as he began his second decade at College Church. The choice was whether to remain in Wheaton or accept an invitation to become the lead pastor of a long-standing, big-city congregation. After wrestling in prayer and receiving the wise counsel of a revered and senior confidante at College Church, Kent resolved to remain in the Midwest. With his feet and heart now firmly established in Wheaton, the years of expansion were underway.

Shortly after Kent's arrival in Wheaton, the people of College Church began outgrowing their facilities. By the late 1980s, prints were being drawn up under Kent's defining leadership for a new space in which the entire congregation could meet for corporate worship. After a protracted series of civic challenges, College Church was finally granted a building permit, and on January 31, 1993, a thoughtful dedicatory service[37] was held in her new, 1,200-seat, Georgian-style building.[38] But the physical expansion of College Church was merely symbolic of Kent's greater desire for spiritual expansion among his people.

With the prospect of a new millennium dawning for the congregation, Kent started contemplating the coming years. As he did, his mind kept returning to a single question: with the forces of postmodernity bearing down on the culture with ever-increasing strength, what kind of person would it take to stand tall for Christ in the year 2000? With that query firmly planted in his mind, Kent began developing a plan for greater gospel growth among the people of College Church.

Kent's strategy evolved in stages and was built on his rigorous biblical reasoning and that of his staff and senior lay leadership. The heart of their effort was twofold: first, to unify the vision of College Church according to the gospel[39] and, second, to strategically bring each ministry into line with that vision. By doing this, the teaching and training at every level of the church, from cradle to post-career, should have a centripetal, gospel pull.

1984), which Kent authored with Ruth Muzzy and to date has sold 150,000 copies, while *Disciplines of a Godly Man* (Wheaton, IL: Crossway, 1991) is his single best-selling book with well over 300,000 copies sold worldwide.

37. The cautionary, dedicatory sermon, "To the Church in Sardis," from Revelation 3:1–6 was preached by Dr. J. I. Packer, and pastor Verl Lindley offered the prayer of dedication.

38. The very first event in the new building was a wedding held on December 5, 1992, two weeks before the structure was completed. The inaugural Sunday morning service took place on December 20.

39. The gospel is understood as the saving work of God in Christ as expressed through all sixty-six books of the Bible.

To begin, Kent preached *Vision 2000: Ministry Countdown to the Next Millennium*,[40] an epoch-making sermon setting forth seven pillar values upon which the future ministries of College Church would be built. Kent's thinking about Vision 2000 was especially refined in the summer of 1994 as he and Barbara enjoyed their second sabbatical, this time in Australia.[41] Upon his return, Kent's disciplined efforts to grow a stronger gospel people began unfolding in earnest.

In 1996 the *Pursuing Christ* document, a catechism created under Kent's leadership, was completed to provoke gospel-centered growth throughout every level of ministry at College Church.[42] This was followed by a series of in-depth discussions convened by Kent, giving birth to a new, gospel-driven purpose statement for the church—"God's people joyfully proclaiming Christ's glory among the nations."

The era of expansion reached its apex in the spring of 1998 when a small band of families and single adults moved from suburban Wheaton to the Hyde Park neighborhood of Chicago. Here, across the street from the soaring bell tower of Rockefeller Chapel at the University of Chicago, Holy Trinity Church was born. Holy Trinity was a source of great pride and excitement for the people of College Church. But there was no one any more elated over the new congregation than the former church planter himself, who had pitched the idea years before in *Vision 2000*.[43] Kent could see that his gospel strategy was not only capturing the hearts of his people, but also moving them out of their comfort zones.

---

40. Preached on January 9, 1994 and followed by "Embracing the Vision: Preparing a People to Stand Tall for the Gospel of Jesus Christ" on November 24, 1996.

41. During his three months "down under," Kent got a front-row look at the many ministries of the Anglican Archdiocese of Sydney. He also began cultivating deep-seated and long-lasting friendships with her leaders. Persons such as Peter Jensen and his brother, Phillip, challenged and sharpened Kent's understanding of the gospel largely through the discipline of biblical theology. At the time, Peter Jensen, who is currently archbishop of the Anglican Church, Diocese of Sydney, was principal of Moore Theological College, and his brother, Phillip, who is now the dean of St. Andrews Cathedral, Sydney, was rector of St. Matthias Church, Centennial Park. Others by whom Kent was especially influenced were P. T. O'Brien, then vice-principal at Moore, and John Chapman, director of the Anglican department of evangelism. The influence of these days became readily apparent in Kent's post-sabbatical preaching which, to this day, continues growing in its biblical cohesiveness and Christ-centeredness.

42. The final form of this document was extensively edited and assembled for church-wide distribution by assistant pastor David Helm.

43. Vision 2000 called for a regular schedule of church plants. Over the next decade, College Church planted Christ the King Church in the growing Fox Valley region of suburban Chicago. In Kent's farewell sermon on November 19, 2006, he announced the approval of the congregation's third church plant.

The Years of Elevation: 1999–2006

Under Kent's leadership, the expanding ministry of College Church was creating an ever-heightening profile. Locally, this became apparent in the ongoing physical expansion of the College Church facilities. In 2000 the much-needed Commons building was opened across the street from the original College Church complex.[44] The completion of this 55,000 square foot structure marked the fulfillment of Kent's dream to leave the next generation of church members with a ministry center suited to take them well into the twenty-first century.

College Church is known for her longstanding commitment to overseas gospel work,[45] but in recent years this dedication to that task has grown dramatically. When Kent arrived in Wheaton, there were forty-two men and women on the missionary rolls who were supported by a budget of $183,000. In 2006 the international gospel force of College Church numbered over two hundred and was backed by a $1.7 million budget. By God's grace, Kent has left "the jewel of College Church," as he refers to the church's missionary program, shining more brightly than ever.

During his days at Granada Heights, Kent developed a thriving ministerial internship program. In 1981 that same model was adopted by College Church. Exactly twenty-five years later, almost two hundred men and women have received intensive training in gospel work through the internship program at College Church. The alumni of this program are helping to realize Kent's vision of elevating the gospel "DNA" of College Church throughout a growing number of ministry settings across the country and around the world.[46]

In the early 1980s, Kent was invited to publish a drastically edited version of his expositions on John.[47] While he was grateful to expand the scope of his gospel influence, Kent was frustrated by the extent of the editing process. A few years later, Lane Dennis, president of Cross-

---

44. The Commons is a compliment to the Georgian-style structure across the street. The building provides the office, classroom, athletic, and meeting space so desperately needed to match the growing gospel ministry of College Church. Over the years of Kent's tenure, College Church grew from a single building situated on a modest street corner to a commodious campus covering well over one city block.

45. So much so that almost fifty cents on every dollar given to College Church goes to missions, and an increase in general spending requires an equal increase in missions spending.

46. Kent's devotion to ministry training for kingdom expansion was especially rewarded when College Church approved his dream of the establishment of a ministerial residency program. This program provides the church with three additional full-time ministers who are working at a level analogous to that of a medical residency. The first class of residents includes two men with earned doctorates and a third with a master's degree.

47. R. Kent Hughes, *Behold the Lamb* (Wheaton, IL: Victor, 1984); R. Kent Hughes, *Behold the Man* (Wheaton, IL: Victor, 1984).

way Books, began attending College Church. Lane was particularly impressed with Kent's series of expositions on the book of Joshua and, with Kent's permission, published them in 1987 under the title *Living on the Cutting Edge: The Challenge of Spiritual Leadership.*[48]

As Lane continued to sit under Kent's preaching, he enthusiastically continued publishing Kent's sermons. "Early on," says Lane, "we decided to call the series *Preaching the Word,* and after [a while], our [steering] committee discussed the possibility of publishing an expository volume for each of the books of the Bible." With the publication of his sermons on Philippians, Kent has contributed seventeen books to the *Preaching the Word* series, with the remaining volumes committed to expositors whose work will be published under Kent's general editorship. During his last era of ministry at College Church, the elevating profile and proliferation of Kent's published expositions[49] was accentuated by three complimentary projects.

The first project involved serving as a member of the translation oversight committee for the English Standard Version of the Bible (ESV). This task combines Kent's love for the biblical languages with his growing concern that English-speaking churches ought to possess a Bible well suited for both rigorous study as well as private and public reading. From the committee's first meeting in 1999 at Cambridge, England, until both testaments were published in 2001, Kent's time and energy spent on the ESV has been a labor of love.

The history behind the second project dates back to 1994, when the inaugural Workshop on Biblical Exposition was held at College Church.[50] The workshop is aimed at helping preaching pastors sharpen their skills as biblical exegetes and expositors.[51] Along with a variety of visiting instructors,[52] Kent has been hosting the annual gathering for an ever-growing group of men. In the late 1990s, he was approached with a plan to regionalize and thereby elevate the influence of the workshop. Within a few years, the third project provided the vehicle to make that idea possible.

---

48. This was the first whole-book series of sermons published by Crossway. In 1986 Crossway released Kent's series of sermons on the Lord's Prayer entitled *Abba Father: The Lord's Pattern for Prayer* (1986).

49. Most are available in audio form at www.preachingthebible.com.

50. The workshop is based on a model forged by Rev. Dick Lucas and The Proclamation Trust in Great Britain.

51. This is done by way of exegetical instructions, model expositions, and interactive, small-group preaching workshops.

52. Past instructors include Dick Lucas, Don Carson, Phillip Jensen, Alistair Begg, John Piper, John Woodhouse, and others. Kent likens the two-and-a-half day meeting for preachers to spring training for baseball players—a chance to focus on and shore up the fundamentals of the game.

In 2001 the Charles Simeon Trust[53] was established with Kent as its founding chairman. The purpose of the trust is to finance a handful of major gospel initiatives, one of which is the regional growth of the Workshop on Biblical Exposition. In its first five years, the Simeon Trust helped Kent and an increasing number of able hosts and instructors to strategically export the workshop to almost ten different locations around the United States and Canada.

The End of an Era

In the winter of 2005, Kent announced that, upon turning age sixty-five, he would retire from the pulpit of College Church and begin a new chapter of ministry. His reasoning, expressed in a letter to the congregation, was put like this: "At midlife I promised myself that when I came to my sixty-fifth year I would transition. I've seen others who, having had a good ministry, made the mistake of holding on too long."[54] Even though his final sermon was almost two years away, the news of their senior pastor's forthcoming departure ran like shock waves throughout the congregation. For some, Kent was the only senior pastor they had ever known.

In time a search committee was impaneled, and the conclusion of Kent's final series of expositions was in sight. With that, the graying pastor informed his people that he would wrap up his tenure two months early, fulfilling his ministry on Christmas Eve of 2006. The end of an era was coming faster than anyone, even Kent, had realized it would.

On the weekend of November 18–19, 2006, colleagues and congregants, past and present, descended on College Church to honor their beloved mentor and senior pastor. After Kent preached a farewell sermon to three packed congregations on the morning of November 19, the College Church family came together *en masse* that night to honor Kent and Barbara. Gathering in the structure designed and built under Kent's inspiration, tears and laughter filled the room as twenty-seven years of ministry were remembered with a stirring series of verbal and visual testimonies.

The four Hughes children and their spouses were present on that night, sitting in the first few rows with Kent's twenty-two grandchildren. A couple of now middle-aged members of the Granada Heights high school group who were on the 1968 river trip were there too, as well as a convert from a subsequent evangelistic river trip. And taking it all in with a sense of paternal pride was the man whom God used to bring Kent into relationship with himself, Verl Lindley.

---

53. www.simeontrust.org.
54. Kent Hughes to College Church, congregational letter, February 18, 2005.

On Christmas Eve 2006, Kent preached five times—twice in the morning, twice in the afternoon, and once at night,[55] all to a packed house. The nighttime gathering was particularly full as many came to sit under Kent's teaching one last time. Other than a brief acknowledgement of his twenty-seven years at College Church and his enduring gratitude for the faithful service of the chancel choir, Kent showed no sign that three decades of ministry were coming to a close.

The customary candlelit singing of "Silent Night" welcomed in Christmas and, as usual, its arrival was heralded throughout Wheaton by the bell atop the College Church bell tower. Kent concluded the service by pronouncing the benediction, blowing out his candle, and receiving an embrace from each member of his pastoral team. Members of the congregation came forward and offered their thanks and affection as well. As Christmas Day was beginning in Wheaton, Kent's career was ending—full, sweet, and blessed.

The Reward of Discipline

If there is one word that particularly describes Kent—now and over the years—it is discipline. It is the term that especially depicts the father whom Kent barely knew,[56] and it is the central theme of his best-selling book.[57] Almost every success that Kent has enjoyed over his forty years of gospel ministry is the result of divinely blessed discipline. In conclusion, here are three areas of Kent's pastoral life in which that discipline has especially paid off.[58]

Discipline of Study

From the beginning, Kent has maintained rigorous discipline in the study. For sermons, the process began with multiple readings of the book on which he intended to preach. Then Kent meticulously

---

55. Service times were 8:00 AM, 9:30 AM, 3:30 PM, 5:30 PM and 11:00 PM. Kent's morning exposition was on Luke 1:46–55, the second sermon in a two-part series entitled "The Song of the Incarnation." His nighttime sermon was a Scriptural meditation entitled "Incarnation's Night."

56. Shortly after his mother's death, Kent discovered from among her personal effects that he is very much like his father. "[Kent's] penchant for orderliness and discipline and his gentle and kind nature are very like his father. In fact, we have an essay his father wrote about being a 'disciplined man.' Amazing!" Barbara Hughes, personal correspondence, October 26, 2006.

57. R. Kent Hughes, *Disciplines of a Godly Man.*

58. Kent's discipline at work matches his discipline at home. To get a glimpse of the latter see Kent and Barbara Hughes, *Disciplines of a Godly Family* (Wheaton, IL: Crossway, 2003).

made a calendar covering the dates and texts for each exposition, factoring in holidays and other special occasions on the church calendar. After consulting a variety of expert sources, Kent went about collecting a cache of commentaries.[59] His accumulated store usually included a combination of classical treatments, critical analyses, pastoral overviews, Jewish works, and even unorthodox treatises of his chosen book.

After carefully analyzing the text for a given week in both English and its original language, Kent determined the main point of the passage and wrote his outline. Only after doing these things did Kent consult his written resources. He then composed a sermon, relying on a vast supply of illustrations to punctuate his points.[60]

Over the years, Kent's discipline in the study afforded him the ability to create a sermon in less and less time. But instead of devoting that time to the other pressing details of ministry, Kent poured it right back into further study. As time went by, this clearly made his messages fuller and richer.[61]

Discipline of Preaching

There are few expositors today who understand the importance of words better than Kent. In a world that increasingly refuses to accept the absolute meaning of words, Kent was all the more disciplined in channeling God's truth by that medium—the very same one through which our Lord reveals himself to the world today. So, like a surgeon who must choose the most appropriate instruments for an upcoming operation, Kent selected words for a sermon with surgical precision. As Barbara once observed of her husband, Kent is a wordsmith.

Once in the pulpit, Kent understood that the power of preaching is in the preaching. That is, all the preparation in the world is of no use to a congregation unless the preacher presents his text in a compelling fashion. That means a sermon must be preached in a manner that is

59. Over his years of study, Kent has amassed a formidable library. J. I. Packer once commented that it is the finest pastor's library he has ever seen.

60. Kent's illustrations are the product of his disciplined habit of collecting and filing stories from a variety of sources. The latest volumes in the *Preaching the Word* series include an index of illustrations, and in 1998 Tyndale published *1001 Illustrations*, a collection of Kent's best quotes and stories.

61. For years, a black-and-white photo of A. T. Robertson's desk adorned a place in Kent's study where only he could see it. The picture was taken just moments after the lifeless body of the aged and august New Testament scholar was wheeled from his office, where he was in the midst of rigorous studies. Kent would say, "That's the way I want to go—with my boots on!"

true to the preacher's personality and prayerfully blessed by the Holy Spirit.[62]

To ensure that he stayed on course and used his pulpit time wisely, Kent preached from a manuscript. That is not to say he preached a written essay, but rather a sermon written as he intended to speak it. This is a distinctive mark of the *Preaching the Word* series—it is a record of Scripture faithfully explained by way of the spoken word before a live audience. In fact, Kent sometimes refused the grammatical refinements of the editor's pen in favor of keeping his printed sermons true to their live presentation.

Discipline of Teamwork

Over the course of his ministry, the discipline of assembling a well-qualified team has served Kent well. This is due, in part, to the following four things.

First, for pastoral positions, Kent hired pastors. He never looked primarily for a "youth guy" or a "music man" to fill his staff. Rather, Kent wanted to work with men who possess the biblically required desire and qualifications to pastor and teach those for whom he was responsible. Once that kind of man was found, Kent viewed him with an eye for a specific ministerial task, and if he was well suited to it, the man was offered the job.

Second, Kent always said that he was looking to hire team members who are better than himself. This unthreatened approach to ministry created an atmosphere of creativity and growth among his entire staff. One area in which Kent especially grew his colleagues was in the pulpit. Rather than hiring out-of-town preachers to speak during his periodic absences, Kent filled pulpit vacancies from among his own staff. This practice not only led to the further development of his assistants, but it also heightened the congregation's familiarity with and confidence in their own pastoral team.

Third, Kent poured time into his team. To begin, he met with the entire staff once a week for almost a half a day. For many years, the morning followed this pattern:

- 7:00 AM Gather in the home of a staff member for an extended season of prayer over the congregation and one another.

---

62. Kent once invited a college professor of communications to come and coach him and his staff on the public reading of Scripture.

- 8:30 AM Shift to a restaurant of the host's choosing. Over breakfast, discuss everything from Monday Night Football to the latest theological conundrums.

- 9:45 AM Reconvene at the church building to work through an agenda of business items.

- 11:00 AM With the congregation prayed for, working relationships refreshed, and business done, the meeting was adjourned and a new week was underway.

The fraternal collegiality engendered during these times was vital in building a hardworking and disciplined staff—one just like their boss!

Another occasion at which Kent poured time into his team was at regularly scheduled retreats for staff and spouses. These five day getaways were held twice a year, and the agenda was simple—a leisurely breakfast followed by a lively time in the Word and then a build-your-own lunch. The afternoon was usually dedicated to free time, while the evening was given to supper, group games, and late-night discussions. In the early days, staff retreats were geared toward doing business. But over time Kent learned that the absence of a formal agenda promoted greater creativity and conversation when business items were informally brought up.

Finally, Kent advocated that many of the professional provisions made for him be made for his team as well. So the pastors at College Church now receive a book allowance, a budget line for continuing education, and (most highly valued) a six-month sabbatical for every seven years of service. These gracious benevolences created a ministerial team in fact, not only in name.

Retrospective from the Family

Kent himself expressed his conviction that the opinion that counts most with him regarding his work is the testimony of his family. It seems appropriate, therefore, to conclude this biographical essay by quoting words that Kent and Barbara's daughter Heather spoke at her parents' farewell celebration at College Church:

> As children, we have been witnesses to Dad's love for this church. As my husband, Jeff, read through my notes for tonight, he told me that one of the ways my father loved the church the most is that he has never shortchanged you on a sermon. His commitment to doing his best for you and before God was evident to us by his very thorough preparation on every text. He has prayed for you fervently and con-

sistently, and I know that as he and mom leave, their prayer for you will certainly echo that prayer of Paul in Philippians 1:9: "And it is my prayer that your love may abound more and more with knowledge and all discernment, so that you may approve what is excellent, and so be pure and blameless for the day of Christ filled with the righteousness that comes through Jesus Christ, to the glory and praise of God."

And lastly, Daddy, we your children want to thank you publicly for being not just our dad but our pastor as well. We have benefited from a lifetime of learning that has been unhindered because we have never wondered about the motives or the heart of the man behind the message. We know you, and you are worthy of our honor because of and only because of the redemptive work of the Holy Spirit in your own life, so all honor ultimately belongs to the Lord God, and we praise Him for you!

Subject Index

Scripture Index